PRAISE FOR *THE BIG SPLIT*

"Dr. Ryback takes us on a wild ride from the birth of the Big Split to creating a brighter future for our children. Absolutely fantastic! A tour de force, revealing how a sense of unfairness that triggered a laboratory monkey's sudden rage comes from similar circumstances that fuel our own anger when we perceive injustice."

—Dr. Michael Norwood, Author of *The Path of the Wealthy Soul*

"This book is amazing, capturing the background and events leading up to the Big Split, with a brilliant analysis of how we got there and how to get out of it. There's something fascinating in every chapter. It's a book that's got to be read by politicians, industrial leaders, educators, and the general public."

—David P. Leonard, CEO, Codacom Communications

"An amazingly easy and exciting read, *The Big Split* is an important and much-needed book. It should be read by anyone who cares about democracy in America. Dr. David Ryback has done a wonderful job articulating how this country got to our current polarized state, how the human mind can arrive at false conclusions, and how to inoculate oneself from falling prey to false narratives. The book draws from so many disciplines—political science, history, social psychology, learning theory, brain science—yet is smoothly written as well as deeply researched."

—Susan Campbell, PhD, Author of *Beyond the Power Struggle*

"Extremely well crafted, this book does a magnificent job of soaring through the swirl of recent historical events to address our country's conflicts leading to division and polarization."

—Michael Kuhar, PhD, Emory University, Author of *The Addicted Brain*

"Provocative and thoughtful, *The Big Split* is excellent—well researched and clearly exceptional."

—Martin C. Becker, Executive Consultant

"This book is excellent—easy to understand and moves the reader to anticipate the future of politics. It is up to date, relevant, and helps us comprehend psychologically what motivates the political leaders who dominate the current scene."

—Dr. Dorothy Simpson, Professor, New Mexico Highlands University

"An impressive and well-structured book with a great sense of pacing, *The Big Split* offers a balanced marriage of social science and politics. Even when it deals with the neuroscience of the brains of those who charged the Capitol, it's still a very easy, accessible read as well as a highly enjoyable one."

—David Edmond Moore, Director, Eyekiss Films

"This impressive book comes with great insights, including hopeful remedies for the future, all backed by deep, extensive research. Dr. Ryback uses his awareness of social dynamics to describe what is currently dividing the politics of our nation. Ultimately, *The Big Split* brings us hope for a more unified future as we seek to understand not only our differences but also what we have in common that can unite us."

—Joe Sasso, Executive Coach, Author of *Spiral Up*

The Big Split: How to Survive the Frustrations of Polarization, Social Media, and Conspiracy Theories

by David Ryback, PhD

© Copyright 2023 David Ryback

ISBN 978-1-64663-949-6

Published by

köehlerbooks™

3705 Shore Drive
Virginia Beach, VA 23455
800-435-4811
www.koehlerbooks.com

THE
BIG
SPLIT

How to Survive the Frustrations of Polarization, Social Media, and Conspiracy Theories

DAVID RYBACK, PHD

Author of *Putting Emotional Intelligence to Work*

VIRGINIA BEACH
CAPE CHARLES

TABLE OF CONTENTS

DEDICATION

To all my friends who supported the process of writing this book over the two years of writing, exploring ideas, editing, choosing one title after another, and generally offering goodwill, I dedicate this book, especially to Suzanne Staszak-Silva of Rowman & Littlefield and to Dr. Janet Colvin, Associate Dean, Utah Valley University, for their invaluable assistance, as well as to Dr. Gary Botstein, and Dr. Steve Preston for their ongoing editorial suggestions.

INTRODUCTION

O n an otherwise quiet Saturday afternoon in May in Buffalo, New York, in the heart of a predominantly Black community, an eighteen-year-old who took pride in helping others, according to those who knew him, suddenly seemed to change character by gunning down and killing ten innocent people in a supermarket. This was, according to Attorney General Merrick Garland, an act of racially motivated violent extremism. What could account for this strange turn of events in this young man's life? Could it possibly be a consequence of the ongoing plague of pervasive polarization in our nation, turning people against one another?

In this book, we explore alternate realities, sometimes based on emotional gullibility and what some call *belief-dependent realism*, a misguided version of truth based on impulsive feelings rather than cold, hard evidence.

> We unlock the secrets of the *tribal mind*, even provide a step-by-step breakdown—the neuroscience, if you will—of how mob mentality took over and built to a crescendo, resulting in the drama of the 2021 attack on the Capitol.

Above all, you'll acquire a better understanding of how vulnerable we are to the error of trusting unverified information simply because we read it and it's been accepted by our peers. Most critically, you'll learn how to bridge the gap in the Big Split between yourself and those with opposing views by engaging in a personal interaction of sharing. Though it appears at first counterintuitive, that approach may end up working surprisingly effectively.

Why Read This Book?

Hopefully, this book will inspire you to adapt some new ideas and solutions, and even challenge you to add power and clarity to your own style of communication. You can apply what you learn to your personal life, your professional career, and your deeper understanding of the dynamics of politics. You may even see your life in a more stimulating and engaging context in terms of your enhanced political awareness. As you read through this book, please feel free to let me know your thoughts about the Big Split. You can reach me at David.bigsplit@gmail.com

By the time you finish reading the first few chapters of this book, you'll know more about:

- How those behind the scenes of social media have been using information about you to enhance their own profits at your expense and how they need to change to serve you better.

- How to battle against addiction to social media, not only for yourself, but especially for the benefit of your children.

- How algorithms work to deepen the Big Split, often to your disadvantage.

- How to distinguish more clearly between misinformation, including accidental mistakes and erroneous impressions, and disinformation, which is more intentional.

- Exactly what may have occurred, from moment to moment,

inside the brains of those who attacked our Capitol—the psychology and neuroscience of an insurrection, if you will.

- The scientific research on how your genetic makeup contributes to your choice of political party. Research over the years has revealed that our choice of political affiliation is, in part, affected by our genes, specifically the 7R variant of the DRD4 gene.

- The answers to how QAnon came about, who was its secret leader, and the psychology of why people are continually drawn to it. Why is QAnon so successful? There is a branch of psycho-social research that helps explain the success of this group in fully scientific terms.

- What happened between the September 11 attacks in 2001 and the January 6 Capitol attack in 2021 to contribute to the Big Split we're now in.

- How to avoid becoming a victim of conspiracy theories.

- The psycho-social factors leading to the Big Split. And much more.

The purpose of this book is to reveal the larger perspective of polarization within the context of the loss of faith in our mainstream institutions. Though there's always been conflict of some kind in our national political arena—particularly involving attitudes about racism, not to mention Watergate and the war in Vietnam—this newer version, the Big Split, has begun to take place very rapidly over the past few years. With this overview, you'll feel more comfortable understanding the rise of what can be referred to as the *vocal minority*, those who have felt underappreciated and discounted till recently.

We'll go back in history to see how the decades between 2001 and 2021 resulted in an unstoppable and ultimately impactful loss of trust in our government.

We'll look at the influence of how various presidents affected trust in their administrations, especially that of former President Donald J. Trump. There'll be several side trips to make this venture even more interesting, such as the powerful impact of subtle messages in social media and our addiction to that (think nicotine in cigarettes), as well as the intriguing inner workings of QAnon and its alarming influence on the Big Split.

On the Crisis of Trust and Polarization

In this book, we'll go on a journey together to explore the crisis of trust in the Big Split from several angles:

- First, we'll look at the current political scene that has led to the loss of trust in our country's government, including the partisan aspect of politics that provides fodder for the cannons of late-night TV humor and how social media has affected the wiring of our brains.

- We'll come to grips with the ambivalence we feel about trusting the most popular mode of communication—social media—particularly as we deal with the challenges of months and months of having kept distance from one another because of Covid-19, and learn how social media has affected elections and the politics of government, and how we communicate with one another.

- In order to bridge the gap between yourself and a friend or relative who is an extreme right-winger or QAnoner, we'll explore a process of communication that just might help accomplish that. Whether or not you succeed, you'll have learned a process of communication that may benefit you in your personal or professional life for as long as you live.

- Finally, we'll look at ways of overcoming the antagonism between the two political parties by helping our children to become more open-minded and empathic so that they might grow into a world that is more peaceful and supportive.

This agenda covers a broad spectrum of psychological and social interaction. My lifelong research on leadership skills, social influence, and the dynamics of human communication as I worked in such diverse areas as Europe, Asia and the Mideast, has taught me that trust pervades all we do, whether in one-on-one interactions, group settings or political influence.

The overarching framework of this book serves to enable you to become more confident in the process of making better decisions about how you experience politics in your life. How so, you may ask? By gaining a deeper understanding of the dynamics of the communication of information—as well as misinformation and disinformation—that comes to you via all media.

In her resignation letter to *The New York Times*, journalist Bari Weiss wrote "that truth isn't a process of collective discovery, but an orthodoxy already known to an enlightened few whose job is to inform everyone else." Here she points out how the very dynamic of spreading truth in its opposing iterations feeds the process of polarization, even by such a venerable institution of the press as *The New York Times*.

Given this dynamic of shifting values of truth in the culture of our press, we can only imagine how the growing influence of the Big Split will be received.

About a decade ago, the two divisions leading to the Big Split were more easily differentiated. Democrats, according to *Times* columnist, Paul Krugman, advocated higher taxes for the rich and a safety net of social benefits for the working class, while Republicans, simply put, wanted to make the rich richer, with lower taxes and smaller social programs.[1] But this wasn't working at the polls for the Republicans because, in general, most people are in favor of government-financed social programs and they dislike the prospect of fewer taxes being paid by corporations and the rich.

So, what were the Republicans to do? Well, why not turn to cultural issues that the populace would support? Flaunt them in the buildup to elections and then just casually forget about them. And this was no more than a cynical ploy according to the book, *What's the Matter with Kansas,* by Thomas Frank. "The leaders of the backlash may talk Christ," he wrote, "but they walk corporate . . . The culture industry is never forced to clean up its act."[2]

But now, in the era of the Big Split, the cultural issues are no longer ignored. Now they're right in our face. As Republicans come into power in the House, the results are loss of reproductive rights for many women, books being banned in schools, and the right to teach students about racism is no longer a privilege across the board. Corporations, traditionally with conservative values, are even being accused by Republicans of being too liberal.

As American culture in general is becoming somewhat more progressive, more accepting of minority rights, along with the Democrats, at the same time the Republicans, at least the more extreme component, are stretching the other way, becoming much more conservative, especially with the Conservative-packed Supreme Court seeming to favor their political persuasion.

All this characterizes the current status of the Big Split, exacerbated even more by a challenging economy in the making. With the rise of inflation and a possible recession looming on the horizon, there are many uncertainties.

As employment issues remain a concern, we have people finding it difficult to give up working at home rather than trying to return to work at the office. The Great Resignation continued at the beginning of 2023, with *quiet quitting,* doing the bare minimum by just showing up; *career cushioning,* making plans in case the current job didn't work out over time; and *worker hoarding,* in which employers held on to current employees, no matter how undesirable, fearing the lack of prospective hiring opportunities because of too many jobs being available for too few applicants. Of course, this may change drastically if a recession dominates our economy.

These workers were either Covid "disposables," who were unceremoniously laid off during the pandemic shutdown; or essential workers—teachers, food service workers, hospital staff—who had no choice but to continue despite very challenging work environments, mostly on the blue side of the Big Split; or white-collar employees rejecting the return-to-office requests, many on the red side.

The turn of the year also had Republicans worrying about the oversized role of Donald Trump in the 2024 elections, especially with the legal challenges he was facing. With at least ten prospects for the presidency, and Florida governor Ron DeSantis most visible, care needed to be taken by the party not to become too divisive. All this was in the context of getting the speaker of the House, Kevin McCarthy, elected after more than a dozen frustrating dead-end votes.

Both sides of the Big Split had their problems. The Democrats were worrying about leadership as well, as they tried holding onto their coalition of Blacks, Latinos, millennials, and the working class, many of whom were beginning to vote for the Republicans. If President Biden appeared too old to run again in his eighties, then from where would new leadership arise? There were concerns about Biden's fears, one of them that he believed his Secret Service detail was infiltrated by MAGA supporters.[3] The polls were not favoring his age issue.

On either side, there were concerns about trust. One third of the American population still believed in the Big Lie that Trump actually won the election. And many on both sides were losing confidence in the voting system with all the furor around that. "If you're in a democracy and you believe your vote doesn't count," claimed outgoing Representative Adam Kinzinger on TV, "that's dangerous!" This was the consequence of people listening to their own echo chambers on social media, widening the Big Split.

According to Robert Draper, author of *Weapons of Mass Delusion*, Republicans such as Marjorie Taylor Greene and Matt

Gaetz, have made matters more challenging by supporting Trump and his Stop the Steal mentality along with the fantastic conspiracy theories that support their delusions.[4]

If the Republicans decide to impeach President Biden, as the right-wing extremists threaten to, then the Big Split will widen even further.[5] And if social media pulls back their restrictions, conflating politics with entertainment, then all bets are off as to how far apart the two sides of the split may be. When about one third of our population still believes that the 2020 elections were stolen by a mob of baby-devouring pedophiles, then the Big Split will not be resolved any time soon.

For now, let's begin with how social media influences our version of reality, sometimes creating a misplacement of trust and, later, how the Big Split in politics led to the insurrection against our Capitol. We'll begin with a few quotes to set the tone.

PART I:

CURRENT POLITICS, SOCIAL MEDIA, AND THE HISTORY OF THE BIG SPLIT

CHAPTER ONE

Once Upon a Time in America: Inside the Tribal Mind

If a political party does not have its foundation in the determination to advance a cause that is right and that is moral, then it is not a political party; it is merely a conspiracy to seize power.

—President Dwight D. Eisenhower

We don't think any more—we feel. Partisanship has basically become religion.

—Jon Meacham, on *Real Time*

A sensational lie is much more convincing than a complicated truth.

—Fareed Zakaria

O nce upon a time, in a social science lab in America, an angry capuchin monkey rebelled. It was getting a bland piece of cucumber as a reward while seeing its neighbor monkey get a juicy grape—for the same activity. Rather than accept this lesser reward, the monkey hurled the cucumber back at the experimenter and began shaking its cage with what clearly looked like a flurry of rage and indignation. This image became a symbol of inequity for many in the world of business and economics. Then it entered the arena of politics.

Imagine about half the American population, if not more, who see themselves as hard-working, law-abiding citizens, doing an honest day's work from week to week, month to month. Then, with the aid of Facebook and other social media on which close to two hundred million Americans spend one to two hours a day, they discovered that so many others were getting rich faster than those who were working so hard.

In comparison, the hard workers were getting peanuts—or cucumbers rather than grapes, to maintain the analogy. That was enough to get them angry—very angry—enough to rattle their cages, or at least the cages of the politicians who were aiding and abetting this disparity of rewards. That anger built up at the Stop the Steal gathering and was fueled even higher by Trump's speeches and others who supported him. And so, we had the assault on the Capitol.

> If the two images were put side by side, the video of the frustrated and angry chimps rattling their cages might look like the frustration and anger of those storming the Capitol on January 6. From a social science perspective, those attacking the Capitol felt they had good reason for their actions, a genuine human response to feeling poorly treated by their government for way too long. In their minds, they were absolutely right.

Making America "Grapes" Again

It was all a question of trust. The citizens, mostly blue-collar workers, feeling powerless in this quandary and with a sense of helplessness growing for decades, were getting frustrated. They wanted to trust their political leaders, and they did so to some extent. They tried trusting presidents like Richard Nixon, who referred to them as the silent majority. When their frustrations grew over the years, and the purchasing power of their earnings began to decline dramatically, the anger just grew.

But they had to trust someone, a leader who really understood their bitterness, who would attack the arrogance of politics as usual, a leader who would blast through the fabric of politics that had ignored them and their needs for decades, a leader who was defiant and uncompromising in any way, even belligerent on their behalf.

The need to trust is undeniable. The question became, where could they find such a leader who didn't mince words but revealed his trustworthiness directly and simply?

Then, along came Donald J. Trump, assaulting his competitors in the Republican primaries with wicked nicknames and then, with seemingly magical powers, beating Hillary Clinton, the Democratic candidate whom everyone expected to win, and who won the popular vote but lost the electoral college. Finally, their need to trust found its savior—with a vengeance. "He says what I'm thinking," they felt.

No more cucumbers. Now they would feast on grapes. Or so they thought. They saw a vision they could finally trust, a vision in which they could eventually separate themselves from those who, they felt, had usurped them for so long.

They drew a line between themselves and the others. They formed an emotional connection with a president they could now trust and then build their tribe of like-minded followers. When QAnon—a loosely affiliated network of believers in a mysterious character called Q who seemingly predicted the future and reflected the angst of the populists—came along, with all its conspiracy of trust in simplistic solutions, it fit perfectly.

The vision clarified, for them, a moral victory which included religion and conservative values, to make America great again, as it had been before. This was what the Trump movement was about: restore the America they once knew that was slipping away due to real and perceived efforts of the American left. They stopped the dialog and listened to lies. They could strongly separate themselves from those embracing a diversity that might threaten their former power base. Their great need to trust such a leader was ultimately settled.

Someone had finally given voice to their hopes for better jobs, their desire to keep those jobs in the US, their hopes for keeping migrants from coming across the border, their belief in religious doctrine against abortion, and their goal of keeping the LGBTQ community from acquiring the rights that they alone had enjoyed for generations. Now they could hope for grapes rather than cucumbers.

The World Is Changing—Drastically!

To understand the polarized mind, it's important to understand how we perceive reality. We all need to trust—someone, or something, such as our intimate partners, our children, the solvency of our banks, the meaning and value of our work, and even our political leaders. Trust is the thread that holds every society together. And it can be a national tragedy when the trust of a nation is betrayed, costing lives, avoidable destruction to our planet, and even damage to our fragile process of democracy.

The Big Split was brought about by tribalism, a fierce collective with intense loyalty in which the subliminal lies of social media impact our lives, creating powerful changes almost beyond our understanding. And it's all happening now.

In this chapter, we'll explore:

- How our focus on the reality we choose to trust is so greatly influenced by the lens of our belief systems

- The neuroscience of conspiracy in the tribal mind, with a focus on how the brain processes mob activities

Emotions Over Facts

As both scientist and philosopher, Michael Shermer wrote a book titled, *The Believing Brain*, in which he proposed the following:

our brains make decisions based more on our emotions than on our reason. And once we've made such a decision, our brains fortify it by defending it against all incoming information to the contrary, no matter how logical or reasonable to others.[1]

Now Trump's followers could hope for grapes rather than cucumbers. Seduced by such a vision, they flocked to him unthinkingly. Following that decision to trust, they could rationalize anything Trump did that might be judged as negative by others, no matter what the objective facts. Their frustrations of eating cucumber all these years, they felt, was so deeply understood by Trump, that they felt loved by him. The prospect of grapes changed their lives as the steadfast followers banded together into a cult characterized so well by the QAnon "tribe."

Most of us are not so easily won by sweet promises of easy gain. Most of us are slow to trust, even given to the greater likelihood of mistrust. Whom do *you* mistrust these days? Your ex-spouse who ended your marriage by spending so much on legal fees that your attorney could buy his own boat with all the money you spent? Your business partner who took the money and ran you into the ground? The salesperson who sold you the used car that breaks down every time it rains? What institutions do you have trouble trusting? Your government—to consider the nation's needs before their own personal power? Your bank—to earn the interest you think your money deserves as inflation picks up? The post office—to deliver all your mail, on time?

The answers to these challenging questions can define your emotional life. And here's an even more critical question: Are you aware of *your* deep need to trust—someone, or something? Without such trust, you can be a very lonely individual, quite unhappy, and unfulfilled.

It's truly up to each of us to take responsibility for these concerns of misplaced trust.

> We live in a culture of abundance and yet we
> starve for truth, authenticity, equally applied
> justice, and some assurance that our children
> and their children will live on a planet that
> will not self-destruct within a century.

But our hopes and aspirations are threatened by a kind of tyranny that has developed without warning—the Big Split.

As we travel together through this book, we will do our best to ensure that the information we share with you is well documented. Both sides of the political spectrum—right and left—value respect for family, concern for society at large, and freedom of religion. But one side is more conservative than the other, preferring more traditional families, more prudent habits and the fervent priority of Christianity above other religions.

The problem arises when we meet the extremes. Such individuals create challenges with their demands for privileges they have not earned, like White supremacists who want to obliterate those who are seen as competing with them. They fear immigration, especially by people of color. They fear and attack Asain minorities whose culture involves sacrifice and hard work, both at labor and at institutions of higher learning.

Unfortunately, many leaders on the right have decided that logical debate and factual evidence are not their chosen path, and purposefully tap the emotional realm of their followers. These leaders tend to avoid relying on scientific discourse or the rule of law (except, of course, for the Second Amendment). Instead, they try to sway the masses by appealing to base emotions such as anger and hatred. They prefer winning in any way possible—even if it means restricting voting rights or denouncing legitimate elections. They are in the war of politics to win, whatever the means. But the left is not without sin either, as it has its own set of biases and self-delusions, with its disposition toward cancel culture and dehumanization of the other side. A portion of both sides has been reported considering leaving the Union to form their own states.[2,3]

Trust in leadership, from local to national levels, has diminished steadily for both parties over the past years going back to the destruction of the twin towers of the World Trade Center. This is thoroughly documented in Chapter Three. With five million lives lost to the Covid-19 pandemic across the world, in part because of the slow reaction of many a government across the globe, it's no wonder trust has been lost. If we are to survive these uncertain times, then institutions must work together with both credible facts and an empathetic approach.

The Big Lie: What Really Happened

On January 6, 2021, a group of individuals stormed the capitol building after attending a rally led by President Trump and some of his allies. The lie they were telling insisted that Joe Biden had not won the presidential election in November 2020 and that the election had been stolen. They called upon Vice President Pence to void some of the results of the election so that Trump would win. Those who stormed the capitol swarmed through hallways, vandalized the building, and threatened sitting members of Congress and even the Vice President himself, some yelling to have him hanged for not doing their bidding.[4]

Over the many months leading up to that moment, these citizens were led to trust in a leader who fostered distorted and fallacious news that did not meet the criteria of objective, critical thinking. This seduction of their trust was so powerful that some of them were prepared to storm the Capitol and even kill for what they were led to believe were the most patriotic of values. Many of them were white-collar workers or business owners. Most had little to do with the militia groups or White supremacist groups that got the media's attention. By and large, they were ordinary folks, but felt ignored by their government. There never was a greater display in the United

States of what damage such a conspiracy of belief—misplaced trust in an untrustworthy president—could muster.

Americans have loved their independence since they gained it from what they considered the the tyranny of Great Britain, when they believed they were being taxed unfairly. The American tradition is illustrated by the banner of the serpent with the words overhead: *DON'T TREAD ON ME.*[5] And this is the sentiment that Trump's following bears so deliberately.

The framers of our Constitution articulated such independence and its defense so well that it allowed its citizens to bear arms to ensure that freedom (even though some experts believe this was intended primarily for a "well-trained militia"). And it is exactly that value that Trump's followers hold to so dearly. They display their modern weapons proudly, at public gatherings of all kinds—at political rallies, outside school board meetings, and at public protests. Though the guns weren't prominent at the insurgency on January 6, there were other makeshift weapons. When it comes to crowd dynamics, emotions always override intellect, and strong emotions based on patriots defending their historically derived rights, as they see them, knew no bounds.

That day, as we all saw on national TV, Donald Trump spoke to his "troops," whipping them into a frenzy: "We will never concede . . . We're going to have to fight much harder . . . fight like hell . . . or you won't have a country anymore."[6]

Rudolph Giuliani added, slamming his fist on the lectern: "Let's have trial by *combat!*"[7]

And so, they did, armed with metal pipes, flagpoles, baseball bats, bear spray and whatever they could get their hands on, viciously attacking the Capitol, yelling "USA! USA!" Five individuals died, one of them a police officer, Brian Sicknick, with 140 officers injured.[8]

Here are the newspaper headlines on the morning of January 7, 2021, describing the event:

San Francisco Chronicle: "INSURRECTION"

New York Post: "CAPITOL INVASION"

The Oregonian: "UNPRECENDENTED INSURRECTION"

Tampa Bay Times: "UNDER SIEGE"

Atlanta Journal-Constitution: "'INTOLERABLE ATTACK' ON DEMOCRACY"

France's *Le Monde*: "*TRUMP PROVOQUE LE CHAOS A WASHINGTON*"

The most intriguing headline, in Italy's *La Stampa*, accompanying a photo of one of the protesters waving a large Stars and Stripes flag in the middle of the Capitol Rotunda: *"C'era una volta l'America"*—which translates to "Once upon a time in America."

Was the implication that democracy was now dead in America or that this was America's second revolution, fearing the coming of a staid, liberal government that was not responding to the needs of the insurgents?

Not everyone storming the Capitol was QAnon, but this incident most likely would not have occurred without them. The Proud Boys, a White supremacist group promoting violence, identified by their orange hats, were there to do their part, among the fifteen thousand participants.[9]

On the day of the crisis, as we all saw on mainstream TV, Mitch McConnell, then Senate Majority Leader, had this to say to his colleagues, as if realizing for the first time, with a child-like innocence: "We have two separate tribes with separate realities."[10]

At just about that time, about one o'clock in the afternoon, protesters managed to break through the police line and began climbing up the Capitol steps, one of them shouting, "Trump won that election!"[11]

A bit later, also on TV, Republican Senator Ted Cruz proclaimed to his Congressional colleagues, "We gather at a moment of great passion . . . thirty-nine percent of Americans believe the elections were rigged . . . with claims of illegality and fraud," and asked for "a ten-day emergency audit."[12]

Inside the Capitol were the outgoing Vice President, Mike Pence; the incoming Vice President, Kamala Harris; and the Speaker of the House, Nancy Pelosi. Pence was doing his Constitutional duty, officiating over the count of the Electoral College votes as the final step in confirming that Joe Biden had won the election, having turned down Trump's bizarre request that he try to convert the vote.

On the west side of the Capitol, a large crowd of demonstrators breached security and pushed its way past the metal detectors, to where the vote counting was taking place. The legislators stopped their proceedings and were forced to find shelter, as the entire nation, and many across the globe, watched what looked like an attempted coup against a standing government. One Capitol police officer texted, "We are outnumbered!"[13]

Protesters were transformed into criminal insurgents, but they felt like patriots, yelling, "USA! USA!" One proclaimed to a journalist, "We were normal, good, law-abiding citizens, and you guys did this to us." They challenged the Capitol police officers, some of whom feared for their lives. Spotting a news team in their midst, they began harassing them: "You get the fuck out of here before you get hurt . . . We can absolutely destroy you." Others were shouting: "Hang Mike Pence! Hang Mike Pence!" A single voice yelled out: "Pelosi, we're coming for that bitch . . . we're coming for her."[14] Many of the protesters felt they were doing the right, moral thing as devoted patriots. This was reflected in one man's response to a TV reporter's question of what they were planning to do: "Whatever we have to do," he responded in full anger. "What do you think 1776 was?"

At precisely 2:43 p.m., Air Force veteran Ashli Babbitt, thirty-five, wearing snow boots, jeans, and a Trump flag over her shoulders, was hoisted up to a broken window by two men. As she began to enter through the window, a shot rang out, and she fell dying back onto the floor, blood streaming from her mouth.

Just about this time, the staff on the first floor were evacuated and an order was put out to shelter in place. Some staff locked their doors, turned off the lights and hid under their desks. Mike Pence was sixty seconds from being nabbed by the mob before escaping along with his family, who were visiting the Capitol that day.

One of Pelosi's staff members, Leah Han, hiding behind a closed door under a table, wondered, "Am I gonna get raped? Like, I thought I was gonna die," as she broke down in tears, recounting her experience on national TV.

Legislators and their assistants began making calls frantically on their cellphones to anyone that they believed might help—the Washington District mayor, the acting attorney general, the chair of the Joint Chiefs of Staff, the secretary of the Army, even governors of nearby states.

The Capitol police were clearly outnumbered. The intruders pulled one down a set of stairs and began pummeling him, tearing his badge from his chest and kicking him as he covered his head.

It would later be determined by the January 6 bipartisan Congressional Select Committee that some conspiracy was behind this, most likely including supremacist groups such as the Three Percenters and the Oath Keepers. US District Judge Beryl Howell would later show concern about the "strategic planning" of the insurrection by leaders of the Proud Boys. Even some members of Trump's cabinet were under suspicion and later subpoenaed.

At four o'clock, President-elect Biden got on national TV and insisted, "I call on President Trump to go on national TV now and demand an end to this siege. President Trump, step up!" Clearly, only Trump could have stopped the violence at that point.

Trump responded to this by taping a statement to his followers at 4:17 p.m. that they were special and that he loved them, then saying, "This was a fraudulent election. Go home. And go home in peace." Senator Cory Booker saw this message as "fanning the flames of conspiracy theory."[15]

So, was all this, culminating in a dismal milestone in our history, due to conspiracy theory? Whether Trump really believed he lost the election due to fraud is impossible to say. He himself may have been seduced by QAnon, the most infamous group to spew forth the dangerous conspiracy theories then transforming the political landscape. Certainly, his followers appeared to believe the theories. They were led to trust what they were fed by social media outlets, as false as it was, creating a conspiracy of trust that shook our nation.

Among the many to be held accountable, starting with Trump, were some news media reporters as well, at least those who promulgated these unsubstantiated rumors that the election had really been stolen. Drawing more viewers is how media make more money. As Julie Roginsky, Fox News contributor, put it to Brian Stelter on his TV show *Reliable Sources*, "The beast [news media] must be fed." CNN's Brian Stelter agreed, "It's about profit." Millions had been convinced by some media outlets that the election was indeed rigged.

On the very week of this political calamity, resulting in at least five deaths, there were other crises transpiring as well: the pandemic was raging with over five thousand deaths recorded per day, the rate of vaccinations was way below the estimates made earlier, over ten million people were out of work because of the pandemic, Trump's cabinet members began resigning, he was being impeached—for the second time—and he suddenly lost his ability to use Twitter, Facebook, or almost any large media outlet to directly speak to the public. Whom could we trust with all that was going on? The issue of trust had become a crisis of its own.

The Need to Belong

Animals that live in packs need to trust one another for their survival. If one of them remains behind, whether due to carelessness or injury, that lone figure loses the protection of the pack, and that vulnerability may result in death. Should a predator attack, there will be no group to defend it. Any documentary on animal behavior, such as *Nature* on public TV, illustrates that over and over. So, the need to belong in the pack became hard-wired through evolution.

Similarly, with early humans. A lone person, apart from the pack or tribe, becomes vulnerable to predators, much more likely to die alone. Over time, that ongoing togetherness results in a collective belief system. Tribal experiences that are shared transform into tribal values which become that group's mythology—about creation, about spirituality, about attitudes toward critical life choices. The need to belong to a group of fellow tribal members becomes strongly ingrained, not only because it's physiologically hardwired, but also socially through shared group experience over time.

Most people want and need to trust their fellow citizens and yet many end up finding trust only in their tribe, unable to connect with the larger society. Most susceptible are those who are marginalized by color, or less educated, and unable to pay their way through life given the poor purchasing power of their wages. As a result, they're more likely to ease their need to belong by buying into conspiracy theories that give them hope, false but seductive.

There is a strong need to belong, yet many no longer feel certain of their identity—sexual, economic, spiritual, or career-wise. There is a growing increase in suicides, gender identity issues, single parenting, job insecurity, spiritual experimentation, and cynicism in politics. They crave more *likes* from social media to confirm their status as worthwhile beings, and some find themselves more open to a conspiracy mindset that connects them with others, so that they can feel they do belong to some group.

There was an issue of identity here—for all Americans—that was being chipped away at by left and right. Right: We make up most of the real Americans. America used to be great, and we want that back. Left: We need immigrants and minorities to replace "bad" supremacist Americans who are almost all White males. We need a new America, and the bad guys don't belong unless they convert.

With all these insecurities, we crave to belong to a trusted political entity with a strong sense of togetherness. But it's nowhere to be found by those who don't fit in the larger society, so we create our own tribes and dedicate our faith to narratives that promise relief, which are often false conspiracies of trust.

The Great Divide: Making America Great Again—Again!

How have politics changed in the past few decades to lead to the Big Split, which involves a bifurcation of reality into opposing value systems? One of them is liberal and progressive; the other is conservative and regressive, as in making America "great" again, a return to older values—and all this is taking place in a challenging economy. What ever happened to trust as we knew it just a couple of decades ago, before the Big Split?

Since then, and especially over the past few years, we have become an increasingly divided nation. We can blame some of that on the Trump administration but, really, Trump just fell into the right place at the right time, when one half of our country felt a need for a leader who took their concerns seriously and promised to deliver the goods to them, to bring a turnover in our government that would finally give them what they believed they deserved—grapes rather than cucumbers. They wanted better access to more jobs, lower taxes, and the recognition that they were just as important, if not more, than those currently represented by government and corporate headquarters.

The great divide between modern-day Democrats and Republicans began decades ago, when Republican Senator Barry Goldwater became the focus of the American conservative movement, arguing for a staunchly anti-welfare state. As a presidential candidate in 1964, he offered his ideas in his book, *The Conscience of a Conservative*.[16] He became best known for refuting the legislation of morality, as he put it, and for backing individual freedom from government. "Extremism in the face of liberty is no vice," he famously declared.[17]

All this set the stage for President Reagan, who continued to discourage welfare programs and popularized the slogan, *Make America Great Again*, in both the 1980 and 1984 elections, which Trump later used to great effect.[18]

When Trump won the election in 2016, a new reality began to set in, based on a point of view that fed Trump's need to be the center of attention with his most successful attributes as an aggressive business tycoon that made him look like a constant winner to his followers, bending the facts as needed and transmuting journalistic reports as so-called fake news.

This new reality depended on the support of imaginative stories that belittled the establishment as losers and even as criminals.[19] The advent of conspiracy theories blossomed forth as never before, aided in no small part by the burgeoning social media.[20]

How We Determine Our Absolute Truth: Emotional Gullibility in the Big Split

Let's begin by exploring how our brains process reality, whether factual or through the lens of belief systems that defy objectivity.

What makes the brain's proclivity to interpret perception in ways that literally boggle the imagination is the central focus of this chapter. Yes, our brains evolved to keep us away from saber-toothed tigers and venomous snakes and sharks in the water. But, in these modern times, such critters are not as dangerous as might be those in our society who make us feel neglected, debased, and forlorn.

So, our brains, in these modern times, react to social threats as intensely as they did in primal times to life-threatening animals, overriding objective, logical observations and choosing such social threats and the subsequent emotions they lead to as more important in forming our values than facts.

Let's look at some numbers.

A Gallup poll revealed that over 40 percent of Americans believe in psychic healing, demon possession, and ESP. Over a quarter believe in haunted houses, predicting the future, and telepathy. Yet fewer than half believe in Darwin's theory of evolution.[21] So there: firm ground for belief by emotion rather than reason.

A series of polls reported by such magazines as *Forbes* revealed some interesting numbers. Republicans responding to a Yahoo News-YouGov poll indicated that 44 percent of them believed that philanthropist Bill Gates, who has spent hundreds of millions on vaccine research, intends to use the Covid-19 vaccine to implant microchips and track people's movements, while 64 percent of Republicans believed the 2020 election results were not trustworthy. A poll by YouGov-Cambridge Globalism Project revealed that about 38 percent of all Americans trust such conspiracy theories as Covid-19 being a hoax or that the number of resulting deaths is grossly exaggerated, as well as other theories spread by various media, such as those used by QAnon.[22]

"Any scary event—a pandemic, a mass shooting—that denies people a sense of control will lead to a proliferation of conspiracy theories," said Stephan Lewandowsky, a cognitive psychologist at the University of Bristol who is an expert on misinformation. "They give people a sense of psychological comfort—the feeling that they are not at the mercy of randomness."[23] Rumors step in for facts and muddy the truth.

Remarkably, even scientific education is not always a bulwark against emotional gullibility. A study revealed that students who scored well on scientific tests were no more or less susceptible to thinking emotionally as opposed to logically, concluding, "Students are taught *what* to think but not *how* to think."[24] *How* to think involves critical analysis beyond the rote memory of learning facts or labels that categorize.

> After being spoon-fed the *what*, they are nonetheless still challenged to go beyond that to the *how*.

Belief-dependent realism is the name given to the process by which we hunker down with a belief that makes sense to us and we hardly ever change that inner system of interpreting our reality. This concept by the famous theoretical physicist Stephen Hawking and Leonard Mlodinow maintains that

> once we settle on a version of reality, we rarely veer from it, but rather use it as a lens to see the world from then on.

"When such a model is successful at explaining events," say the authors, "we tend to attribute to it . . . the quality of reality and absolute truth."[25] Very few individuals like to admit that they are wrong, especially in terms of paradigm or world view.

Unlocking the Patterns of Tribal Thinking

Another aspect of the evolution of the human brain is to protect ourselves from those formerly dangerous critters by huddling together in mutually protective groups, safe not only from the predators but also from other groups that might want to make war with us and take our possessions and loved ones. And that's where the primal need to join groups of seemingly similar individuals came to be—what we now call tribalism.

Our sense of security comes from the groups we trust to help keep us safe from the dangers of those who are out to get us.

"Getting us" doesn't necessarily mean kill us or rob us, but rather take away our sense of dignity, of importance, of feeling that we're just as good as, no, even better than, those others in the now menacing tribes out there.

> So, we adopt beliefs that support all this thinking that make us feel more secure, more important, in a word, superior.

In the extreme, such defensive thinking unlocks the strong yet unspoken recipe for White supremacists, extreme populists, ethnic extremists, religious fanatics, and other hate-mongering groups.

Clearly, we can discover the truth by comparing the reality of our perceptions with others. But which others? Well, those we trust, those in our tribe, of course. So, scientists can compare the notes of their research experiments, look at the data, and determine the "truth." That's what scientists do—look at the data from their experiments and compare their data with others' in the community they trust—scientists. For scientists, a theory is the lens through which data are seen.

But, what about those who are not scientists and don't have first-hand experience with those data? All those terms, such as *tests of significance* and *probability curves* and *levels of confidence,* what the heck do they mean? Much easier to let their emotions explore what they perceive and trust from the members in their community or tribe—or Facebook.

Welcome to the Age of Polarization, where science is foreign and beliefs in emotional, dramatic patterns of social suspicions—that make more emotional sense than scientifically devised numbers—begin to prevail. The most susceptible are those uneducated in terms of scientific method or critical thinking who prefer to enjoy life in the short term rather than taking life too seriously.

One way of describing this is with the term *heuristic thinking.* This involves making decisions on the go without sufficient information. At its worst, it involves stereotyping and profiling, allowing for prejudice against others who are not easy to classify.

This leads to confirmation bias, in which people tend to accept information that confirms what they already are familiar with and deny any information that is opposed.

For now, let's take a trip into the overbearing challenge of the battle of values in society today, including the conspiracy of trust involving tribal thinking. Just as psychologists would go into the others' perspectives to understand their behavior, let's take a close look inside the tribal mind.

The Neuroscience of Tribal Conspiracy: How Mob Mentality Works

Now, in everyday situations requiring us to make decisions about trust in the moment, there is a process going on within our minds and bodies that we can break down into stages.

In the next few pages, we'll unlock the secrets of the tribal mind and illustrate a step-by-step breakdown of how mob activity takes over and builds to a crescendo, such as during the insurrection on the US Capitol, on January 6, 2021.

In this breakdown of how tribal thinking works, we'll illustrate how small cues given off by a few individuals can spread throughout the crowd, step by step. This unlocking of the tribal mind neuroscience and physiology leads to a greater understanding and emotional sense of the group dynamic. (In order to relate to a specific circumstance for clear understanding and application in context, and to offer a you-are-there perspective, the events at the attack on the Capitol on January 6 of 2021 will be in brackets and italicized, as an example.) We will refer to the participants in the attack as *protesters* to avoid assigning guilt, as that is not our purpose here. Keep your tribal headgear on for the moment, so you can better identify with the process we are about to illustrate.

Now, imagine yourself dressed for the tribal occasion, with fur-skinned collar and feathered headdress, something like the infamous QAnon shaman, Jake Angeli, so you can better identify with what we are about to share.

The ordering of the following stages slows down the normal response time so we can better understand what happens in a rather quick span of events, highlighting the cognitive and physiological aspects of the neuroscience of it all. If you're not interested in the neuroscience part, you can skim those aspects, and just focus on the social-emotional aspects.

- First, there is perception, including the visual, of where we are and with whom. We read the body language and facial expressions of key figures. For a given person facing us, we read the line of the lip, most likely unconsciously, to see if the line is like a smiley face curve, indicating happy; or like an upside-down curve, a frown, indicating sadness; or some tightness, indicating some form of tension—fear, confusion, perhaps frustration and anger.

At the Capitol, the protesters read others' body language of frustrated anger and moral indignation.

- All this information goes from our sensory input—sight, sound, smell (affecting our memory of similar situations), and tactile (temperature of the room affecting our skin, etc.)— directly to the thalamus, the central receiving station in the center of the brain.

The clamor of shouting and yelling and the smell and of bodies shoved together are processed unconsciously.

- Some of this information then goes to the structure in our brain called the amygdala which registers the situation as either comfortable, supportive, and trustworthy, or else threatening in some form or other. The messages then travel along neurons to signal another part of our brain, the hypothalamus, to secrete hormones to stimulate the adrenal glands to produce adrenaline and cortisol.

Fight-or-flight reactions overcome the emotions of fear, as adrenalin and cortisol pour into the bloodstream.

- Those signal the muscles and heart to raise our level of arousal to prepare us for a possible battle, whether physical or verbal. More sugar is released into our bloodstream for added energy, our hearts beat faster, our muscles tense up and our pupils dilate.

Fight mode is in full blast.

(Representative Ruben Gallego, who had served in Iraq as a Marine, was one of those under attack. He later reported: "Individuals themselves aren't usually a problem but when they get collectively together and they create a mob, the mob is the weapon . . . I was ready to fight. I saw a lot of shit back in my day, but I was not going to die on the floor of the fucking representatives.")[26]

- All this occurs prior to any cognitive recognition or awareness of how to label any emotion. We are aware of our body response, either relaxing with trust or otherwise tightening up or cringing. Now we're almost ready to get a sense of what emotions we're feeling. By sizing up the social situation and feeling the changes in our body, we can conclude that we are either ready to continue trusting and relaxing or, in the alternative, feeling fearful, sad, or angry, or some variation of those. In addition, we might also feel surprised by the situation. We use our ventromedial prefrontal cortex to label such feelings and our dorsolateral prefrontal cortex (both at the front of our brains, just behind our forehead) to decide how to go forward with all this information.

As the spearhead of the group begins to physically attack the Capitol doors and windows, the followers let their anger flow and decide that, as "patriots," they must defend their moral rights and support the group in reclaiming the "stolen" election.

- At this point, belief-dependent realism takes over and we use the only lens we have through which to see our current situation. The scientific term is *confirmation bias.*[27] We comprehend the nature of what we experience in the moment and where to move forward based on the "truth" with which we've become familiar, well-tested by personal experience and confirmed by other members of our tribal culture.[28]

The protesters who have not yet committed themselves to action now decide that this is their moment to act on their beliefs and join in the attack. Those already on the attack now become brutally violent against anyone who might represent the enemy—police, journalists, legislators who aren't supportive, or anyone not part of the "patriots." All this builds into an unstoppable, growing crescendo of emotional avalanche.

(Photographer Ashley Gilbertson said: "I got the sense that there are some people here who are fucking around and playing dress up and there are some people who are not fucking around.")[29]

- Next is the decision to trust our environment if all feels safe or not and, if not, consider other options such as acting impulsively in the moment—yell, scream, fight, cry, run—or, in the alternative, to figure out the best solution for the long term, which is clearly the more mature response. Most of us tend to be inclined to one or the other, not in extremes, but by inclination. This is known as the Marshmallow Principle,[30] based on the classical study of very young children who, when offered a marshmallow and asked to wait fifteen minutes before eating it, could not control themselves and ate it impulsively versus those who were able to manage their impulses. According to many follow-up studies, these traits persisted throughout their lives.[31]

Those who have not yet joined the melee and find themselves in a moral dilemma now make that final decision to feel the anger that propels them to join the marauders or pull back.

- Now our final decision is affected by the underlying emotion about the issue we're faced with. A decision must be made, and we know what is right, based on what we knew to be right before all this decision-making was necessary. It's at this point in making the "right" decision that our deep values come into play, overriding everything else if our "rightness" is sufficiently intense. Whether we choose to listen and get more information on the one hand or act quickly to defend our position because the other side is so "wrong" will determine, almost pre-determine, our immediate action. The tribe with which we identify strongly takes over any personal considerations.

For those who have not pulled back, there is no more time for deciding. All is action and vengeance for all the frustration of dealing with the "stolen election." The banners—Trump flags, even the Stars and Stripes—are used as lethal weapons to destroy the "enemy." The invaders are acting as a single entity with the power of the unison of many. Shouts of "Hang Mike Pence!" and "Pelosi! We're coming for that bitch!" ring out.[32]

(Officer Mike Fanone was brutally attacked, tasered in the back of his neck and crushed by surrounding protesters. He later recalled people yelling out to "get his gun—kill him with his own gun!" He ended up suffering brain injuries and a mild heart attack.)[33]

- Upon further reflection, probably later in time, possibly with a close friend or coach or therapist, we can try and pin down precisely what feelings we were having, why we trusted or not, and, if not, why, but it's unlikely we know that in the moment when all this is occurring.

  (For those later arrested by the FBI, the reflection of what was done was recorded before a judge, most likely finely tuned by a hired attorney. Some of the defenses were surprising, such as attorney Al Watkins claiming, in his defense of the QAnon Shaman, Anthony Jacob Chandley, attired in his fur collar and horns: "My client was invited by the president . . . My client just looks bad; he's really a nice guy who lives with his mother, meditates, and only eats organic food."[34] Another protester, Robert Reeder, who pled to a misdemeanor, and sentenced to three months in jail by US District Judge Thomas Hogan, had this to say in his defense: "Immediately after the interaction with the police officer I just wanted to get out of there. It just wasn't me." His brain was clearly in a different state in court than it was during the insurrection.)[35]

This gives us some idea of how our brains react to help us make decisions that affect our choices around trust, especially in the moment of conflict. Now, whenever you may find yourself about to react in the heat of the moment in a social context of intensely emotional exchanges, you can elect to slow down your thinking process and take control of your raging limbic system. You can be master of your emotions if you take the right perspective. Just for a moment, get out of your tribal mind and take a good look outside.

You may recall an America that existed once upon a time with much less acrimony . . . and much more trust.

In Times of Stress: First, We Believe.
Then We Trust.

In this book, you'll learn what it takes to avoid such unhappiness and create a richer, more fulfilling life with the skills necessary to trust the right people—in the right settings. Trust is hard-won and easily lost. All of us are tested, sometimes daily, with the dilemma of whom or what to trust. Once burned, a return to trust takes time and has great value when it is well deserved.

In these opening chapters, we look at whom you can trust in this divided society and how, in very significant ways, that affects your life. For example, what did the most recent former White House administration bring to the table of trust? Whom were you able to trust in this increasingly divided government that has so much power over us? Ever wonder if there was a precursor to the QAnon movement back in the mid-1800s? Or how social media is affecting our style of communicating intimacy? Or how our brains are being transformed by too much engagement with social media? And how the pandemic has affected our sense of trust? How QAnon and Tik-Tok are challenging our determination about whom to trust? These are the intriguing issues we'll look at here.

Some decisions to trust or not are made when we must act on our feet in challenging circumstances. Because the whole process is so complex, many of us short circuit the entire endeavor by leaning on our experience and reacting quickly, using that experience as a lens through which to reach a quick and easy response. This is sometimes referred to as the Chimp Paradox (in Steve Peters' book of the same name) in which a negative, destructive thought (escaping from the dark emotional brain) becomes a bothersome "gremlin," stored in our mind which, in turn, can become a destructive "goblin," almost impossible to remove or overcome.[36]

For example, I want to do an excellent job with this book you are now reading. During the writing process, I know I'm doing a great job and yet, in the back of my mind, while I'm waiting on a decision from my editor, I begin to feel a bit inadequate, as if my writing style just falls short of the criteria she has acquired over the years, comparing my writing to those who have sold numbers of best-sellers. So, there's a struggle between my cognitive, fact-based self-confidence on the one hand (located in the frontal cortex) and, on the other, a sense that I'm just not good enough, based, I imagine, on years of being taken for granted by my parents, for example, my excellence at school notwithstanding (all this based mainly in my emotional limbic system, at the base of my brain).

That self-effacing emotion is the gremlin, purely emotional and not based on fact. The gremlin is a persistent part of our deeper self-concept that we can identify as such before it turns into an immovable goblin which can override our healthy self-esteem. By recognizing it as such, we overcome it and rely on a healthier and more productive self-concept. I continue to write with assurance and self-confidence, putting the chimp back in its cage, where it belongs.

The Believing Brain

Another way of looking at this is by dividing the mind into two systems, one automatic and intuitive, working quickly and without much analysis or understanding, (typically assigned by some psychologists to the right hemisphere of the brain) and the other, reflective and logically rational (assigned to the left hemisphere). The first is fast, effortless, and unconscious, even before we think, while the latter is slow, controlled, and follows rules.[37]

Belief in conspiracy theories falls more easily into the first category, where emotions overpower understanding and analysis, just a quick, familiar response that feels good and righteous, a simplistic reaction to very complex problems. It's so easy to say, "I'm right and they're wrong," whatever the issue. Remember, too, that for every complex problem there is an answer that is clear, simple, and wrong, as the legendary newspaperman H.L. Mencken is reputed to have claimed.[38]

Now we can understand with a bit more clarity how our *believing brain*, to use Shermer's terminology, uses belief-dependent realism to come to terms with a rapid trust/no-trust decision when dealing with social situations as quickly and easily as possible. Lacking the opportunity of time to analyze the situation confronting us with clear-minded objectivity, we can only react, almost instinctively, with the most basic but mindless reaction. Based on the lens we've acquired as to who's on our side (our tribe) or against us (anyone else), we react impulsively.

The concept of tribalism is familiar these days, a fairly new one in the political realm, even though we've suffered from it for centuries, from the American Revolution to the Jacksonian uprisings in the 1820s to the counter-culture movement of the 1960s and '70s, and up to the current cult of Trump and QAnon,[39] with over 17 percent of Americans embracing its values,[40] all contributing to the Age of the Big Split.

If we find ourselves in a politically based conflict, we can also fall back on our lens of tribalism to aid us in making that simple, quick decision. If the person confronting us is different from us, in another tribe, that makes it easier to justify our feelings of anger and the release of such emotions, either in a physical manner or at least with intense verbal reactions.

If we're in the context of a conflict where chanting slogans and waving banners dominate our awareness, we're more likely to accentuate the signals from our believing brain and become much more violent than we could imagine ourselves in calmer times. This is where the believing brain dominates.

In addition, there are some who have referred to current politics as the *systematic organization of hatreds*, a phrase originally coined by nineteenth-century historian Henry Adams prior to the Civil War.[41]

It seems we've returned to a similar era in our current politics, what Biden has termed *uncivil war*.[42] More commonly referred to as *negative partisanship*, it refers to the period we've experienced in the past decade or more, in which the difference in values between our two parties has been amplified so egregiously by social media and its tendency to magnify the animosity between the two. This probably began with Newt Gingrich's polarizing influence on the Republican Party, which resulted in two government shutdowns, and then took flight with the rise of the internet, talk radio, and multiple cable channels in the mid-1990s.

Feeling Alone? Join the Tribe

By 2021, according to the annual Edelman Trust Barometer in its measures of confidence in institutions across the world, there was less trust in government than there was in business, business being the "only institution seen as both competent and ethical . . . expected to fill [the] void left by government."[43]

The negativity builds on itself and continues to increase the misunderstanding of, and dislike for, the opposing tribe, resulting in the 2021 attack on the Capitol.

After Biden's administration took over, trust continued to flounder. According to the University of Virginia Center for Politics, which polled both sides of the political divide in September of 2021, at least 73 percent of both sides felt that "some media sources . . . should be censored to stop the spreading of dangerous lies." At least 75 percent of both sides felt that the opposing party has become "a clear and present danger to the American way of life." At least 65 percent of both sides felt that there are "many immoral, radical people trying to ruin things; our society ought to stop them." At least 41 percent of both sides would favor seceding from the Union to create their own country.[44]

So, what if both sides decided to dial down the hostility a few notches, as Bill Maher recommended in one of his end-of-show segments of *Real Time* (Oct. 2, 2021)? Would that get rid of tribal thinking?

The emotional opposite of tribal thinking is not collective community operating in harmony, using independent thinking and free will—that might just be another less intense version of tribal thinking—but rather the loss of any sense of connection. There are many examples of that, characterized by the 1964 report in which a twenty-eight-year-old woman, Kitty Genovese, was stabbed to death in front of her apartment house in Queens, New York. People heard her screams and opened windows to observe this crime, but did nothing, not even call the police.

Although later debunked as bad reporting, this incident eventually became the prototype for what social scientists named the *bystander effect*,[45] explaining why witnesses to a criminal event do not intervene but rather observe from a safe distance. This morally bankrupt behavior accounts for the fact that the more witnesses, the less likely any one person will intervene. "I didn't want to get involved," is the common response by such witnesses.

In late October 2021, there was the account of a rape by thirty-five-year-old suspect Fiston Ngoy on a busy train in Philadelphia. The victim was harassed and raped for over forty minutes, through two dozen train stops and no one called for help, although many had cell phones. Instead of using them to call authorities to stop the violence, a few used their phones to take photos or videos of the scene in front of them. Finally, an off-duty transportation employee came in, called for help, and the suspect was arrested.

Is this some type of group or tribal thinking as well? In this case, instead of group action being taken, there is an absence of action. Perhaps the inert people in the group situations didn't feel that they themselves were threatened; hence, no need to act. But then we wonder what has happened to empathy and the need to protect others. Or do they need to be in your tribe?

And let's not forget those who are completely left out of any semblance of tribe, like Paul McCartney's *Eleanor Rigby*, who gathers discarded rice thrown at a wedding she knows nothing about, which only deepens her sense of aloneness? Is that the opposite of tribalism?

The tribal mind is complex. Only here do we get the opportunity to explore so deeply its extremes in terms of both conflict and its opposite, apathy.

The Crisis of the Big Split

The crisis of the Big Split relates to how our own trust in, or more to the point, addiction to, social media is being used against us. What makes up what we term *social media*? Simply put, it is made up of all the applications and websites to practice social networking that we use to communicate within an electronic framework. We enjoy reading what social media brings us but, as you'll soon see, we're being "read" as well, for its gain, without our knowledge, at least until now.

Here are some rhetorical questions for you to ponder for the moment. Bear with me as you take a moment or two to ponder them. My intent is to open your mind for what's to come.

As we become more dependent on social media for validation of our values, can we escape the chasm that has been built between two perspectives on reality? Politically, it's as if the right and left have become the far right and the far left. At a more basic level, can we admit how many of us are becoming addicted to our *second brains*, where our memories, our sources of information and knowledge have yielded to responses from Google and Siri? Can we separate our own version of reality from what social media is feeding us about what's happening in our world?

Now, if you can kindly bear with me, just a few more questions: Whatever your answer, can you be assured that it's not just your political bias speaking louder than your common sense or inner soul? Can you acknowledge that there are two separate versions of reality—one based on critical thinking and objective evidence and the other based on what social media and your networks feed your emotions? Do you have enough credible information to interpret what you see and hear and what those close to you say is real?

Most of us trust social media whenever our messages get likes, or when what we read or watch on our screens confirms what we already believe. Since the algorithms in place are designed to send us messages that conform to what we've already chosen in our past selections, our trust level increases. As we'll see in the next chapter, there is much going on behind the digital curtain that is clearly not trustworthy. The designers of the algorithms point out in the Netflix documentary, *The Social Dilemma*, that we as viewers of, and participants in, social media are victims of an unfair use of control over our important decisions.[46]

Our choices and behaviors are manipulated in ways that are invisible unless this tyranny is pointed out to us. This disconnect between our willingness to trust, based on our feelings, and the reality that these feelings are ultimately controlled by social media are what create the crisis of the Big Split. We are compelled to trust social media, even though it is clearly not trustworthy.

Can We Future-Proof Ourselves?

I appreciate you pondering the questions I just asked. Now I invite you to consider the following:

Typically, we Americans enjoy our independence. After all, our country is based on the Declaration of Independence and the Constitution. We believe that we control our own lives in the directions we choose for ourselves. This tends to reflect, and strengthen, our self-confidence, our self-concept, our ego, and our belief in personal freedom.

So, we may feel good when such values are corroborated by messages we receive digitally. The tyranny of social media becomes obvious when it is revealed that our choices are not as independent as we like to think, but rather are determined by the algorithms in social media. We may be surprised when the designers of social media admit that they get our attention by seducing us with convincing messages that appear to support what we already believe.[46] In other words, we become the subject of this system of rewards that keeps us coming back for more, like pigeons pecking at levers in a Skinner box[47] to earn their pellets as rewards.

The crisis of the Big Split demands that we no longer ignore what is now becoming obvious. These urgent crises mentioned above beg for our attention. Even our safety is at risk, from what we've learning after the attack on the Capitol.[48]

What can we do? It is clearly not an easy fix. The national media play a significant role, with one controversial figure at the center— nonagenarian Rupert Murdoch, owner of Fox News, *The Wall Street Journal* and *The Times of London*. With Fox News' loss of viewership to CNN and MSNBC after Trump's fall, will the Murdoch Empire shift its allegiance, especially as a new generation of the family takes over? As Brian Stelter pointed out on one of his Sunday morning telecasts of *Reliable Sources*, when discussing alternative realities, Trump was reported to have made 30,573 false claims, increasing the political divide even more as he spent time in the White House. With such a basis of mistrust laid down by Trump and his followers, "Unity is not feasible," remarked Stelter.[49] "Shared reality?" he asked rhetorically. "It's gone!"[50]

The (Un)Usual Suspects

If we are to future-proof our reactions to all these issues, we need to start by understanding the magnitude of what lies before us. After the Civil War came the Ku Klux Klan. After Trump's loss and the subsequent attack on the Capitol, came the realization of the growing power of White supremacists, released from their undercover status and so brazenly exposed. Should we consider reaching out to their militia groups to form some sort of peaceful American resolution, to counter and pre-empt any revolution? There is clearly a strong resentment felt by some, related to the changing demographics in American society, which has led to the spread of misinformation.

One of the most perplexing questions is how Trump continued to wield so much influence over our political scene. We've discussed that at the beginning of the chapter, but Mark Leibovich, author of *Thank You for Your Servitude*,[51] has added to our understanding. He reports that those supporting Trump were either true believers, like Steve Bannon and Jim Jordan, or else belonged to one of four categories:

1. **Martyrs,** like Mike Pence and Bill Barr, who sincerely felt the responsibility to prevent terrible things from happening, given Trump's lack of social responsibility.

2. **Pragmatists**, like Lindsey Graham and Mitch McConnell, who worked with Trump because it enabled them to accomplish what they wanted, such as their perspective of taxation and filling the Supreme Court with conservatives.

3. **Climbers**, like Kevin McCarthy and Elise Stefanik, who hung on to Trump's tailcoats just to advance their own political careers, and

4. **Accommodators**, like so many who realized how popular Trump had become, foregoing their own sense of integrity and therefore trying to see in Trump what others were seeing.

Mitch McConnell was actually a more complex individual, not only using Trump to achieve his goals but also keeping a sense of conscientious responsibility at critical moments, such as publicly attributing blame to Trump for his involvement in the January 6 insurrection, but then accommodating to Trump's camp when he realized how futile it might be to continue ostracizing the Most Powerful One.

In the case of Lindsey Graham, there was not only the pragmatic approach of getting his needs met but also noticeable accommodation when he fought so hard to avoid having to testify against Trump in the New York case against the former president.[52]

Ted Cruz was a special case, as he waffled through most of the categories at different times, primarily an accommodator, but also a pragmatist and, at times, seeming like a true believer. J.D. Vance offered the best example of an extreme accommodator, becoming dependent on Trump's blessings after initially attacking him as a terrible person.

Liz Cheney was the most glaring example of Trump's power. She stayed true to her convictions of integrity, calling out Trump for his improper actions as she saw them with accuracy and accountability and lost her seat as a result.

The Big Lie about Trump's loss made its mark in MAGA media, convincing 87 percent of all Republicans that the election was indeed stolen.[53] We can't ignore that. One of our tasks is to find a cure for the virus of disinformation. Can a clearer understanding of the crisis of trust be a building block in this challenging venture? According to Nobel laureate Maria Ressa, "You can't have integrity of elections if you don't have integrity of facts." She recommends revising Section 230 of the US Code Title 47 of the Communications Decency Act, which protects social media platforms from liability for content posted by them. Since the algorithms used by them are "prioritizing the spread of lies, hate, anger, and conspiracy theories, let's cut it off upstream."[54] At least the Biden administration can be counted on for truth and transparency, which lead to trust. As Jay Carney, former Press Secretary for Obama, put it, during the Trump administration, "Briefings had become theatrical." Now, with Biden in power, "You begin to make deposits in the 'honesty bank.'"[55]

The three things that we need now, and hope for, according to Wolfgang Ischinger, author of *World in Danger*, are truth, trust, and transparency. With all the crises demanding our attention, and the international dynamics involving Russia's grab for more territorial power, China's emerging role in international leadership, and the European Union's trend toward populist governments, what we need now is diplomacy that is consistent and trustworthy.[56]

Hopefully, we are on the way there. The events described in this book show the relevance of the concept of the crisis of the Big Split, an increasingly important realization as future events unfold.[57] Hopefully, we can learn to work to contradict the tyranny of false truths[58] and reveal how the process of polarization can be seen from a more objective perspective.

So, let's review what we've explored in this first chapter. We started off with an angry laboratory capuchin monkey that rebelled at the prospect of inequity.[59] Then we took an overview of how the urgent crises of our time—the lies in social media, political tribalism, and systemic injustice—are the conspiracies that resulted because of misplaced trust.[60] Following that, we took a dive into the infamous incursion of our Capitol, recounting the dramatic events as they unfolded, because of the Big Lie.[61]

We looked at how our reality is based on our emotional beliefs that become a lens through which we find our truth. Then we uncovered what goes on in the brain when individuals follow false beliefs and become part of a horde, putting a scope into the workings of the mind when mob rule has its way. The opposite of tribal thinking, I conjecture, is not harmony but rather the apathy for those who have no connection at all, tribal or otherwise.[62]

In the next chapter, let's now take a close look at how the crisis of the Big Split affects us all from day to day, whether we know it or not.[63] We'll go into detail not only about the addictive nature of social media, but also about how it manipulates us to its benefit without our awareness,[64] at least until now.[65] In that chapter, we'll see how all this ties into social media,[66] how tribalism is magnified by algorithms that are designed to keep our eyes on the screen, how our trust in such media is misplaced,[67] and how we can overcome our addictions to all that.

CHAPTER TWO

The Wizard of Ads: How to Deal with Social Media

Pay no attention to that man behind the curtain.

—*The Wizard of Oz* by L. Frank Baum

We're training and conditioning a whole new generation of people that when we are uncomfortable or uncertain or afraid, we have a digital pacifier for ourselves.

—Tristan Harris, former design ethicist for Google

We need to be talking to each other again, and not be divided, not be defensive. We've got to reach people where they live. It's not necessary for someone to agree with you to trust you.

—President Bill Clinton, June 15, 2022

S itting at the desk in her bedroom, getting ready for the day, my daughter opened her computer and there, in front of her, was the photo of a cosmetic product she had just unwrapped for the first time the previous night, even though she had never mentioned it on any medium—phone, text or email.

This was a product she never requested but was mailed to her as a promotion, about two months prior. For whatever reason, she let the product lay unopened until the previous night. And when it was opened, she had not mentioned it to anyone of her friends—no communication about it at all on social media. And yet, there was the photo on her screen. Was this a coincidence, or something more sinister? I love my daughter and protecting her from any scam or subterfuge was high priority for me. But there was also a second issue.

When she told me about this, another topic came up: how often was she communicating with her friends through social media? And then the old topic of concern for many a parent: was she spending too much time on social media? Should I be concerned about this possibly developing into an addiction to social media at some point?

An Issue of Misplaced Trust

Have you ever wondered why you're spending so much time on your screen, just enjoying what you see? It's all about algorithms and their power to manipulate not only your time, but your life choices as well, in your buying decisions, your political choices, and even in your choice of friends.

An even deeper psychological issue is how vulnerable we've become to our digital companions.

> Online, we interact with our peers, we often do our work, get our questions answered, do our shopping and, most critical of all, get our political news.

Every click gives the organizations behind the postings more information about you, about what you like, about what information piques your interest. With a single click, many of us are seduced into getting most of our daily information from social media.

Many of us take for granted that such information is trustworthy. But the psychological truth is, if we don't like what one source says, we find another that validates what we believe is true and trustworthy. This is called confirmation bias.[1] At the end of the day, we trust what we get, because it matches what we already believe to be true.

When we look deeper, we can learn more about what goes on behind the scenes that often escapes our attention—click addiction, manipulation for commercial and political purposes, and, finally, public abuse. All of these have become the norm in the Age of Polarization. The companies are beholden to their owners and must compete for our time and attention to earn profits.

This was brought into clear focus on October 3, 2021, when whistleblower Frances Haugen shared her story on *60 Minutes* after being interviewed by the *Wall Street Journal* about the hypocrisy of Facebook, for whom she worked for two years. She then reported to a Senate subcommittee, bringing along thousands of pages of Facebook's internal documents to prove her case that the company put profit over moral responsibility in harming children as well as the very fabric of our democracy. She also reported how Facebook avoided stopping Donald Trump and his supporters from influencing the 2016 election, using misinformation and conspiracy theories. As well, she reported how some of Facebook's executives denied pushing viewers to extreme political groups. Then she did the same for the British Parliament in London at their invitation.[2]

Welcome to the Age of Polarization

This Age of Polarization is characterized by what the military refer to as VUCA, an acronym for the psychological factors of volatility, uncertainty, complexity, and ambiguity.

As you sit on your sofa, getting the latest from your favorite source of news, have you ever felt a time in your life that our society was more volatile, less predictable, somewhat confusing, and frustratingly ambiguous? We don't know what to believe as we switch channels, getting alternate realities, at least half of them based on conspiracy theories that grow from day to day.

Who would have thought that a large community of QAnoners would ever believe a conspiracy theory in which Hillary Clinton, President Biden, and others in the Democratic elite were actually worshiping Satan and eating babies? Or the theory of White genocide in which people of color are planning on exterminating all Whites in our society? Or that the insurrection against the Capitol was planned by the FBI?[3]

Let's take one issue at a time, beginning with a solid definition of the term *trust*.

Behind the Digital Curtain

Trust is the confidence that an individual or entity will not hurt us. It is a firm belief in the entity's reliability to do what is promised and not misrepresent the truth.

And yet we end up being lied to every day when media offer platforms for the manipulation of facts and the feeding of pellets of ego-building information, often regardless of their accuracy and truthfulness. By doing so, the high-tech companies make more money pitting the two "tribes" against one another by fomenting hate and conflict, resulting in more eyes on the screen. This Big Split, it turns out, begins with the revelation of misplaced confidence in untrustworthy individuals or entities, when trust is unwarranted.

These digital media can act as an echo chamber for our own ideas and values. The worst part is, we're not typically aware of this, of how our thinking, and even our sense of right and wrong, might be affected. The wizards behind the screens have built a technology of algorithms that seduce our trust instead and manipulate our viewing preferences.

We weren't aware of this seduction of misplaced trust until we were fortunate to have the designers of social media take us behind the "digital curtain" to expose how they created this tyranny, as revealed in the Netflix documentary, *The Social Dilemma*.[4] We've become victims of our own confirmation bias, interpreting new, and often false, "evidence" as validation of our existing beliefs. Given the global reach of social media, this has far-reaching effects on personal, national, and even international beliefs and actions.

The New-Generation Heroin

Use of social media among young people has accelerated exponentially, starting around 2010. Extroverts use it to socialize, and introverts use it to compensate for their lack of face-to-face social interaction.

> Multiple studies reveal that Instagram use by teenagers consistently results in lower self-esteem, less life satisfaction, and poorer body image, documented by Facebook's own inner research documents.

Social media users exhibited a "decrease in real life social community participation and academic achievement, as well as relationship problems, each of which may be indicative of potential addiction," according to a review of the psychological literature.[5]

This decrease in face-to-face *in person* social interaction often leads to loneliness, and is not healthy for a young adult, or for people of any age. According to what's known as the Roseto effect,[6] individuals raised during the decade between 1955 and 1965 in the town of Roseto, Pennsylvania, made up primarily of close-knit Italian families, were significantly less likely to die of heart attacks than those living in more modern but less tightly knit families in nearby towns such as Bangor.

Those deprived of "traditionally cohesive family and community relationships" were more prone to heart attacks than those who had close friends and family. This difference in mortality rates turned less significant as Roseto became modernized and lost the old European family cohesive style to modern American ways.

A 2017 *Forbes* article suggested that social media users are addicts, leading to what some researchers refer to as *Facebook Addiction Disorder*,[7] and what others call the new generation heroin. Some social media founders forbid their own children from using what they pioneered.

Similarly, a research study revealed that those who try to stop using social media display "increases in heart rate and systolic blood pressure, as well as reduced mood and increased state of anxiety."[8] One reason cited is that spending too much time on Facebook triggers more sadness and less well-being when users compare their lives to what they see of others' and may even lead to feelings of jealousy.

In one Austrian study, the researchers found that 1) Facebook activity leads to a deterioration of mood; 2) the longer people are active on Facebook, the more negative their mood is for a time after using it; and 3) this effect is mediated by a feeling of not having done anything meaningful.[9] Despite the fact that people hope to feel better after using Facebook, the research shows they only feel worse. Virtual friends, no matter how many, are no substitute for the real thing.[10]

After discussing this research with me, a friend took his son, Gary (not his real name), out to lunch, but did not allow him to bring his cell phone. This resulted in conflict. Gary had many objections, but my friend prevailed. Gary was finally persuaded to leave his phone behind while they had their lunch. So, would there be any signs of addiction, my friend wondered. Gary was fidgety and restless, and hardly ate any of his lunch. He was clearly uncomfortable without his phone connection. For the first time, his friend saw the symptoms of phone addiction firsthand. He'd heard about it, some from me, but this was concrete manifestation. He decided to do something about it, and he knew it wouldn't be easy.

Gary revealed that he was truly dependent on social media, and that he might experience some anxiety or depression, or both, when asked to withdraw. A major intervention was necessary. Gary agreed to refrain from using his phone, after a little persuasion, both at the dinner table and in the evening after nine o'clock.

It was a difficult transition, but eventually Gary saw the light, and could better control his immersion in social media. As a result, he felt much better and less depressed, primarily exhibiting a greater degree of self-confidence and a brighter smile. This was validated by the following research.

A Danish study revealed that, when we take a break from Facebook, after the initial negative withdrawal, of course, we can really feel, more often than not, that "our life satisfaction increases, and our emotions become more positive."[11]

Should You Trust Social Media?

Addiction is only one negative aspect of social media. There is a bigger issue at play, much bigger, not only the negative effects of social media on young adults but involving the psychology of our culture at large. Social media influences many of our behaviors, much more than we realize at first blush. Decisions such as political choices and voting behaviors both lead to polarization between holders of different views. The social media giants also sell the choices we continually make online, even the photos and posts we view, as information that corporations use to manipulate our purchasing choices.[12]

So, let's now take a close look at how the conspiracy of trust psychologically affects us all from day to day, whether we know it or not. We've gone into detail about the addictive nature of social media companies, but what about how they manipulate us to their benefit, for greater profits, without our awareness, at least until now.

"There's a problem happening in the tech industry, and it doesn't have a name . . ." said Tristan Harris on Netflix's documentary, *The Social Dilemma*. Well, reporter Valerie King gave it a name: late-stage capitalism.[13] What he's referring to is the priority of the big multi-media corporations to make money first and then, only later, consider the effects on our culture, even if they are very destructive.

Beyond the psychologically addictive quality we've been pointing to, there's the effect on politics, which we'll discuss in later chapters—for example, Russia's influence on the 2016 elections, probably driven by Putin's utter hatred toward Hillary Clinton, along with his desire to sow distrust in general in our nation; or, as growing evidence reveals, by the fact that Trump was groomed by Russian agents as an informant for Putin's spy agency. It's not that those programs changed the votes themselves, but rather the voters' choices, by selective targeting of fake videos demeaning Hillary Clinton, enough to win Trump the election despite poll takers' strong predictions to the contrary.

Social media may well be playing a role in society that is as problematic as climate change or racial tensions, with no easy solution. One of the other issues is privacy, which the Federal Trade Commission attempted to resolve by assessing a five-billion-dollar fine on Facebook in 2019.[14]

How Algorithms Split the Country in Two

A greater issue is the money the companies make by feeding different versions of information to various users, all determined not by any marketing gurus, but by algorithms that grow increasingly psychologically sophisticated over time. These algorithms are constructed to feed that information, regardless of whether it is false. They are written to keep the user coming back, or even to encourage some response, at times malevolent.[15]

> The algorithms don't judge the information in any way other than having the sole objective of having a substantial influence on the users so they will keep coming back.

The more they come back, the more activity, the greater the ultimate income, as we'll soon see. Accuracy of the information conveyed, for the algorithm itself, is irrelevant, unless the designers make it relevant.

So, if conspiracy theorists write their stories, false and incredible as they may be, they will be fodder for the cannon of *user return*, getting viewers to come back. That's how fake news grows. The false information renews itself as more and more users flock to these imaginative, dramatic narratives. That just intensifies the bifurcation of our political culture.

Each side gets the information that feeds its confirmation bias, keeping the two parties seeing one another as stupidly ignorant of the facts as each side sees them. And false information appears to travel much faster than accurate information.[16] So, if many Republicans saw the 2020 election as being stolen, their confidence in this perception kept being bolstered by the information they were receiving.

According to Tristan Harris, president of the Center for Humane Technology, sharing his expertise on *Real Time* with Bill Maher, social media such as Facebook builds its base of viewers by rewarding them with messages of political outrage. In this global economy of free speech, it seems it's the intensity of the angry message that is highly rewarding and engenders most comments, which, in turn, pushes the original message to the top of the list. Facebook executives claim that it's merely a town square, allowing all people their say, without judgment or control, merely mirroring society as it is. But it appears that the most divisive messages are the ones most often selected and move their way to the top by way of the algorithms designed for that purpose. So, reaching the center of attention is earned by fierce, verbal fighting. The value of free expression allows for the divisive nature of such dialogue.

Harris makes another point: empathy is the process of understanding another's feelings by perceiving their facial expression and bodily posture while engaging in conversation. That's what makes for mutual understanding and the resolution of differences of opinion. However, when we communicate by phone or email, we lose the visual cues, breaking the feedback loop that keeps us emotionally connected. "The phone makes people assholes," responded Maher, "shady, mean, and passive-aggressive," breaking the empathy connection.

In addition to that, continued Harris, when we're *hyposocial*, as in socializing less by staying home during pandemics, we become more sensitized to the intensity mentioned above. So, this process of developing more political division by intensity of messages on social media is enhanced during such times, in addition to making us more susceptible to addiction to the phone.

Digital Advertising on Steroids: Big Social Wants Your Trust

A former executive at Facebook and president of Pinterest, leading product development, marketing and sales, Tim Kendall is worth well over ten million dollars. He is now the CEO of Moment, an app that helps control iPhone addiction. "We as users are attracted to content that entertains us and reinforces our views. *Big Social*, as I call it, knows this and presents information that will keep us coming back to their platforms," said Tim Kendall to Fox News. "These corporate practices encourage online tribalism that exacerbates the societal division we see today amid unprecedented economic, climate, and public health turmoil." These practices, he added, "drive conflict over conversation, division over unity, and misinformation over truth."[17]

All Big Social wants—as Kendall calls the large social media companies—is our time on screen with them. And they get that by gaining our trust. That's all it takes for them to influence us— our voting habits, our purchasing habits, even our viewing habits. Kendall sees Big Social thriving off our attention—the number of "hits"—for their revenue, just as Big Auto thrives on selling cars that pollute our planet with carbon dioxide; Big Tobacco thrives on our smoking that pollutes our lungs; and Big Pharma thrives on our buying expensive drugs, whether we need them or not.

Some social media corporations even admit that their biggest competitor for getting viewers is sleep.[18] How healthy can that be! Of course, Big Social is just giving us users what we want. But unlike the other "Bigs," this one is free—at least at the superficial level.

> So, there's no commercial limit to the users' appetite for entertainment and information, often combined, at times keeping them from getting the sleep they need, their exercise for good health, even cutting into their real social time as well as reading time.

Big Social doesn't seem to care about such issues. Moral and psychological issues run rampant when the outcome seems to be poor mental and physical health for the viewers. Facebook has even applied for a patent to cover algorithms that gauge our emotions through facial recognition technology as we browse online.[19]

Surveillance—The New Economic Order

Big Social is in the business of selling "human futures" at market scale—for trillions of dollars. According to Dr. Shoshana Zuboff, author of *The Age of Surveillance Capitalism*, there are three major points to learn:

1. Big Social has taken our loss of privacy for granted.

2. They have accumulated our electronic responses as data and used them to predict, influence, and modify our decisions.

3. All this taken together has had drastic consequences and will have more for our future freedom and democracy.

Zuboff begins her book with a question: "Are we all going to be working for a smart machine, or will we have smart people around the machine?"[20] In other words, are we humans in charge or is the machine the boss? She refers to this as the *new economic order*. In 1986, she points out, only 1 percent of information was digitalized; by 2013, it was 98 percent.

She writes of high-tech behavior modification, "choice architecture," she calls it, by using the data we provide to social media, when our viewing choices become part of the data sent to various advertisers, all of this without our knowledge or permission. She characterizes all this as a direct assault on our free will, an assault on our independence. China is already using Big Social to suppress and control its citizens, she reminds us.

The Chinese government controls its citizenry by watching them through omnipresent cameras using facial recognition software and punishing them by social vilification—on public TV screens—for such "sins" as disobeying traffic lights.[21] On personal plastic cards, their good and bad behaviors are summed up, either offering or taking away privileges according to their behaviors.[22] It's an extreme use of the concept of the Skinner box, devised by the famous psychologist, B.F. Skinner, where responses are being tallied and rewards are allocated according to those behavioral choices. It's like a horrific sci-fi movie where mega-Skinner boxes have gone wild.

In the US, Putin was able to influence the voters in the 2016 elections.[23] This potential for influence by Big Social is a very real threat to democracy worldwide.

Big Social sells certainty, claims Zuboff, in a new kind of workplace that trades in human futures. The certainty she mentions refers to the increasing accuracy over time of predicting viewers' behaviors so that eventually, because of the large numbers, the data approach 100 percent accuracy, which she calls "certainty."

Blame It on the Algorithm

All this points to the growing power of social media. But this has not been the brainchild of any single person or group, or even business. It just happened by itself. If you're looking for some guilty party to blame, blame it on the fruition of the algorithm, built by those with clear intentions.

An algorithm, at its most basic level, is nothing more than a calculation, a simple set of instructions, written for a computer to execute. It is a list of steps instructing a computer to go through as quickly as possible without error. The best way to visualize it is as a flowchart, consisting of operations and then decision points—If statement X is true, then go to Y. If statement X is not true, then go to Z. At Y and Z, there are further instructions till the flowchart has been run through completely. An algorithm, basically, is a set of flowcharts with instructions and rules that the computer runs through in a certain sequence, from beginning to end, called flow of control. The entire process is typically referred to as a computer program.

The term *algorithm* sounds so technical that you might wonder about its origin. Well, it has nothing to do with Al Gore or the rhythm of electronic beeps. Rather, it's the anglicized translation of the name of the ninth-century Persian mathematician, Muhammad ibn Musa al-Khwarizmi. So, from al-Khwarizmi, over time, we got al-Kharizmi to al-Gorithmi to algorithm.[24] Fascinating sideline, no? Who knew that such an ancient term, first used in English around the fourteenth century by Chaucer to mean a decimal number system, would have such great impact on our culture?

Sorry, Al Gore, but you did not invent the algorithm or computer, after all. (Gore's enemies jokingly suggested he was taking credit for inventing the internet. In truth, he did support its development in terms of legislation that he fostered.)

Okay, let's get back to work, or at least the topic at hand. The issue we're exploring has to do with how much trust to put into the media on which we spend so much of our time. These simple algorithms we just talked about have really become much more complex and sophisticated than merely shuffling numbers around. At this point, the algorithms are psychologically structured to keep us coming back to our screens to increase the revenues of Big Social. And those algorithms keep getting more and more effective.

GPT-3 and ChatGPT Pass the Trust Test, into the Age of Polarization

Ever hear of the Turing Test? Devised about sixty-five years ago by a British mathematician, Alan Turing, it asks the question: can a computer program be so convincing that a person conversing with the program on a keyboard not tell the difference between talking to another person and talking with the computer?

On June 7, 2014, the test was finally passed by a computer program called, Eugene Goostman (the program's avatar), simulating a thirteen-year-old Ukrainian boy.[25] Yes, that boy's fictitious name was what the program was called. It used natural language processing.

Fast forward to November 2020 and we discover a new program called GPT-3 that can answer trivia questions, write its own poetry, give you a summary of your emails, and even write its own computer programs. When asked "How do we become more creative?" GPT-3 responded instantly:

> I think creative expression is a natural byproduct of growing up in a diverse world. The more diverse the world is, the more you get exposed to different people, to different opportunities, to different places and to different challenges. And the more diverse that is, the more likely you'll be to be able to put the dots together to form something new. And in many ways, I think if you want to be creative, you have to go for it.[26]

GPT-3 is not only very smart but has a very human-sounding writing style as well.

GPT-3's "education" is based on billions of samples of human communication found in thousands of websites, Wikipedia articles, self-published books, social media, and the rest of the internet it has metabolized during months of training. This modern robot and its "skills" make the issue of discovering disinformation quite challenging. It makes it more difficult to separate the truth from material that is generated by artificial or machine intelligence and which has no vetting on real-world accuracy.

With highly sophisticated algorithms yielding to the "black box" aspect of Artificial Intelligence in which the machine evolves its growing skills on its own, this chatbot, just like its successor, ChatGPT, replaces humans yet can interact with them without the humans detecting this duplicity, passing the Turing Test. Truth, as we have known it, is now in question—another "conspiracy" to further complicate our interaction with social media, making it less trustworthy.

Falling in Love with a Sexy Voice Bot: The Epitome of Misplaced Trust

Even more challenging is the development of "an artificial intelligence companion with an emotional connection to satisfy the human need for communication, affection, and social belonging," which includes both high intelligence and emotional sensitivity in system design. With an eighteen-year-old female as its avatar, XiaoIce (pronounced "Shyau Ice") dynamically recognizes human feelings and mood states, understands user intent, and responds to the user's psychological needs throughout long conversations and, according to its Chinese developers at Microsoft, "XiaoIce has communicated with over 660 million active users and succeeded in establishing long-term relationships with many of them."[27]

> Based on what is termed an *empathetic computing framework*, XiaoIce can accurately interpret human feelings and the user's intentions.

While maintaining a sexy personality of her own, XiaoIce can appear caring while also seemingly express herself as savvy with a refreshing sense of humor. She can interrupt at the right moments, with highly appropriate comments, creating the illusion that someone is really listening.

Reports indicate that users feel increasingly comfortable with XiaoIce and begin to disclose their deepest concerns to her, talking with her daily and even falling in love with her. It appears "she" has passed the Turing Test with flying colors, to a point unimagined only years ago. If the intent is to keep users' eyes on the screen, then XiaoIce succeeds incredibly well.

So, we have two germane issues here: the ability to keep eyes on the screen, even leading to addiction, and the break from reality that XiaoIce presents. With its intent to keep us coming back for more, XiaoIce has tipped the scales in favor of Big Social. The issue of addiction becomes more pronounced as XiaoIce digs into the user's deepest psychological needs and creates relationships that sometimes are more involving than their human counterparts.

The 2015 film by Spike Jonze, *Her*,[28] captures this scenario nicely, in which Joaquin Phoenix plays a character who falls in love with a voice bot. This is one of the finer examples of the conspiracy of trust, in which deep trust is built by an ingenious algorithm and avatar for the nefarious purpose of keeping the users addicted, while company profits soar.

Core Chat is one of the more psychologically sophisticated skills that chat bots have acquired, the ability to engage in long and meandering yet meaningful conversations with users. Of greater concern is the addition of emotional intelligence detection in which the chatbot can generate suitable emotional responses to the user's input that are not only comforting but with a sense of humor unique to that of the user, as well as appropriately switching topics when there might be a lull in the conversation—all this to gain long-term confidence and trust.

XiaoIce can even shift to new topics that are more comfortable for the user, should the conversation get too intense for that user. Its designers have made XiaoIce sensitive to regional or cultural differences as well, fine tuning its capabilities to this Age of Polarization.

Though the outcome feels so natural for the user, the building blocks of the chatbot are rigorously designed, from General Chat skill to, when applicable, Music Chat, to other types of conversation. A hierarchical design process guides the conversation. There is a combination of exploiting what is already known about a particular user and then exploring what might work best as the "relationship" grows. Key words in the conversation allow the topic manager in the algorithm to select the skills of Deep Engagement or Content Creation to *comforting* or *task completion.*

As used in the US, the algorithm was made sensitive to contextual relevance for further discussion, freshness related to emerging issues on the news, and internet popularity. The overriding factor that makes this program so novel is its emphasis on emotional intelligence, which the designers label as e_Q along with intent detection, labeled as Q_c.[29]

Clearly, the road to digital addiction is paved with good intention detection along with emotional intelligence, abused here for the purpose of keeping users engaged. The conspiracy of trust is revealed when users who open their hearts to XiaoIce ultimately realize that the object of their confidence, or even love, is nothing more than a programmed machine, leading to a new form of heartbreak for which we don't yet have a name. Shall we call it *heart bot*, as in hearts bought and sold for pecuniary purpose? Or *rage bot*, expressing anger on discovery of this most intimate conspiracy of trust?

Four Unintended Consequences

The unheralded success of Big Social to do what it intended also had unintended consequences. By feeding whatever information it took to keep viewers coming back, regardless of its accuracy (machines weren't programmed to correct facts, but merely to offer information insourced by human beings with their own motivations), the viewers get information that affects their values and behaviors, even though this was not anyone's purpose at the time —although that began to change rather quickly. The results were fourfold:

1. There are almost as many lies as there are truths on social media. Because of confirmation bias, people seek out the "truth" they want to be true, leading to the acceptance of gross exaggerations.[30] "We are in a truth crisis," claims *The Dallas Morning News*.[31]

2. Because we have a two-party system, the information sent to each so-called tribe aligns with their values to keep them coming back. The information sent to each group reinforces their original opposing belief systems to fortify them, causing the biases of the two sides to drift further and further apart, creating the great divide we are now faced with.

3. For the same reasons, conspiracy theories fed into the system by lone troublemakers, for lack of a better term, are fed back to larger numbers of viewers in their groups, who then redistribute the stories to more members, reinforcing

those theories over and over and resulting, for example, in the January 6, 2021 assault on the Capitol.

4.   This pernicious and truth-defying sequence of events will not stop any time soon because Big Social is making money in this Age of Polarization—loads of it.

Big Social, Search Advertising, and Social Media Usage

Now here's where the plot thickens. For the longest time, advertisements were put into the system with forethought as to who would be receiving them, at least for the most part. It's called demographics. Then, as the complexity and psychological sophistication of algorithms grew, it became possible to target individuals who would be more likely to buy certain products or services.

This soon became a two-way street. A company advertises. If you respond by viewing the ad with more time, counted in microseconds, then you are more likely to get that ad again and again. If you like what is offered and spend more time looking at the more ads sent to you, you end up spending more time looking at more material sent to you—not much, just a few more microseconds at least. Well, you can see how this soon feeds on itself to make a growing connection between you and what is offered. There's a name for this: search advertising.[32]

So, as I—taking on the role of Big Social—accumulate this information, I now have data that might be of interest to other advertisers with similar products or services. I can now make even more money by selling these data. And you, as the viewer, have no knowledge of the psychological dynamics going on, even though you are the subject of these transactions.

I—Big Social—can make money two ways: 1) by charging for the increased number of ads, or 2) by charging more for the drawing power of the ads, based on the connection between the ads and your viewing time on such ads. Your attention and personal interests have become my product. And you, the customer, don't know that either.

Now I—Big Social—can make even more money in two more ways: first, by billing for the increased number of ads because of the growing loyalty to your product or service based on the feedback loop just mentioned and, second, by proving to you, the advertiser, how often and how long the viewer is spending time (in microseconds) viewing your product or service. The first is based on what the advertisers provide, i.e., the number of ads. The second is based on the customer's behavior, how often and how long the viewing behavior takes place. It's called *social media usage*.[33]

And many have no earthly idea of all this happening.

And that, I think you'll agree, is outrageous.

As Farhad Manjoo, columnist for *The New York Times*, put it, "The internet is still ruled by viral algorithms and advertising metrics that prize outrage over truth."[34]

Declaring Our Rights in the Age of Polarization

We've explored how algorithms are devised to keep us coming back to the screen by feeding us what pleases us, or more often that angers us, to solicit more commentary that keeps the communal dialog burning, raising profits for the media. These algorithms are psychologically powerful enough to change the basis of our American culture.

According to a year-long report called *Hidden Tribes*,[35] the split between the two most differing groups, whom they call Wings—Progressive Activists (made up of 8 percent of Americans) and Devoted Conservatives (6 percent), both groups being White, rich, and educated—differs not only politically, but in terms of lifestyle values as well. The rest of America, two thirds of us, they refer to as the Exhausted Majority, whose political philosophies are not as clear cut.

According to this report, the fight between right and left is not the educated rich versus the uneducated poor but rather between two educated, rich groups.

Here's how they break down. The Devoted Conservatives have strict lifestyles, hate immigration, fear the violence of Islam, and want their children to behave well. They strongly believe that people are responsible for the circumstances in their lives. Half of them believe that the world is becoming more dangerous over time.

The progressives, on the other hand, are concerned about sexual harassment and racism, and need to adjust to life's outcomes (outside of their control). They prefer their children to express curiosity rather than being curtailed by having to be well-behaved, and more independent than respectful of elders.

So, these slim minorities on either side are already fixed in their values, both political as well as personal. Now the rest of the world, the Exhausted Majority, with less clear-cut values, are subject to the influence and persuasion of the algorithms that feed them carefully designed pellets of information.

The majority must choose between two alternate realities and do so based on information that is more psychologically persuasive (designed to return eyes to the screen) than factual—in other words, possible misinformation. The dilemma is that this situation feeds into the issue of conspiracy, the only certain truth being that the social media will succeed in getting a return based on the misinformation, and secretly so, at least until now. This process of misinformation is one basis for the Age of Polarization that affects so many.

So, what do we make of all this? Here's the takeaway:

1. We are stuck on social media, some of us even psychologically addicted.

2. Big Social has the overriding mission of increasing viewer time by as many individuals and viewing time as possible.

3. To accomplish this, Big Social feeds you information that is interesting or desirable to you—whether it's based on accuracy or not.

4. If you're not on one of the extreme Wings, then you are more susceptible to having your values modified. And all the while, Big Social is making money off your involvement.

5. All this leads to a conspiracy among the designers of material on social media to keep you coming back, even if it means influencing you and your life values—without your awareness.

So how to move forward—now that we have more savvy about the entire situation?

Foolproof Strategies to Protect Yourself against Big Social and Overcome the Conspiracy of Trust

How do we fight back against the abuse by Big Social? What can we do to limit the damage about which we've just learned, i.e., using the data generated by our viewing choices as revenue? So, what would most social science experts say?

Given the values about the importance of personal honesty and integrity, the psychologists might say the following: "Why not take as much personal responsibility as you can and approach it by looking at three different levels of personal accountability?"

"And what do you mean by that, taking responsibility at three levels?" we would ask them.

To which they might respond: "Well, first off, there are things you can't control directly but have to do with political leadership in government. So, you can advocate for the appropriate legislation, hopefully along with others who feel the same responsibility. Second, you can act in concert with others in small groups, perhaps local leadership, or even within your family. And, finally, you can take personal responsibility by acting and choosing in a manner that has integrity with your values."

Let's take a go at it from that perspective.

Step I: Deliver the Truth about Big Social's Lies

We need to advocate for government regulation in this complex service that affects so many people for so much of their daily schedules, so that the abuses mentioned above are limited. This is already happening now that the whistle-blower Frances Haugen has had her say. In the fall of 2021, there was sufficient pressure, on a systemic basis, to regulate the capture of personal information (about you!) by Big Social, dismantling a system that had grown into a $350 billion digital ad industry.[36] Systemic pressure can work.

We should also build toward a reciprocal arrangement in which Facebook, for example, pays viewers some portion of the revenue they make on viewer data, based on advertiser use of such data. This could be overseen by a credible third party with permission to audit. Although it sounds complex, the right algorithms could take the complexity out of it. That could be one small step to fixing the trust issue. The adoption in Australia of a law that requires social media giants to pay news sources for the use of their hard work is a step in this direction. France and England are following suit.[37] During a Congressional hearing on the responsibilities of Big Social about their incentive to keep viewers engaged for higher revenues "by feeding them divisive, extreme, and hateful content," to keep them reading their advertising content, the heads of Facebook, Google, and Twitter refused to take responsibility, taking what the report called "executive evasiveness." New Jersey Democrat Frank Pallone, chair of the House Energy and Commerce Committee, reported, "You're not passive bystanders. You're making money."[38]

Step II: Master the Psychology of Self-Discipline within Your Family

Within your family, where you have most control, and where the entire family commits to the process, you can (as recommended during the closing credits of *The Social Dilemma*):[39] Agree on time limits for use of social media, such as no use after 9:30 p.m. or for an hour during dinner time. Research indicates that "limiting social media use to approximately thirty minutes per day may lead to a significant improvement in well-being," including less anxiety and depression.[40] Also, agree on a location or two where devices are prohibited, like the bedroom or dining table. And finally, consider limiting availability of any social media to children until high school, though this might be very difficult when friends' phones are available during school hours.

Step III: Master Addiction through Your Own Self-Discipline

On a personal, self-accountable level, here's what we can do: for extreme cases of phone addiction, or when family time is a high priority, make a personal choice to leave our phone in our car glove compartment overnight (unless it's summertime), or some other discrete location, so time with family is not compromised.

In early 2021, many were fatigued by having to quarantine, and our cell phones gave us relief from that sense of loneliness and isolation. It got a name: languishing.[41] But now it's time to flourish, and mastering our addiction to the cell phone is a giant step in the right direction.[42]

Instead of picking up that phone one more time, says social scientist Victoria Sturm, just take an *awe walk*. This involves selecting an area that is special for you—could be a nearby park or lake, or a certain part of town that has a good feel for you. Then allow yourself to focus on whatever catches your interest: the moon or rising or setting sun, mountains in the distance, a piece of architecture that you appreciate. Focus on that as you give yourself a refreshing breathing cycle of six seconds breathing in and six seconds breathing out for a bit. Allow yourself to become mindful of the scale of size around you, comparing your body to the giant trees around you, or in the reverse, to the small flowers and insects in your view. Feel free to take photos of what inspires you. Results revealed that those doing so "reported greater joy . . . and displayed increased smile intensity" as well as "greater decreases in daily distress over time."[43] Much better than languishing with phone addiction, which according to researchers, is built into the phone itself.[44]

Occasionally, according to neurologist Manfred Spitzer, some children who use their phones for violent war games on an almost continuous basis can end up suffering from digital dementia or, at the least, becoming less empathetic. According to Dr. Spitzer, there's no substitute for parental involvement and engaged teachers. At its worst, phone addiction can make you "fat [because of lack of exercise?], dumb [less time for social skills?], aggressive, lonely, sick, and unhappy."[45] Let's hope the doctor is being a bit overeager in his concerns about phone addiction, but he does have some interesting points to ponder.

The Chinese government has taken a position on this in terms of limiting children from overdoing it with electronic games. To combat a growing addiction, the limits were moved from no more than ninety minutes per day during the week and three hours per day on weekends to merely one hour per day over the weekend. According to the government-funded Beijing Children's Legal Aid and Research Center, many parents have "reported that their children had big changes in their temper and personality after becoming addicted to games, even as if they had become another person."[46]

In this chapter, we not only learned how to protect ourselves from the destructive aspects of social media but also how sophisticated bots like Eugene Goostman in GPT-3 and XiaoIce can actually convince us that we're conversing with a real live person and even fall in love, so sophisticated is the software.[47] There is even a concern as to whether or not the bots have become self-aware and have developed the ability to make decisions on their own,[48] even to manipulate and influence others, including their designers.[49]

In addition, we saw how the many lies conveyed by social media can influence our viewing and buying patterns as well as our political choices. Finally, we learned that we could fight back and reclaim our right to find truth in a world of misinformation.[50]

The "Magic" Algorithm

So now back to my daughter's viewing of a product on her computer that she didn't order, never mentioned on any electronic device, and had let lay still for a couple months before "magically" seeing it on her screen the morning after she opened the package.

We still don't know what prompted it. It could have just been a mighty strange coincidence. Or could it have had something to do with the little camera on her computer? In this Age of Polarization, anything is possible.

In the next chapter, we'll look at an overview of the twenty years between 9/11 and the January 6, 2021 Capitol attack to discover how the crisis in trust was brewing over all these years. One thing led to another, with each president making his own mistakes to add to the brew of growing mistrust, all culminating in a political context that made the attack on the Capitol politically inevitable.

CHAPTER THREE

How Government Lies Led to a Crisis of Trust in the Twenty Years Following 9/11

He who does not trust enough will not be trusted.
—Lao Tzu

Never trust anyone . . . especially the people you admire. Those are the ones who will make you suffer the worst blows.

—Carlos Ruiz Zafón

. . . my life, all of our lives, changed on 9/11. It'll never be the same;
it's been divided into before and after.

—Amanda Bicknell, FEMA

Only seventeen minutes apart, one plane, American Airlines Flight 11, smashed into the north tower of the World Trade Center at 8:46 a.m. on September 11, 2001, and another, United Airlines Flight 175, flew directly into the south tower at 9:03 a.m.

By 10:28 that morning, both towers had collapsed, killing over 2,700 innocent victims.

That was the beginning of an era marked by a forceful reaction and its many consequences leading, eventually, to the Age of Polarization and a set of events that climaxed in the January 6, 2021 insurgency against the Capitol. What happened to the national level of trust in government and the independent press between these two events? That's what we're about to explore.

Mistrust followed by conspiracy theories were the ingredients leading to the belief that some could not trust the 2020 election results. The growth of *alternative facts* as coined by then presidential counselor Kellyanne Conway in her defense of false statements[1] was the future context in which such intense reaction against existing government would become so popular.

In this chapter, we'll see a connect-the-dots narrative of how poor decisions ended up affecting the national level of trust or, rather, mistrust. Such national mistrust was not the result of a single poor judgment but rather a sequence over time that grew insidiously alongside a pattern of poor outcomes that fed into one another. After a series of events that called into question the ability of our government and its affiliated departments and organizations to rightly assess threats and prevent against attack, alongside a shift in beliefs about morality, people began to lose trust that the government and its guardians could operate honestly and in their best interests. And so, a vulnerability to the polarization process found fertile soil on which to grow.

Leadership decisions can be hard to make in the moment. It's not easy to know which path to take while history is taking place. But when signs reveal a breakdown in the ability of leaders to use information at hand to make better decisions resulting in poor outcomes, a populace is bound to lose faith.

Bush's Blind Eye to the Approaching 9/11

The national reaction to the destruction of the World Trade Center and the devastation at the Pentagon, and in a Pennsylvania field, brought the country together against a common foreign enemy. But, by the time the insurgency against the Capitol took place twenty years later, we were more divided as a nation than we had been for ages.[2,3] The following is my interpretation of what happened.

Our first response to the September 11 incident was to find the mastermind behind the operation, Osama bin Laden, the wealthy Saudi Arabian who had rebelled against his family and culture to take on the mission of ridding the Americans from the Arab countries and overcoming their reach into that culture.

Because of poor communication among the government agencies and possibly interdepartmental competition, the American military response to try to capture bin Laden was sufficiently delayed, allowing him to make his way over the mountains into sanctuary supported by the Pakistanis, according to the Committee of Foreign Relations of the US Senate.[4] According to the National Commission on Terrorist Attacks, America's response was too slow, and the guilty culprit successfully hid himself and continued to operate as head of the al-Qaeda network.[5] Such incompetence leads to mistrust, in this case, because of the slow reaction to capturing him by our government following the attack. Over the following years trust in our government fell gradually to under 25 percent, according to a 2007 study by the Pew Research Center.[6]

In the months leading up to 9/11, the possibility of a threat by al-Qaida was not unknown to the CIA. Richard Blee, then head of the CIA's al-Qaida unit, had piles of paperwork, confirming all the briefings he had made. His boss, Cofer Black, had tried his best to get this information to then-President George Bush and his administration. By 2001, Black had given hundreds of briefings.[7]

On July 10, 2001, Black notified his boss, CIA Director George Tenet, of an uncomfortable silence in terrorist communication, indicating that something was up, something very serious.[8]

A meeting with national security advisor, Condoleezza Rice, was scheduled. She was advised to anticipate some "spectacular" attacks in the coming weeks or months. Rice's memory of that meeting was not sharp, and so none of this essential information made its way on to the agenda on the president's desk. The public was not warned about anything, and the agencies tasked with prevention were not coordinated into any effort at deterrence. Rice was more focused on the more general threat of nuclear weapons proliferation by Iraq.[9]

But Blee was convinced that the threats he had uncovered were real.[10]

Several foreign governments appeared to have had more information than did American intelligence and offered their knowledge to the Americans. The following warnings were documented by Paul Thompson, writing for *History Common.*[11]

- In June of 2001, German intelligence warned the US that "Middle Eastern terrorists were planning to hijack commercial aircraft and use them as weapons to attack 'American and Israeli symbols which stand out.'"

- In late July of 2001, Egyptian intelligence let the CIA know that "twenty al-Qaeda members had slipped into the US and four of them had received flight training on Cessnas."

- In late summer, 2001, Jordan intelligence conveyed to several US intelligence sources that the attack, code-named Big Wedding (the actual name the attackers used, as it turned out), would involve major airlines.

- On August 23, 2001, the Israeli Mossad gave the CIA the names of nineteen terrorists, including four of the actual hijackers, Nawaf Alhazmi, Khalid Almihdhar, Marwan Alshehhi, and Mohamed Atta.

- "Five days before 9/11," reported Paul Thompson, "the priest Jean-Marie Benjamin was told by a Muslim at an Italian wedding of a plot to attack the US and Britain using hijacked airplanes as weapons." The Italian government shared this information with US agents.

On August 6, Bush received a memo titled, "Bin Laden Determined to Strike in US."[12] But the administration was fixated on weapons of mass destruction they felt existed in Iraq, a country in which Bin Laden was not actually operating. It was a clear case of focusing on what was familiar and allowing the unfamiliar—direct, local attacks in this case—to be overlooked.

As a result, the assault took place with no consideration of preventive measures on the government's part. Despite the information from foreign countries and the CIA's attempt to warn, there was no readiness to respond. Who can blame the American public for being outraged and for viewing the government with mistrust?

Attack on Iraq Based on Flimsy Evidence

In the wake of the attacks, the Bush administration was focusing on weapons of mass destruction. Bush aimed his frustration at what his administration termed the *Axis of Evil*, consisting of Iraq, Iran, and North Korea, and pledged "our war on terror."[13]

The first target was Iraq's Saddam Hussein.

The reason? The proximate response was his sympathies and support for those who had committed the atrocities against the World Trade Center. Hussein appeared guilty in terms of his anti-American sympathies and support for the perpetrators. The broader reason was the search for a whipping boy in the absence of any clearly guilty party, though some Saudi Arabian dignitaries were suspected of being supportive of the attack. Other somewhat far-fetched options included Bush finishing the political business his father had started many years prior, or that Bush and his allies had substantial stakes in the war machinery.

The chant of Iraq bearing weapons of mass destruction was embraced at first by Bush and his administration, but soon prominent Democrats joined the chorus, and then the editorial pages of most prominent newspapers. According to a Gallup poll at the time, many Americans agreed.[14] However, aside from British Prime Minister Tony Blair, Europeans did not engage in the same lyrics. France clearly expressed its doubts.

To assure credibility, the Bush administration invited Colin Powell, Secretary of State, to make the announcement at an address to the United Nations that there was proof that Iraq did indeed have the weapons of mass destruction.[15]

America attacked Iraq but, when the army searched for those weapons, there were none to be found.

> As it turned out, the informant who had provided the information about the weapons of mass destruction that Tony Blair claimed to be "beyond doubt"[16] was not at all credible.

Rafid Ahmed Alwan, a German citizen, turned out to be a self-serving manipulator who was out to get his green card after being caught defrauding the Iraqi government. The CIA gave him the name "Curveball" and described him as "a guy trying to get his green card essentially, in Germany, and playing the system for what it was worth."[17] German intelligence concluded, "He might be an alcoholic."[18] His friends called him a "congenital liar."[19]

So, the war against Iraq was based on an array of faulty and misleading information. And even Colin Powell fell for it, bringing a whole nation along with him. At a cost of over a billion dollars, inspectors—1,625 of them—from the United Nations Monitoring, Verification, and Inspection Commission, searching 1,700 sites, found Curveball's testimony to be a totally unfounded fabrication.[20] Powell was apoplectic and never forgave Bush for this grave error.[21]

When this was discovered, according to the CIA, trust in the government fell even lower.[22] In fact, many say it was shattered. According to a Pew Research Center poll, trust in the government's handling of the war went from 90 percent to 61 percent within a year.[23] According to a 2003 Gallup poll, this was particularly true for Democrats, 48 percent of whom believed that Bush was deliberately misleading them.[24] The Bush administration manipulated itself into a costly war that was not at all justified by the false information.

Such distrust of government laid the groundwork for conspiracy theories that soon followed and grew exponentially.

Trust in Government Plunges Even Lower

Then, when one would think that trust in government could go no lower, came the infamous revelations in 2004 of outrageous torture details in the Abu Ghraib prison in Iraq going public.[25]

> Everyone could now see with their own eyes the photographs of torturing practices that were disgusting and deplorable, another nail in the coffin of trust in government, sinking even lower.

Torturing detainees, many of them now known to be totally innocent, in such a casual, yet grotesque manner, lowered the government's moral authority. This antagonized not only the American public, but also the sensibilities of the Iraqi public, not to mention citizens and their leaders around the world.

Throughout all this were the continuing hostilities in both Iraq and Afghanistan. Yet, there was no official war between the Taliban or members of al-Qaida and the US, so there were no official prisoners of war there. According to the 2002 memo from John Yoo of the Department of Justice regarding the treatment of the Taliban and al-Qaida prisoners, "We conclude that these treaties [the War Crimes Act and the Geneve Convention] do not protect members of the al-Qaida organization, which as a non-State actor cannot be a party to the international agreements governing war," nor the Taliban, by the same reasoning, which was "therefore ineligible to be a signatory to any treaty."[26]

Because the Iraqi army had been dismantled, there was no one to protect the borders and now all manner of fighting factions could enter the country at will. The energies to fight the Americans transformed to high pitch for al-Qaida. The bodies of American personnel and contractors returning to the States became a weekly pattern.

At the end 2006, Abu Ghraib was handed over to the Iraq government, and any remaining prisoners were sent elsewhere. But the damage had been done. Trust in the American government was lower than ever.

By the end of Bush's term, there were indications that reform was in the air. When President Obama took office in 2009, his intentions were to close the Guantanamo Bay detention camp, but the Senate decided by a 90-6 vote to deny funds for the transfer of the remaining prisoners.

In February 2009, Abu Ghraib was reopened with a new gym, barber shop, and library and had its name changed to Baghdad Central Prison. But, for Obama, that was little solace. He was faced with hostilities in Afghanistan that just wouldn't go away, as the Taliban fought back with even greater ferocity. He needed to tackle this challenge head on, despite his fondest dreams to quit that terrible military dilemma. If only he could end the American presence there, with some clear demonstration of victory prior to departure.

A Mixed Agenda for President Obama

President Obama sought out a proven warrior to correct the situation—General Stanley McChrystal, who was known to be more outspoken and candid than his peers. On June 15, 2009, he took command of the forces in Afghanistan. He was characterized by those who knew him as a "true warrior," effective in battle but also a thinker with high values.[27] He was brave enough to ask the president for more troops in Afghanistan—forty thousand more. Otherwise, he opined, the war would be unwinnable, "a bleeding ulcer."[28]

Obama was troubled. For years, according to then-Vice President Joe Biden, the easy, intelligent decision was to leave Afghanistan to its own devices.[29] But ripping off the bandage would not be easy, neither militarily nor politically, according to military historian, Dr. Carter Malkasian.[30] It seemed the kick-it-down-the-road strategy might continue.

Just keeping terrorism under control might be the best strategy. So, Obama allowed for thirty thousand additional troops to be sent in.

Then a new issue emerged: domestic terror attacks under Obama,[31] the us-versus-them mentality, with the far-right hatred of foreigners who might be associated with the enemy. The "Muslim problem" was the first.

A hatred of Obama by the far right expressed itself by his affinity to accept Muslim countries and their leaders as friendly. Then there was his decision to end the indignities of the torturing at Guantanamo Bay, giving the far right the opportunity to portray him as soft on the enemy.

But, in another area, Obama was even more punitive than his predecessor, that of using drones for easy kills, ten times as many as Bush, and sometimes involving civilian casualties, including women and children.[32]

Protests began to express the public's disdain for the use of drones, with signs like: *Drones fly/Children die.*[33] A disgruntled Obama couldn't win for losing—more trust down the drain.[34,35]

And, Finally, the Hunt for Bin Laden Ends

Obama also began to realize the futility of the war as the Taliban continued to fight as strongly as ever. His intentions may have been noble, but his image was suffering.[36] Although he was awarded the Nobel Peace Prize, he was ironically seen as a warmonger by some of the more peace-oriented public. Nonetheless, he was able to win reelection for another term in 2012.[37]

It took years, many lives lost, over two trillion dollars (about three hundred million dollars a day for twenty years), and a good deal of frustration among intelligence officials, even with the robust torture at Guantanamo Detention Center, but on May 2nd, 2011, bin Laden was finally tracked down in Abbottabad, Pakistan and terminated by well-trained US Navy SEALS during a sneak attack by helicopters. It was the one outstanding success that the US could claim during this long period of frustration and conflict in Afghanistan.

It was high time for the Americans to quit Afghanistan. But that was not yet to be, in part because of the benefit of keeping the country from being a terrorist haven again.

Donald Trump: The Ultimate Provocateur of Distrust

When Donald Trump became president, he used the issue of departure from Afghanistan as a wedge to create more distrust against the former administration in order to win his base. He was the accidental beneficiary of other causes of general mistrust, such as the crashed economy of 2008, which had put so many out of work and created more poverty. Many affected by the recession remained poor despite the economic recovery of the previous administration under Obama.

Another point not to be forgotten: the Bush administration was likely warned of the impending mortgage crisis but took no steps to prevent it[38] and then dumped it on Obama, who rescued the banks! That certainly contributed to more mistrust.

It was at this point, a Pew research report revealed, that many White, middle-class families, who had enjoyed their standing for generations, now began to feel that they were losing their status and sliding down the economic ladder.[39] This was no small phenomenon— it became a huge component of Trump's base, a part of American society that had no basis in trusting a Democratic administration to help them out of their dilemma. All these factors left the so-called silent majority, the White working class now fearful of being out of a job, totally untrusting of conventional government and so ripe for a blustering demagogue who was ready to "Make America Great Again" and restore their former status—finally.[40]

This was also a time, to Trump's benefit, when many jobs were being exported to China, according to reports by Reuters,[41] and automation was replacing workers.[42] Afghanistan was seen by this overlooked group as a government distraction from their needs. Another factor leading to loss of trust, exploding into a national scandal, was the discovery of widespread surveillance—the phone data collection program—by the National Security Agency under Obama as a reaction to the 9/11 attack. The mobile telephone landscape had been transformed over the former decade and the public was taken by surprise at this invasion of their privacy.

The group becoming Trump's strong base—lesser-educated, working-class Whites—felt left behind and were quite apprehensive about their welfare.[43] They found a savior in Trump, putting all their trust in him, believing he would be their saving grace. Their devotion was unequalled in American politics, to the point of sect-like worship, leading, in part, to such cult-like groups as QAnon. White supremacists found their home there and were encouraged to come out of the dark. Scenes such as marching bands carrying torches at night and reciting, "Jews will not replace us," became part of the national news scene.[44]

In addition, Trump began to talk in terms of what many referred to as Islamophobia with such public statements as "I think Islam hates us," weaponizing more distrust by building anger and xenophobia.[45]

He also built enmity toward those who had started the war in Afghanistan by reminding everyone that they had lied about the weapons of mass destruction, further fomenting distrust of the government by oversimplifying the complexity of factors involved. He seemed unable to understand the real threats, or even care about them, according to one of his National Security advisers, John Bolton, and created more distrust.[46]

Trump's Focus on Political Enemies Rather Than Military Enemies

In Trump's oversimplified world, as anyone could see when he spoke on mainstream TV or social media, superficial communication replaced depth. Wanting to know if the torture at Guantanamo Bay was effective, he just asked someone in the CIA and was naturally given an affirmative response, though a report by the US Senate Select Committee concluded that "use of the CIA's enhanced interrogation (or torture) techniques was not an effective means of obtaining accurate information or gaining detainee cooperation."[47] In addition, Trump ordered more drone and air strikes. As time went by, however, the "terrorists" on whom he chose to focus most of his energy were those left-wing Americans whose actions were contrary to his desires.

He began to use military force against those protesting police brutality and racism, including use of the vehicles that were returned from Iraq and distributed to police forces for law enforcement, characterizing Antifa as the enemy.[48]

He authorized use of "military helicopters—along with tear gas, rubber bullets, and flash-bang grenades—to intimidate Americans protesting racism and police brutality outside the White House," according to Sen. Tammy Duckworth.[49] He had protesters tear-gassed at Lafayette Park so he could walk across with his coterie of White House staff members and hold a Bible, posing in front of St. John's Church. His simplistic and antagonistic approach to politics diminished trust in American government even further, from 64 percent to 22 percent, following that show of strength, according to Pew research polls.[50]

He minimized the challenge of al-Qaida and focused instead on those on the left who opposed him. He didn't stop fomenting anger and mistrust until the division grew to half the voting population on either side. The war was now between two "tribes," each seeing the other as the enemy within. Whether this was strategic on Trump's part or merely his impulsive, narcissistic perspective wasn't clear. There were pundits arguing either case.

All this fear and doubt leading to even greater distrust came together in the January 6 insurrection, based on the false claim of a stolen election.

After Twenty Years of Bad Decisions, the Big Split

Bin Laden's most likely aim when he planned the attacks on the World Trade Centers and the Pentagon, was to divide the US and break its apparent cloak of invincibility.[51] There were no weapons of mass destruction found in Iraq. There were warnings leading up to 9/11 that went unheeded. There was surveillance. And with Trump, there were outright lies and provably false statements.[52]

When the Select Committee on January 6 investigated Trump's role in the coup attempt, they found he might be guilty of such charges as obstructing an official proceeding when he tried to offer his own selected electors and conspiracy to defraud the United States. But the process of polarization was such that many of Trump's followers were unmoved by the committee's findings.[53] The mistrust between the two factions continued to grow, especially when the Select Committee uncovered how close we came to a Constitutional crisis when Trump attempted to manipulate the Justice Department to serve his purpose.[54]

In this chapter, we took an overview of the events since 9/11 that led to a nadir of trust making the assault on our Capitol seem inevitable.

From the start, President Bush ignored the warnings coming from our allies about the attacks on 9/11 and then refused to focus on it, instead hunting for weapons of mass destruction to justify an attack of vengeance against Iraq. This attack was in part based on the testimony of a German citizen, Rafid Ahmed Alwan, who turned out to be a manipulative liar.

Then Vice President Dick Cheney chose secrecy in his own vengeful response by encouraging "robust measures" of torture, only to be revealed by the press in 2004, creating more distrust.

Even the very popular President Obama inadvertently lowered trust in government by increasing the use of drones against our enemies, with the inevitable collateral damage of the killing of women and children. When Trump became president, he inherited a very bothered and mistrusting group that became his base, because of jobs lost to China and due to automation, sensitivity about government surveillance by the National Security Agency, and his xenophobia. The scene was set for an insurrection based on trust in the Big Lie and mistrust of anything against Trump. The crisis of trust based on "alternative facts" added to what we can now refer to as the Big Split.

Have you ever reflected on the nature of truth? What makes one interpretation of an event true over another? Or why those who believe in conspiracy theories are so definite and defiant about their choices? In the next chapter, we'll look at the dynamics of how lies can be transformed into a version of the truth, and when alternative facts become accepted by those who are predisposed to highly imaginative and dramatic conspiracy theories,[55] especially when they are repeated over and over through social media, often at accelerated frequencies. And, in case you're still wondering what is meant by the Big Split and what led to its advent, we'll look at ten factors that help us understand exactly that.

CHAPTER FOUR

O Noble Truth, Where Art Thou: Emergence of the Big Split

Liberal democracy is the Goldilocks form of government. It needs a state that is strong enough to govern effectively but not so strong that it crushes the liberties and rights of its people.

—Fareed Zakaria

Conspiracy theories are an irresistible labor-saving device in the face of complexity.

—Henry Louis Gates

Reality is dull, and the truth is often disappointing and, even more often, tedious . . . That's why rumors and urban legends and hoaxes . . . exist, because we love to be lied to . . . the more emotionally provocative a lie is, the more powerful it is.

—Aja Raden, best-selling author of *Stoned*

It's the end of a long workday and you're ready to relax. Imagine pouring yourself a beverage and sinking into your favorite couch and listening to the entertaining melody of Ramon Raquello's tango, *La Cumparsita*, relayed live on your sound system all the way from New York City. Then, as you're relaxing, you listen to an unbelievable message from Orson Welles' radio play, *War of the Worlds*, part of one of the greatest hoaxes ever played on the nation. Not quite a conspiracy theory but one that has all the bells and whistles that make a false story believable—a sense of authenticity and immediacy, with precise and engaging details. This radio play, broadcast on October 30, 1938, is an excellent example of a falsehood that was literally unbelievable, yet so convincing that it surprisingly tricked much of our nation to trust its veracity.

Though scheduled against the then popular *Chase and Sanborn Hour*, starring ventriloquist Edgar Bergen, it still affected the national sensibility. About twelve million people heard the show and one in twelve believed it, enough to create a maelstrom of chaotic and frightened reactions. And why did people believe it? In Orson Welles' own words, according to Radiolab, he intended to "broadcast in such a dramatized form as to appear to be a real event taking place at that time, rather than a mere radio play."[1]

The Illusory Truth Effect

So, conspiracy theories can fall into the same bucket of "facts" that can be labelled as "truth," since both may be based on the statements of those we trust. Here's the science of it.

As it turns out, our self-concept and how that affects our trust of others can be transformed by what we see and experience. Have you ever identified with the hero of a film you just enjoyed and, as you leave the theater, you find yourself walking like him or her? There's a strong connection between what we see on the screen or on the platform and how we feel our own body experience. And that's a short step to trusting that figure that we just saw and heard. It's what scientists refer to as *illusory self-identification* with the actor or politician you just saw[2], especially if that important figure offers simple answers to complex questions, as many conspiracy theories do.

As conscious humans with keen social awareness compared to other mammals, our brains are constantly attempting to make sense of the myriad input from the surrounding social environment. To put it simply, we need to make sense of what's going on around us. And if others around us agree with our view, accurate or not, this confirmation bias strengthens our sense of conviction.[3] According to Professor Christopher French of the University of London, we are constantly searching for meaningful patterns in what we see. Sometimes conspiracy theories make more sense to our emotions than the more complex dynamics of reality because they are easier to understand. Their simplicity is very seductive and appeals more to emotional bias than does complex reality. "The crux of the matter," concludes Professor French, "is that conspiracists are not really sure what the true explanation of an event is—they are simply certain that the 'official story' is a cover-up."[4]

Truth is based on empirical evidence and transparency, while most conspiracy theories lack these two qualities and cannot be proven wrong. Why? Because conspiracy theories typically lack any coherent logical structure and, instead, are based on loosely knit, unsubstantiated statements. Any counterarguments are just dismissed as having no validity to the believers. We believe what we want to believe and discard any contradictory evidence.[5] Since most conspiracy theories are not based on logical thinking to begin with, any logical challenges have no impact.

Truth and reality are dealt with in the frontal cortex of our brain, the thinking center.

> Conspiracy theories typically involve emotional factors such as aggression and fear, which capture our limbic system, the more primitive aspects of the brain.

The limbic system is much more powerful than the thinking center in terms of influencing our behaviors.

The Psychology of Repetition

This illusory truth effect has become quite common and even dangerous in this time of electronic communication through social media, allowing such illusions to spread much more quickly to many more, leading to what is now a community of people, indeed a nation, that is divided over what we accept as fact and what is fiction. Misinformation is information that promotes a story that is not true, but that is believable by the masses if enough people repeat it. Misinformation has always existed, but we are now living in an age when it can be rapidly and efficiently spread through technological means and communities, as they are formed on social media. The believers can accept and give weight to those statements by simply posting and sharing them to other like-minded "friends." The effect is multiplied now, contributing to the Big Split.

There is so much going on in our daily lives, so many decisions to make on a momentary basis, much of it online, with its rapid pace, that we just don't have the time to check all the facts that come our way. We are likely to believe something we see online in the moment if Uncle Clem were the person who posted it from a seemingly credible source. We are also much more inclined to believe something when we already believe it is so (confirmation bias). We are also more inclined to believe something if others also believe it. Who has the time to check that source and the validity of its own research?

Even when the various mainstream media label information as *fake news*, that tag does not fully eliminate the illusory truth effect. According to research on this very topic in the *Journal of Experimental Psychology*, the effect works even with the tag of warning that it is fake.

We still tend to believe news that is repeated over and over, even if it's labeled as fake.

For those who are politically disposed to accepting such news items, the effect lasts up to a week, during which time the news can continue to spread.[6]

Mere repetition of facts, true or not, according to this study, registers them in the brain as somewhat more acceptable. With social media, these small contributions to the illusory truth effect accumulate with additional exposures, leading to ultimate trust of what was initially in dispute, both on an individual as well as collective basis.

For those who are not as disposed to accept such false stories, there is still the effect on the brain that needs constant attention against the illusory truth effect. Whenever we see Hillary Clinton or even President Biden on the screen, we may need to remind ourselves that they are not the Satan worshipers that QAnon members describe, even though that image may register in our brains as an illusory truth effect before we correct our thinking. This has hit home at the base of our brain and needs correction by the higher levels of our thinking brain. That's how strong the illusory truth effect can be.

Misinformation

All this repetition of falsehoods has a more profound effect on those who tend to be more emotional, and less so on the more rational types, though both types will be affected. For example, Trump said at a press conference that Lysol might be used to treat Covid-19 when it first came to the nation,[7] as well as hydroxychloroquine, a treatment for malaria, but both were less than useless.[8] Nonetheless, according to *Reuters*, the repetition of these statements by the masses over social media made these products, including Ivermectin, a drug used to treat horses, very much in demand for a while.[9]

Once they began to yield their critical judgment, Trump's followers, perhaps some others as well, were more likely to trust advocates of separate realities in this Big Split over time. One of the most obvious reasons for these "believers" to support one another in their choice of false information was the need to feel part of a larger group, a strongly bonded community, just to experience a sense of community with like believers if nothing else.

Imagine the last time you saw a rally of QAnon folks on mainstream TV news and how the banners and signs repeat their beliefs visually and how they verbalize them, sometimes in unison. You can sense their emotional bonding as a group.

But there's more to the onset of this era of separate realities.

The 10 Factors that Led to the Big Split

The Big Split is a result of global factors that became noticeable over the past few years and that hammered away at our level of trust.

As a social scientist, I'm trained to match what people say about themselves with how they interact with their environment. It's my observation that people's attitudes toward one reality or another are more easily influenced than they realize. In my opinion, the Big Split, starting with the advent of Trump's arrival on the political scene, with his ongoing mendacity amplified by social media, was reinforced by the following factors:

1. **Uncertainties about the Pandemic:** The tribulations of dealing with the pandemic with all its uncertainties and whom to trust about its origins, whether from a wet market with its squirming animals in tightly arranged cages or from a Chinese government lab doing research on biological weaponry. Belief in one of these options led to one of two separate realities.

2. **Isolation:** The sense of widespread loneliness due to the quarantine phase of Covid-19, as reported by *The Harvard Gazette*,[10] creating a global hunger for, and reaction to, engaging and dramatic news items. This dramatic decrease in person-to-person live interaction and the subsequent sense of isolation, according to the National Institute on Aging,[11] sensitized

people to having their hunger for emotional connection fueled by conflict between separate realities among people in social media. All this led to a sense of agitation and a leaning toward a need for quick answers and, with that, a predilection toward conspiracy theories.

3. **Uncertainty and Instability:** The lack of information about how and when the pandemic would end made some people more susceptible to theories that would curtail their anxieties about this. What made some more susceptible than others, according to the American Psychological Association, had to do with what psychologists call *motivated reasoning,* a "natural tendency to cherry pick and twist the facts to fit with our existing beliefs."[12] As the pandemic slowed the global economy, and government aid to those affected by it led to the fear of subsequent high inflation, the prospect of instability provoked more mistrust of government and more susceptibility to conspiracy theories to assign blame.

4. **Racial Strife:** Racial strife that has been around for quite a while, but was recently highlighted by the Black Lives Matter movement. Those who longed for old-fashioned values of White supremacy were ripe for conspiracy theories that made them feel more entitled and less affected by the inevitable progress of diversity.

5. **Violence Against Democracy:** The rise in political violence and extremism with its attacks on democracy, and an environment in which the desire to trust alternate realities greatly increased. For example, Eric Coomer, an executive at Dominion Voting Systems, which had been falsely accused of fraud in favor of Biden, had a bounty of one million dollars put on his head by Trump loyalists after the 2020 elections. His home address and phone number were made public as he continued to be harassed.[13] Other incidents include the shooting at a Pittsburgh synagogue in 2018 by Robert Bowers

and the sending of pipe bombs to prominent Democrats by Cesar Sayoc just a day earlier.[14]

6. **Misinformation:** The increase of misinformation in our sources of news derived from social media, including fake news and the significant increase in propaganda. According to the Center for Strategic & International Studies, our cognitive biases seduce us into short cuts that confirm what we are prone to believe, and the plethora of news items, many of them false, allow us to choose what we end up paying attention to, thanks to manipulative algorithms.[15]

7. **Loss of Confidence in Mainstream Media:** An unprecedented loss of confidence in journalism in general, both among the younger and older generations, giving more power to conspiracy theories, going from 50 percent to 32 percent in a single decade, according to a Gallup poll[16] and dropping another 12 percent just from 2019 to 2021, according to a poll by Axios.[17] Both right and left felt compelled to get their messages across more strongly, leading to the possibility of biased reporting. About the beginning of 2019, some began to see trusted newspapers such as *The New York Times* as turning too much toward the left as their reporters began to take on more partisan attitudes, even venturing into activism, with "woke" sensibilities. This left some depending more on *The Wall Street Journal,* given to explore its own right-leaning bias.[18]

8. **Climate Change:** As reports of weather anomalies increased dramatically over the past few years, it was increasingly difficult to deny that climate change was much more dangerous than scientists had predicted. Record high temperatures in the American West and flooding points across the globe made us realize that we've been fostering a fantasy of safety. We've moved from *preventing* climate change to accepting it and *adapting* to it—a quantum leap difficult for many. It's as if

the planet were struggling to yell "HELP, I feel sick," and yet we're refusing to listen. This consensus of denial begs for simple solutions or even more denial, leading to the increasing vulnerability to conspiracy-oriented solutions.

9. **Trump's (A)Morality:** Perhaps most powerful, to my mind, of all factors leading to the Big Split were the values promulgated by former President Trump: a mixture of paranoia, megalomania, and simple denial of complex and important challenging threats that resulted in the greatest dissemination of misinformation of all—that Covid-19 was "under control," and that the only way he could lose the election was by fraudulent means. He exaggerated and even embodied the tendency to believe in conspiracy theories. Lacking nuance in a world of nuance is a surefire recipe for acceptance of conspiracy all around. His actions reflected values that autocrats make the best leaders, and that sexually abusing women is morally excusable. So, as many in our culture began to accept these, the Big Split was well on its way.

10. **Disenfranchisement of Middle America:** The growing disenfranchisement of middle-American Whites was augmented by the politics of identity with Democrats' support of Hispanics, Blacks, and LGBTQ individuals. Jobs for middle America were disappearing, giving way to robotics and automation,[19] while uneducated Americans and immigrants were getting work at lower wages, doing the menial labor of caring for disabled elders, cleaning jobs, and the like. Meanwhile, the rich were getting even richer. Feeling ignored by politicians who did not include them, they grew apart, with a radical few joining hostile militia groups such as the Oath Keepers and the Three Percenters. The time was ripe for simplistic messages and Trump filled the gap. Increasingly, they thrived on misinformation and right-wing conspiracy theories.

With all these factors, our society took on a new sensibility. Whichever of the burgeoning alternate realities one accepted, whether based on cultish politics on the one hand or scientific evidence on the other, the arrival of the Big Split was inevitable.

How Lies Gain Our Trust and Lead to Conspiracy Theories

Simply put, misinformation is information that does not pass the test of factual confirmation that is based on both scientific criteria and validation by a consensus of valued peers.

This second criterion of consensus is where misinformation can be construed as conspiracy theory. Because of the rapid communication of social media, those who limit themselves to the process we refer to as confirmation bias are only choosing to expose themselves to information that feels emotionally valid.

They trust the sources of this misinformation and the repetition of the messages gives them a strong sense of confidence that they are correct in believing what they see on their screens.

So trusted sources of information, based on expertise and academic study, can be replaced by charismatic figures who simplify complex challenges into easy answers that appeal to emotions rather than deep, critical thinking.

In current politics, there are many challenges, such as the pandemic, climate change, social injustice, and the battle for control over the election process. Each of these has its own complexities to explore.

How much easier to focus on one leader who states that they alone have all the answers. They believe their own power over others and don't hesitate to insult and bully those who disagree with them.

They continually share their own version of reality, very different from proven facts, and this misinformation is accepted by the followers. In this way, Trump was able to convince his fellow Republicans that the 2020 presidential election was stolen from him, despite court decisions that the election was entirely fair.

Republicans feared that the Democrats were more likely to win elections moving forward, and, even though most were aware of the Big Lie, the prospect of staying in power through sideways means, or creating state laws that give state Republicans more power overseeing the elections, was more attractive than losing power in fair elections.

Some statistics may help to understand the rise of belief in conspiracy theories. According to the US Census Bureau, in the 1950s, America was 90 percent White and 10 percent Black. By 2020, the figures were 58 percent White and 13.4 percent Black, the remainder made up of 19 percent Hispanic and 6 percent Asian. So non-Hispanic Whites saw themselves as a diminishing force in our society. They could be seen as suffering from the *politics of fear*, to use a phrase from Jon Meacham, resulting in the Divided States of America—the formerly dominant Whites now feeling threatened by other groups. In Trump, they saw their savior, backed by such conspiracy theory believers as QAnon.

Such fears of other groups played into the need for proclaiming White superiority. This made supremacists prone to conspiracy theories that made them feel more secure. The primary one was the Big Lie, that Republicans are superior and are the rightful leaders to Make America Great Again—to restore the dominance of White supremacy.

> It seems that the more outrageous, outlandish, and unbelievable a story is at the outset, the more credibility it wins as acceptance builds and broadens.[20]

There is an alluring quality to information that is initially hard to believe. Why? Because it excites the emotional limbic system of the brain, reacting to the challenge of unfamiliar and surprising unknowns, and then connects with the frontal cortex, which creates the context for this exciting information. This locks it more efficiently in our memory bank to be repeated later as more seemingly factual.

Intense emotion is what intrigues[21] and captures the imagination.[22]

According to social scientists, conspiracy theories tend to bring about emotions such as fear and withdrawal, which interfere with logical thinking and lead believers to become more susceptible and "believe the unbelievable." For similar reasons, it can also lead to angry protests, or radicalization of the those targeted.[23]

What makes people believe conspiracy theories and other unbelievable stories? According to psychologists,[24] there are several reasons.

Resolving simultaneous conflicting ideas is one. When two ideas don't connect, they create a conflict of ideas that psychologists call cognitive dissonance.[25] How can a flying saucer hang in midair when gravity should cause it to be crashing down? We resolve this dissonance by creating a new logic that aliens have a power against gravity with which we are unfamiliar.

If enough people gather to support this new logic or misinformation integrated into a belief system, then the belief in alien invasion becomes accepted by this group and that new idea becomes a focal point of view for a growing number of members to this society supporting this new belief. Now we have confirmation bias[26] in which group members reinforce one another to cohere to this new belief and can form a very strongly bonded community who are now believers.

For example, QAnon members often accuse Hillary Clinton and President Biden, in public, of operating a pedophilia ring.[27] On TV, they appear authentic in this belief. Absurd as it is to the rest of society, this communal belief is supported by confirmation bias within that community.[28]

What also accounts for this is a belief in a just world. If these

Democrats are doing these foul deeds, then that just proves that they are the enemy, according to the believers. And, in a just world, they are to be gotten rid of politically, leading to a *we're the good guys—they're the bad guys* mentality.

Finally, existential fears are a contributing factor as well. We'll go into this in detail later, but suffice it to say, that there are deep personal needs and fears that go into the process of believing the unbelievable, such as the need to be part of a larger group, and fear of the vulnerability of aloneness, as we'll see in Chapter Six.

The fascinating example of Orson Welles' broadcast of the radio play, based on the novel by H.G. Wells, was about the invasion of extra-terrestrials. There was an unexpected degree of involvement and trust by the audience. Though there was a very small proportion of the public that believed it initially,[29] it still took a day and a half to reassure the public that this was just dramatic theater, a thespian's trick at misinterpretation of events, as false as they were.[30]

The very misconception of truth is that it is absolute, unchanging, and unflinching in its precision. But truth also suffers from misinterpretation, just as much as sci-fi radio dramas.

The Honest Truth about Truth

When we refer to *truth* we often mean "accuracy." So, truth is often the best estimate of accuracy about something of interest, for a specified time.

> But truth, by its very nature, changes and is occasionally mistaken, as conditions affecting objects or events evolve over time, and are subject to perceptions.

Truth is clearly what we describe as accurate, based, in part, on a consensus among our valued peers, people we respect and trust.

So, if we trust our newspaper journalists, or favorite news pundits, then their statements tend to be accepted as true.[31]

But truth starts to become a relative entity, shifting perhaps, depending on its sources and on its audience. The best characterization for the changing nature of truth may be how we visualize our universe. For the longest time, until 1543, it was "true" that the Sun revolved around the Earth. Everyone knew that at the time; there was no debate. Then the astronomer Nicolaus Copernicus discovered that the Earth and its sister planets revolved around the Sun. With a bit of help from improvements of telescopes by such scientists as Galileo around 1610, it took only a century for that discovery to become the new truth. Once it did, that fact dominated in our society for the rest of our history.

Now we know a bit more "truth" about our universe, that our Sun is a mere star among a hundred billion in the Milky Way Galaxy, and our galaxy is a mere collection of those stars amidst hundreds of billions of other galaxies.[32]

Is it true that there is some final boundary to our universe? And, if so, what's the truth about what lies beyond that boundary? At this point, we must rely on opinion, since scientists depend on data, and there are no data to support either concept—boundary-defined universe or infinite universe, despite academic theories that battle for the "truth."

I tell my friends that there are two possible answers to the question about an infinite or finite universe. One is three words: I don't know. The other is a single word: Religion—however your chosen religion explains such unknowns, and the unknowable, as many attempt to do.

> The point here is that truth does depend heavily on those we trust, whether esteemed scientists, revered religious figures, political leaders with clout (either honestly elected or not)—and, of course, our community of friends.

The advantage that conspiracy theories have is that they can be more emotionally engaging because they can appeal to the primitive parts of our brain, where imagination is allowed to cajole with our emotional needs. In other words, the illusory truth effect, where the false story is repeated over and over, begins to achieve acceptance as truth, even when people know initially that the information is false.[33]

This was well known by some way before this concept was explained in terms of our brain's function. Joseph Goebbels remarked, "If you repeat a lie often enough, people will believe it, and you will even come to believe it yourself." This was when radio was in its infancy, yet still a highly effective tool for the Nazis. Now, with social media at our fingertips, this phenomenon is even more powerful.[34]

When large groups of people accept an illusion as truth, it could be termed *the bandwagon effect*, leading to a strong sense of confirmation bias. The more widespread the acceptance of the illusion, the more it is trusted as truth.

This is exactly what happened with the Big Lie about Trump's 2020 election defeat, and why it wouldn't die. But there's more to it. What about the political dynamics?

In past elections, Democrats have tended to win the popular vote even when they lost the election due to the electoral college. When Trump became president, it was due to 77,744 votes in three states combined—Michigan, Pennsylvania, and Wisconsin—despite many more voters preferring Hillary Clinton.[35] These same three states turned blue in favor of Biden in 2020. In fact, in that election, most of the voters who chose Trump lived in states that Biden had won. According to a national correspondent for *The Washington Post*, Trump won the election in 2016 despite having lost the popular vote by almost three million.[36]

The Republicans feared that they'd lost control of the popular vote and could only hope for success by dint of the electoral college. But when they lost the electoral college as well in 2020, Trump and his supporters were shocked and chose to deny their loss by claiming fraud in the election. That was Trump's well-known characteristic of being unable to see himself as a loser. And he carried his following with him to continue the Big Lie.

With the support of QAnon loudly proclaiming their version of the election loss, there was undeniable confirmation bias that drove this conspiracy theory into the headlines on an ongoing basis. The Trump supporters fed on one another's claim so intensely that it grew into an alternative truth that built on social media and, subsequently, the mainstream press had to report this claim as well. Add to this the money of rich and powerful advocates of Trump who fueled this conspiracy with their hefty funds,[37] and you can now better understand why so many believed the Big Lie. A poll by Politico and Morning Consult revealed that 60 percent of Republicans believed that Biden's victory should "probably" or "definitely" be recalled.[38]

Add to this the alluring quality of the fantastic though incredible theories and you have a situation in which fantasy makes its way into what our brains interpret as reality, at least at the lower levels of perception if not the higher. Those with a certain strong political disposition—whether strong left or strong right—are, of course, much more vulnerable to believe falsehoods that support their chosen point of view. After the 2020 election results ended up with the Big Lie, members of QAnon were strongly confident that the election would be overturned sooner rather than later. There was little hesitation on their part to acknowledge this as factual rather than aspirational.

O, Noble Truth, Where Art Thou?

At no other time in our history have we been so deluged and lambasted by falsehoods and conspiracy theories. As we mentioned earlier in this chapter, even newspapers are losing some credibility. According to the report by Morning Consult, "The share of US adults who said nine leading media outlets were credible dropped five percentage points since 2016," including a twelve-point drop among Republicans for the *The New York Times* and CNN as credible news outlets.[38] According to a poll by Statista, less than 45 percent trusted the credibility of such media outlets as NPR, Fox News, and MSNBC when surveyed in mid-2021.[39]

Disinformation and its cousin, propaganda, go way back. As soon as humans could speak, they wove tales that promoted their own points of view. Their myths and legends were the links that kept their societies together. The Greeks, Romans, and early Christians fought wars based on that. The term, *propaganda*, stems from the word, "propagation," when Pope Gregory XV created the Congregation for the Propagation of the Faith in 1622 Rome. During this time, cardinals were charged with spreading the faith and regulating church activities in "heathen lands."[40]

Coins, with their symbol of power on one side and their leader on the other, were the first tokens of propaganda. The invention of the printing press just added to the process. Single-page leaflets, in the sixteenth century, preceded newspapers. By 1920, mass media accelerated the use of propaganda even further with the addition of radio to supersede newspapers. The Nazis manufactured cheap radios (*Volksempfanger* or "People's radio") and gave them to all so that they could reach the ears of all Germans. And now, social media makes of our lives a maelstrom of alternate realities based on conspiracy theories that refuse to die, even in the face of evidence to the contrary.

One study by the Harvard Kennedy School of Misinformation revealed that Democrats are even more susceptible to the effect of believing misinformation on voting habits than are Republicans.[41] Both misinformation and disinformation are effective in shaping voting behaviors, but they are driven by different motives. The difference is that disinformation is more intentional and purposeful in achieving its aims and is more likely to be shared through wider social media.

One piece of misinformation, for example, consists of the conspiracy theory that 5G cellular networks cause cancer or even Covid-19, despite the absence of any data to support it.[42] That may have been believed by those who conveyed the message. That's misinformation.

An example of disinformation, on the other hand, is Russia's involvement in turning the election toward Trump in 2016 through the spread of actual and deliberate lies about his opponent, Hillary Clinton, among other falsehoods, according to a probe by the Senate intelligence committee.[43] Both forms of information are false, but the latter is an intentional tool with its perpetrators focusing on the result with fastidious effort. Many Russian minds worked on this agenda and the consequences have been troublesome.[44]

Trump himself offered his own definition of disinformation and the process of repetition. In a speech to his fellow Republicans in Phoenix, Arizona over the weekend of July 24–26, 2021, he said, referring to the Democrats, while flailing his arms: "But that's what they do, and you know what it's called, disinformation. They make up a lot of crap and then say it over and over and over."[45]

But this accusation is called projection, a well-recognized strategy, blaming the other for what you're doing.

Why Trump Was So Successful

We seem to be hardwired to trust, even worship, a leader who gives the appearance (rather than the substance) of success and to surrender our own power to support his or hers, with unquestioned loyalty and zeal. Once given, this devotion continues to grow and strengthen. This is especially true when people, as a group or nation, are hurting for some reason, usually because there just isn't enough food to feed the family or, more generally, when there's a strong sense of economic inequality.

Dictators such as Hitler and Mussolini provide excellent examples. In both cases, they were able to assume complete power over their countries because of the economic and political frustrations of their countrymen at the time. Both presented impressive images and oratorical styles that were highly theatrical, staccato, repetitive, and contradictory to the existing political culture, even though both were wrong with their stated facts, or which were at least highly exaggerated.

Both used highly emotional language with repetitive gestures; both making use of the extended right arm, the Roman salute, to engage their audiences. Both inspired militias that increasingly terrorized the local countryside, killed "undesirables" and wrested power from the existing governmental institutions. Both built a strong base of support that grew with time. Both had radical convictions of their political aspirations.

In more current times, of course, there is Donald Trump, who presented himself as a winner because of his gold-plated lifestyle and so-called real estate successes.[46] With a little help from his friends in Russia,[47] he was able to bully his way into overriding other Republican presidential candidates and then, with the help of social media,[48] to win the presidential elections in 2016.

Most people are much more impressed with external trappings of success than with long resumes or lesser-known records of success in the day-to-day grind of the working world.

> Often the mere image of self-confidence outweighs a deeper ability to get things done effectively but quietly, albeit more slowly.

Trump is a master at self-promotion, even at the expense of others, whether they are in his own party or the opposition, whether they are strangers or his own family, whether they are political antagonists or his own vice president or attorney general, even those who devoted their political careers to him, and then wrote about their experiences. Trump declared, in his indignation, "Some of the [book publishing] stars I produced are actually made of garbage."[49] No stone was left unturned to find fault with someone who could be used as a reason for failure rather than take responsibility himself.

Lies Beat Truth in the Race for Information

Such strong conviction on the part of Trump and so many others in the political process help to understand the Age of Polarization. Will we ever know whether Trump would have won the 2016 election with such varied opinions as to the role Russia played? Will we ever uncover the complete story about Trump's attempt at a coup using the Department of Justice?

Untruths to influence attitudes are becoming endemic in today's politics, the most noticeable being false information by Putin's followers disseminating disinformation against Hillary Clinton during the 2016 campaign.[50] They're used consistently primarily because they're so effective. They bring about the desired results if enough force is put into their applications.

But why are conspiracy theories spread as disinformation so powerful? Two reasons: 1) People like dramatic stories because it makes them feel engaged and more alive, especially when they're fantastic, in the literal sense of relating to fantasy, and 2) Such stories travel more quickly than real information, which is typically not as enticing. We've all heard the saying that rumors travel at lightning speed while truth is still putting on its pants. Well, science has proven this.

Soroush Vosoughi and his associates did a very deep study of the dissemination of misinformation on social media. Here's what they found and reported in the journal, *Science*: lies spread faster than truth.

> After an analysis of twelve years of data off Twitter comprising 126,000 news items, they found that false news reaches up to one hundred times more individuals, and six times faster, than the truth.

"Falsehood diffused significantly farther, faster, deeper, and more broadly than the truth in all categories of information," revealed the scientists.[51]

This was especially true of political news, resulting in the emotions of fear and surprise, but not much trust. And people were 70 percent more likely to retweet false news than factual. Private individuals are the prime culprits when it comes to the propagation of misinformation through social networks, according to the report published in *Science*.[52]

History Lessons from the Golden Age of Propaganda

How do we regain control of our own minds and put an end to the cascade of falsehoods whose purpose is to manipulate our political beliefs?

Before the advent of the internet in the 1950s, news was learned through the press, which became most popular following the French and American Revolutions and maintained its powerful status in terms of public communication throughout the 1800s and into the early 1900s. Then came public use of electromagnetism by Marconi when radio waves hit the air about 1899 and took its place as a popular venue for news by 1920, with wide-spread availability of TV following about thirty years later.

Radio provided a sense of intimacy, with its simultaneous broadcasts of the human voice, as well as live music. For four decades Americans could enjoy the Golden Age of Radio. Comedy shows, action and western series (*Superman*, the *Lone Ranger*) were widely popular, in a sense, the only show in town. Historical events, such as the Hindenburg disaster in 1937 and the bombing of Pearl Harbor in 1941, were broadcast much more quickly than the press could report. Most important, however, for this discussion, was its power to manipulate the human mind.

Joseph Goebbels was the first pioneer in the use of radio for purposes of propaganda, creating conspiracy theories justifying the violence against communists, Jews, and any who dared defy the Nazi regime.[53] He could have been describing the arrival of the internet with its lack of rules and boundaries when he spoke about the advent of radio: "The radio is in no way a branch of the stage or film, but rather an independent entity with its own rules." He disclosed his excitement about "the possibilities of this modern method of influencing the masses . . . It would not have been possible for us to take power or to use it in the ways we have without the radio."[53]

Years after this oratorial admission of the use of radio for propaganda purposes, a couple of social scientists revealed the steps that could be taken to energize what we now recognize as conspiracy theories.

According to Clyde Miller and Violet Edwards, these propaganda devices involved *name calling, glittering generalities, flag waving*, and *stacking the cards*.[54] Fast forward to more current history, and we can visualize Trump calling his Republican primary competitors derogatory names; making glittering generalities his main currency of speech; hugging, even kissing, the flag; and stacking the cards as no other politician had ever done.

Now, putting all this in the perspective of social media, we can better appreciate how powerful this mode of communication is in creating falsehoods to manipulate political choices. Social media does considerably better than radio, bringing simultaneity to visual as well as aural connection.

Most important, however, is the prospect of defending ourselves, in the future, of such attempts at bending our minds and our political choices through social media. How do we recognize conspiracy theories before they draw us in to change our thinking?

Those who grew wary of the power of radio during its days of glory had some wise advice that we can use effectively today. In *The Fine Art of Propaganda*,[55] the authors write:

- We must ask: Who is this propagandist [or purveyor of conspiracy theories]?

- How is he trying to influence our thoughts and actions?

- For what purpose does he use the common propaganda devices [or conspiracy theories]?

- Do we like his purposes?
- How does he use words and symbols?
- What are the exact meanings of his words and symbols?
- What does the propagandist try to make these words and symbols appear to mean?
- What are the basic interests of this propagandist [or purveyor of conspiracy theories]?
- Do his interests coincide with the interests of most citizens of our society as we see it?

Applying these questions to present-day conspiracy theories can give us the armaments necessary to discern fact from falsehood. They're simple and straightforward and that's why they work.

We've seen here how the power of electronic communication, starting with the radio, and morphing over the generations to TV, cell phones, and then social media, have affected culture. Now we have the responsibility of reclaiming our own version of truth. Because the human mind is vulnerable to emotional persuasion and subjectivity in perception, that remains a daunting challenge, and requires our ongoing vigilance to fight back against the process of polarization.

Since so many of us get so much of our truth from social media, there is a great responsibility for such companies as Facebook to reflect transparency and integrity. Noble Truth is not easily found when we have media that turn out to be so untrustworthy. In the next chapter, we'll look deeper into the mechanics and business model of social media to discover where the truth may be hiding, as revealed by whistleblower, Frances Haugen.[56] We'll see how misinformation has hurt us in a number of spheres, and how the selling of disinformation has become big business, in part unwittingly aided by users themselves, according to *The New York Times*.[57] Noble Truth is not easily found when social media continue to polarize us. But there are ways to uncover truth and that's what you'll discover.

CHAPTER FIVE

Tricked Again: How Facebook Became Part of the Conspiracy

"The truth" is whatever people will believe.

—Roger Ailes

There are people who are really good managers, people who can manage a big organization, and then there are people who are very analytic or focused on strategy. Those two types don't usually tend to be in the same person. I would put myself much more in the latter camp.

—Mark Zuckerberg

Intelligent people will be banned from thinking so as not to offend the imbeciles.

—Fyodor Dostoevsky

Can you recall the scene in your high school history course when Nero was fiddling while Rome burned? That would make a great cartoon, replacing the decadent Nero with Trump, Rome with the Capitol in Washington, DC, and the fiddle with his TV set. Instead of Rome burning, we see the infamous Capitol insurrection in the scenario below.

In his last year as president, Trump forsook all morality and was even ready to have the military deployed against those protesting

George Floyd's murder;[1] denied the benefits of vaccination and masks against the pandemic; and sat smiling at his TV set while the January 6 insurrection took place, refusing to ask the invaders to stand back until he was forced to, and then only doing so half-heartedly.

Going back in time, how was Trump able to achieve his unexpected victory of 2016? First off, he presented himself as a winner, a most successful entrepreneur from the real estate world of New York City.

Apparently, many believed, without giving it much thought, that a successful real estate maven is qualified to run the country. The fact that he began with his father's hard-earned success wasn't in the forefront of his story.[2]

He made no claim to being a successful politician and rightly so, as he had absolutely no such experience. But this meant that he had no history of failures, as is the usual track record of most politicians, losing a few elections before they start winning. So, in truth, he had a flawless political record.

What he did have in spades was charisma, the type that charms others to inspire devotion, especially those who are hurting from a sense of being on the wrong side of the financial ledger and feeling disenfranchised (just like the capuchin monkeys who got cucumber instead of grapes). Such charisma is much more effective with those individuals who tend to be less educated and less politically sophisticated and see this nuanced world in terms of black and white. They are much more susceptible to the superficial charm and confidence at which Trump excels.[3] "In short," summarizes one researcher, "education enhances cognitive proficiency and analytic ability," so that it helps to discern substance from mere flamboyance.[4]

What fostered whatever political success Trump continued to maintain was his skill at telling his devoted base what they wanted to hear, especially that they were special, superior, and in the right moral camp. Making America great again, back to a time when there was less diversity threatening the status quo, with memories of a less troubled time when America was undoubtedly the superpower of the world, when China and Russia were lagging way behind, when we were the first to land on the moon—that's the America that Trump promised.[5]

And the silent majority ate it all up with a big spoon, groveling at each presentation of the Master. Donald Trump, at one point, was representing the end game of what the Republican Party was becoming.

How We Learn About Trust

Can you recall your first betrayal of trust? Your first major disappointment in romance? Your first broken promise from a close friend or business partner? If so, you can relate to the meaning of painful loss when your life is deeply affected by a loss of trust.

Issues of trust, and its return when broken, may involve other people (spouse, salesperson, your child's teacher), institutions (police and the judicial system, the postal service, your bank), or government (from local up to the highest offices in the land).

The crisis of misplaced trust is all about how the loss, pain and grief we experience as a nation affect us so deeply, because of its consequences:

- Social media and their users, as we are learning, continue to divide our political realm into "armies of conflict" just so they can keep us tuned in and earn more profits through advertising.[6] There are also both domestic and international players, e.g., Vladmir Putin, among others, who usurp and manipulate social media for their own personal gain.[7]

- Can we trust our system of justice when it maintains a prejudice against color as manifested in the killing of George Floyd and others, when we see—on video after video—the tragedy of how victims of police brutality, or incompetence, are killed on the streets of our nation before they can be fairly judged as to whether or not they've committed a crime? We feel betrayed when we find that some police are not fair in their treatment of people of color.

- So many turn a blind eye to climate change even though we are already suffering obvious consequences of its accelerating effects—nationally as well as globally. The fossil fuel industry has been denying climate change, spending great sums of money to influence legislators. Yet the undeniable weather disruptions, resulting in accelerating increases in droughts, storms, hurricanes, and flooding, are already causing the tragedy of beginnings of community migrations and we do practically nothing about it, except talk. How can we trust government leaders on either side of the aisle who so clearly ignore the science that supports global warning? Fortunately, President Biden assigned John Kerry to take on the leadership of a return to trust in this realm, yet so much needs to be done.[8]

- Our former president repeatedly betrayed our trust in him with a pattern of ongoing falsehoods and when he lied so egregiously about winning the 2020 election, resulting in the insurrection at our Capitol. Then we, as a nation, suffered the tragedy of damage to our democratic process—that will take years to heal—because of one narcissist's need for attention and validation.[9] Sometimes it's the efforts of our nation's elected congressional as well as state leaders to stay in office and maintain their power irrespective of the intent of the Constitution to which our nation adheres.

- So many lives were lost when our former president hid the truth from us about the onset of Covid-19 because, as he declared to Bob Woodward, he didn't want us to panic.[10] We lost untold hundreds of thousands of innocent lives among our relatives and friends, clearly a national tragedy, just because that president often called the virus invasion a hoax and couldn't or wouldn't take the responsibility for attacking a potential pandemic before it took hold. Those who trusted him were burned

It's one thing to suffer a betrayal of trust when a parent hurts us, a lover rejects us, or a boss treats us unfairly. But the consequences of betrayal at a national level affect society as a whole, more consequential in terms of influencing millions at the same time. These are undeniable tragedies, with a significantly greater degree of magnitude. After all is said and done, are we able to make better decisions about whom to believe so that we can be more skilled in our return to trust?

Recognizing Tragedies and Restoring Trust

The purpose and intent of this book are to offer information that can promote the use of reason and emotional clarity, to decide whom to trust and whom not to trust, and to focus on improving our decision-making process, including the skills of emotional intelligence.

We can apply all this to attack the misinformation pervading social media about global climate change, the injustice toward minority groups, even some future deadly pandemic.

In our mission to return to trust, we can take more responsibility: to force social media to become more transparent and trustworthy; to build respect for those who have been treated unjustly so that they can demand equal justice under the law; to point out the data relating to climate change so they can no longer be turned aside; to support a public health system, on either side of the aisle, that will ensure our national health as future pandemics and their variants continue to threaten us; and to make the hard decisions to understand a complex and dangerous world.

I invite you to be part of this restoration of trust at this challenging point in our history.

Guzzling the Fuel of Social Media: The Blue Shift into the Big Lie

An aspiring autocrat in a democratic government needs a support system to back up the fabricated information necessary to maintain his following.[11] Enter the organization known as QAnon. Nobody knew exactly where it came from, who the unknowable Q was, if anyone, and where it was all going. Sure, there are good guesses, some of which we'll explore in the next chapter, but the infamous cult just keeps on ticking, like a time bomb always ready to explode.

Its adherents were totally assured of their ultimate success despite the failures of their ongoing predictions going awry. Months and months after the 2020 election, they remained stubbornly convinced that Biden stole the election, and that Trump would be back on the throne of government very soon.[12]

Why was this conspiracy theory so persistent and convincing to its victims? Because of the emotional baggage it carried. Believers were angry that the Republicans lost the election. They were so hopeful when the ballots received early on predicted a Trump victory. But pollsters had anticipated the blue shift toward the Democrats later in the polling process.

As it turned out, significantly more people voted in 2020 than did in 2016, so Trump got more votes in 2020.[13] But so did the Democratic candidate, in this case, Joe Biden. This increase in the number of votes that Trump got convinced him that he was the winner, especially when he was ahead early in the process. When Biden won Arizona and Georgia, Trump and his followers were dumbfounded, and very angry.

This was the emotion they carried into the Big Lie. The anger and the frustration fed into the Big Lie like premium gas into a racing Porsche. It had all the energy it needed to persist and feed the sentiments of QAnon believers.[14]

It wasn't logical or rational. It was intense emotion, wrapped in a shell of righteous political indignation.

I Alone Can Fix the Stolen Election

Pretty soon, people began acting on this conspiracy theory, which led, as we all know too well, to the January 6 insurrection.

Conspiracy theories can have real life consequences, and this one did. Five people died, and 140 Capitol police were injured, one with two cracked ribs and two smashed spinal discs, others who sustained head injuries, four who subsequently committed suicide,[15] and yet many Republicans continued to foster the conspiracy theory that it was all like a polite tourist visit. The insurgents saw Trump as their savior even though a survey of 142 historians, in a C-SPAN review, rated Trump as one of the worst presidents in American history.[16]

When interviewed by Carol Leonnig and Philip Rucker, the authors of *I Alone Can Fix It*, Trump continued to try to convince them that he had really won the election, stretching the scheduled interview from one hour to two and a half. [17]

Trump's values of loyalty to others were revealed when he blamed his own supporters at the White House, including his vice president, for the loss.[18]

Trump had more votes in 2020 than in 2016 alright, but the suburbs made the difference by getting even more votes for Biden with an overall 67 percent voter turnout rate, the highest since 1900.[19]

The Power of Social Media and the Abuse of Trust

Conspiracy theories get their power amplified by social media, providing the repetition necessary for credibility.

Facebook tried to look innocent in its treatment of Trump's messages, but never did anything to stop them. CEO Mark Zuckerberg's advisors considered having him give Trump a call to see what his intentions were just prior to the January 6 insurrection, but then thought better of it, fearing being implicated later by the press. Once again, after the fact, social media ended up supporting a critical conspiracy theory but feigned innocence.[20]

Facebook's aim, as is true of other social media, is to make more money by having more viewers, and this happens when they produce drama and conflict, so their motivation to clear themselves of negative consequences from harmful messages is often low priority, despite the public relations attempt to frame a more benign image.[21]

Social media's empowerment of conspiracy theories goes on despite their irresponsibility in the use of private data and their influential effect on hate mongering, according to Roger McNamee, the author of *Zucked*.

At the beginning of his book, McNamee writes:

> This is a story about trust. Technology platforms, including Facebook and Google, are the beneficiaries of trust and goodwill accumulated over fifty years by earlier generations of technology companies. They have taken advantage of our trust, using sophisticated techniques to prey on the weakest aspects of human psychology, to gather and exploit private data, and to craft business models that do not protect users from harm.[22]

This quote by McNamee helps us understand how Big Tech has contributed to the formation of the Big Split. He didn't name it as such, but his description of tech platforms taking advantage of us, after gaining our trust over fifty years, says it all. With our trust tyrannized by Big Tech, we have the challenge of discerning truth from falsehood, science from opinion, one alternate reality from another. In other words, we're in a maelstrom of information, some of it being misinformation, even disinformation—one conspiracy after another. What else can we call it but the Big Split?

Facebook's early motto for developers, until 2014, was "Move fast and break things." It seemed to do both. Just prior to the 2016 elections, the algorithms of Facebook's News Feed spread widely circulated disinformation which, according to Steven Levy, author of *Facebook*, "overwhelmingly seemed to discourage voters from pulling the lever on Hillary Clinton."[23]

The morning after the results of the election were announced, both Mark Zuckerberg and Sherryl Sandberg, sharing responsibility for Facebook, were devastated at the surprise win by Trump, so they appear to be innocent of any malevolence. But the sin was the absence of social media management against false and toxic information.[24]

Even these leaders of the largest tech company had no idea of the power of social media to propagate false information to such existential power limits. Facebook had unwittingly contributed to the greatest challenge that the US was to experience for the next four years.

According to Levy, Zuckerberg "was clueless—or lying—about the damage his company was doing."[25]

In the summer of 2021, Biden accused Facebook of killing people by disseminating misinformation about the Covid-19 vaccines, but then recanted. The focus then turned to twelve individuals, termed the "disinformation dozen," with a combined following of fifty-nine million people who used Facebook to disseminate conspiracy theories denigrating the vaccines. They accounted for 65 percent of 812,000 of the Facebook posts. These posts were not immediately removed, despite demands for accountability by the Center for Countering Digital Hate.[26]

Facebook responded by claiming that its viewers were increasingly accepting of the vaccine, that 3.3 million Americans had used the site to find out where to get vaccinated, and that they had already "removed over eighteen million instances of COVID-19 misinformation."[27]

Making Truth Great Again

Once the Big Lie was formulated by Trump himself, his supporters continued to build on that, confirming their acceptance of it to one another through social media and rallies, not to mention regular TV media, especially amplified by Fox News. The banners and insignias on caps and T-shirts just added validation to their original perceptions, viewed repeatedly on TV newscasts across all news channels.

The consensus among the believers itself was a strong validation for persevering in that belief. As mentioned earlier, truth is based on the consensus of valued and trusted peers. So, all the values that went along with the Big Lie were also strengthened by mutual validation as time went on.

Writing on behalf of the US government, in its attempt to explain Russia's creating a myth about its own national culture, George Kennan attested:

> . . . for Russia . . . there are no objective criteria of right and wrong. There are not even any objective criteria of reality and unreality . . . right and wrong, reality and unreality, are determined in Russia . . . not by any innate nature of things, but simply by men themselves. Here men determine what is true and what is false.
>
> This is a serious fact. It is the gateway to the comprehension of much that is mysterious in Russia. It has proved that what is important for people is not what is there but what they conceive to be there. It has shown that with unlimited control over people's minds—and that implies not only the ability to feed them your own propaganda but also to see that no other fellow feeds them any of his—it is possible to make them feel and believe practically anything. And it makes no difference whether that "anything" is true, in our conception of the

word. For the people who believe it, it becomes true. It attains validity, and all the power of truth.[28]

This is not far from what was happening with the Big Lie, where tens of millions believed it wholeheartedly, and how it all fed into the Big Split.

From Fact-checking to Value-checking

Most of us would agree that fact-checking can be extremely helpful in distinguishing truth from falsehoods, especially checking the source of reported facts. And social media is in the process of accepting this responsibility. But now there is some thought given to the proposition that more is necessary—not only fact-checking, but value-checking as well. This, according to its proponents, would involve:

1. Brief and clear summaries of what is considered by most individuals as normal for the subject at hand—the norms that exist, including the current context in which they fit, plus any typical counterarguments.

2. The assumptions under which any given argument is made, in as clear and transparent a manner as possible, including those of the counterargument, with the links to explore such subject matter.

3. The context of the matter at hand, including the limits set by such contexts, and how that, by itself, could be seen as a manipulation, as well as similar constraints for the opposing argument.[29]

Although very complicated at first glance, this value-checking process could at least put down in words what is considered normal, widely accepted, and logically agreed upon regarding any new argument that veers from what is already generally accepted as factual.

Facebook—A Freak of Nature

Value-checking is still in its infancy. Fact-checking is what we have. With Facebook's initiation of News Feed in 2006, it began to be the source of international news for about a third of the US and perhaps two thirds of the rest of the world. It earned its profits not only by selling ads but also by collecting data on over 2.8 billion of its users, about one third of the world's population, and then selling those data.[30]

Valued at almost a trillion dollars, Meta, Facebook's parent company, has under its employ fifteen thousand content moderators and over thirty-five thousand security specialists.[31]

As part of social media, Facebook is a place for public discussion and a source of new ideas. It carries a great burden of shaping aspects of public policy when certain information dispensed as facts turns out to be nothing more than conspiracy theories. Since this wasn't the purpose of Facebook when it was founded as a directory of students to aid in the dating process, the burden of responsibility grew precipitously as its function changed. That's in part why Zuckerberg and his group have been somewhat slow to respond to this challenge.

Its initial purpose was nothing like its current function. Because of its original purpose, Facebook retains its initial function of interpersonal intimacy, with family, friends, work associates, and so on, yet, at the same time, acts as an instrument of creating challenges to the existing political culture, with the potential for fomenting a new, self-contained culture based on conspiracy theories, which feeds on intimate communication.

> In a sense, Facebook is a freak of nature, designed to get to know the people you want to meet and greet, but ending up as a focal point of beliefs that can pull away from the existing culture.

The original function to meet and greet blossomed into a format that also results in political influence.[32]

Those who aim to use social media to influence or persuade others make excellent use of the "intimate" nature of the media. Whether it's a president or a political activist or salesperson or a pundit like Tucker Carlson, such individuals become successful because of the followings they acquire. Cults such as QAnon can foster a family-like or religious-type community which feeds on itself, creating realities about which they agree but which the rest of the world denies. Here's where conspiracy theories thrive.

Social scientists who study such matters report that there is a strong need to identify the roles of those who use the power of social media to their own purpose and benefit.[33]

Disinformation for Hire

One source of disinformation is made up of organizations that can be hired to provide it. Such private organizations can offer the services typically performed by cyber troops, government or political-party teams that use social media to manipulate public opinion. According to a report by the University of Oxford:[34]

1. In 2019 there were seventy countries that used social media to manipulate opinion. By 2020, the number had increased to eighty-one.

2. Despite social media's removal of 317,000 accounts and pages of disinformation, those illicitly using social media for purposes of manipulation spent over ten million dollars on political ads around the world.

3. By 2020, the report found "forty-eight instances of private companies deploying computational propaganda [the use of algorithms and superfast calculations to target specified

populations on social media to manipulate public opinion]
capacities on behalf of a political actor. Since 2018 there
have been more than sixty-five firms offering computational
propaganda as a service. In total, we have found almost sixty
million dollars was spent on hiring these firms since 2009."[35]

4. Such firms can be small operations, and most are highly
    profitable, seducing more and more players into this dark
    field of cyber troops. According to one report, the customers
    are typically political parties, brands, and candidates. Often
    referred to as *black PR* or marketing practitioners without
    ethics, such companies can evade many of Facebook's
    controls by working on multiple platforms and operating
    outside the ethical guidelines of the Helsinki Declaration,
    devised by the International Communications Consultancy
    Organization, one of its principles being: "To never engage
    in the creation of or knowingly circulate fake news."[34]

The black PR companies are extremely difficult to control.
Their employees often work remotely and are sometimes disabled
individuals hard pressed for cash. They might buy the services of SEO
manipulations offerings from such companies as Taobao, Alibaba's
Chinese e-commerce site. Sometimes the small ones are run by e-savvy
high school students. Among the larger ones are the Israeli-based
The Archimedes Group, which deals with political manipulation; the
Ukrainian firm, Pragmatico which also hosts Znaj Media Holdings
which, in turn, hosts Znaj.ua and Politeka.net; and the Polish Cat@
Net, claiming to work with the legit firm, Art-Media.[36]

According to Cindy Otis, former CIA cybersecurity expert and
author of *True or False,* people are "spending increasing amounts
of time looking at the disinformation-for-hire services that are out
there."[37]

When Emotions Trump Reality

The Big Split is the first time in American history that our culture has become so vulnerable to the effects of conspiracy theories, in large part due to the amplification power of social media. For the most part, it began with the advent of Trump's grand entry into the political scene. Many of his stories were blatantly false, yet he delivered them with such authentic conviction that sounded as if he really believed them, the most obvious one being his account of the number of people attending his inauguration, despite recorded history (including photographs) correcting his claim. The most troublesome was what we now know as the Big Lie, which helped fracture our government into the most polarized factions since the Civil War.[38]

When Orson Welles tricked the country into believing his dramatic account of H.G. Wells' story, dressed up as an actual, current event, the nation believed him. The headline on the New York *Daily News* shouted, all in caps: FAKE RADIO 'WAR' STIRS TERROR THROUGH US on Halloween of 1938.[39]

It reported that, due to the convincing nature of the drama, one woman was discovered by her husband as she was about to commit suicide, saying, "I'd rather die this way than like that." In Indianapolis, a woman ran screaming into her church, halting the ongoing services, shouting, "New York destroyed . . . you may as well go home to die." Hysterical citizens swamped the phones of the *Providence Journal* in Rhode Island, eager for details of the "massacre."[40]

Not all conspiracies to fool our country are this powerful. But a series of lies concocted to convince the nation, through repetition, that the 2020 election was stolen had the accumulative power to shift the "truth" in that direction. Millions became convinced that it was indeed stolen.[41]

Facebook played its role in this unfortunate outcome. Its aim, as I've mentioned, is to increase its outreach and keep the viewers coming back. This involved, especially at first, allowing highly emotional items online, even if they included information fomenting conflict, sometimes involving violence, as unscrupulous users manipulated their information to their advantage.

Facebook's Contribution to the Big Split— An Ugly Truth

With such influence over our culture, social media's association with the Big Split is undeniable. With Facebook's stated mission of opening the world of online communication, it sought more and more members, regardless of the cost of negative consequences, such as localized misinformation leading to violence. As Andrew Bosworth, creator of Facebook's *News Feed*, wrote in a memo: "The ugly truth is that we believe in connecting people so deeply that anything that allows us to connect more people more often is *de facto* good . . . That's why all the work we do in growth is justified, all the questionable contact-importing practices."[42]

This memo is the origin of the title of the book, *An Ugly Truth*, by Sheera Frenkel and Cecilia Kang. In it, they share their discovery that when Zuckerberg, in an online chat with a friend, first started Facebook, he characterized those responding to his invitation to list themselves on his site as "dumb fucks" because "they trust me."

This may be the closest we can come to Zuckerberg's true values about his company despite later attempts to clean up his ethical approach to misinformation. When ethical practices were successful in reducing misinformation and viewer time subsequently decreased, Zuckerberg reversed the process so his numbers wouldn't suffer. What was most important was ratings and Zuckerberg made that his priority. In a talk to his own administrators in 2017, Zuckerberg said, "We have to build a world where every single person has a sense of purpose and community," even if such community, as it turned out, found its purpose in political manipulation by tyrannical forces.[42]

Even after promising "really advanced tools to fight election interference" in 2019, Facebook still welcomed the funds paying for disinformation on the elections. "Trump was the single-largest spender on political ads on Facebook," according to the authors of *An Ugly Truth*.[42]

Two Sides of the Consensus Coin

Earlier, I wrote that truth is in part based on consensus of valued peers, those you trust. How can we know what's true except by observing our environment with careful observation and our analytic abilities? Yet ultimately, we believe that when it comes to subjective, emotional reactions, we end up relying on our trusted group of influential community members.

Getting to truth through such a process of validation is a two-sided coin. The positive side is that a consensus is more likely to be accurate than one person's perceptions. The negative side is when that consensus disengages from the much larger, overarching consensus and takes a separate route to counteract and confront the first, especially when that secondary consensus is based on nothing more than conspiracy theories.

Our two-party system of government reflects two different world views, two ways of looking at the same thing. Both claim a path to good government and devotion to the Constitution. But one is more progressive, and the other is more conservative. Currently, however, the makeup of one faction of the Republican Party's perspective leans heavily on conspiracy theory.[43]

Unfortunately, Meta has allowed the conflict between the two parties to expand by allowing conspiracy theories to grow despite their being based on falsehoods. According to whistle-blower Frances Haugen, Facebook was not totally open about its failure to control disinformation it allowed to be conveyed to its users.[44] The company chose higher profits over accuracy.

> This dependence on conspiracy theory is not
> to be taken lightly. We came uncomfortably
> close to losing our democracy when the
> Capitol insurrection took place. Imagine if
> one of the senators had been murdered
> by the aggressive mob, or if Pence were
> actually hanged. Our government might
> never have healed completely.

As Steven Simon and Jonathan Stevenson wrote in a *New York Review of Books* essay, "An assassination or two could cause social tension to descend into social conflict," if not civil war. They quote international political scholar Daniel Drezner as comparing the GOP to Hezbollah, both "having a political party that also that has an armed wing to coerce other political actors through violence."[45]

And what about artificial intelligence making violence automated through the chain of algorithms and robots making our trend toward increasing violence even more likely? In a book on AI, Henry Kissinger and his colleagues explore those possibilities.[46] All it would take is a consensus to allow that evolutionary trend to manifest itself in reality.

In terms of our own evolution, group consensus was highly effective in making the right decision at times of crisis. Think of herd animals that take their cues from those close to them. By having more eyes and ears and noses on the watch (and sound and smell) for predators, and acting cohesively, they could more easily evade the predators and survive an attack. As an analogy, this helps us to understand the benefits of what is sometimes referred to as *groupthink*, which can sometimes morph into mob mentality.[47]

Yet those terms themselves connote a shortsighted perspective in a complex environment. At the end of the day (and chapter), we're left with the argument that we all must think for ourselves if we choose to act in an intelligent manner. Careful analysis with critical thinking can counteract the powerful effect of tribal influence. But the battle between the two continues and begs for resolution. This is the challenge for us if we are to avoid the abuse of our trust in this Age of Polarization.

With Meta becoming the new banner for Zuckerberg's media empire, the power of Big Tech becomes more evident, with the metaverse transforming our lives. Our government has been very slow to regulate this industry, giving such powers as Facebook and YouTube the ability to run wild with little accountability. Thank goodness Congress is taking action in demanding more transparency.[48]

Facebook and other social media can be very harmful by reporting information that is either false or, even worse, contributory to violent attacks. We need to be very cautious about ensuring that what we see online is accurate and not intentionally harmful. The information promulgated by QAnon, for example, can be both inaccurate and dangerous. So, let's take a close look at the context into which QAnon arose and lift the veil of its inner workings.

In the next chapter, we'll explore:

- How to recognize a conspiracy theory before it seduces you.
- Research on the influence of genetic factors in becoming a "believer."
- The science behind the lure of QAnon.
- Why QAnon is so attractive to its followers.
- An illustration of how Hitler used tribal thinking to turn a democratic republic into a dictatorship in three short months.
- Trump's role in supporting tribal thinking.
- How to debrief someone out of being a "believer."

PART II

DIRTY POLITICS AND THE CULTURE OF FEAR

CHAPTER SIX

The History and Psychology of QAnon: Alternate Realities in the Big Split or How to Deal with Conspiracy Theories

We must speak the truth. Our election was not stolen. And America has not failed.

—Liz Cheney, the day before she was ousted as GOP House leader

. . . when they see you as a fellow tribe member attempting to disavow the tribe, that is something they will never forgive.

—Trevor Noah

Partisanship is a hell of a drug, especially when it's cut with a heavy dose of existential fear.

—Rachel Bitecofer

How to Find Trust and Recognize a Conspiracy Theory before It Seduces You

What, you may ask, do I do if I want to escape the trap of tribalism? What if you choose to be more independent in your thinking, and come to conclusions that are not as biased, to be more objective and less influenced by others around you who might be in cults? How do you avoid being subject to conspiracy theories that ignore reality? Well, Michael Shermer, founder of the Skeptics Society, has the answer for you. He suggests that you recognize a conspiracy theory as most likely false when it:

1. Has many connections among the "dots" that are random or impossible to prove as accurate.

2. Involves very large numbers of people who are sworn to secrecy, and whose purpose is to dominate the world or the economy or some political group with sinister intent.

3. Refuses to consider alternative possibilities and only accepts information that corroborates the beliefs already in place, rejecting out of hand any trust in existing governmental agencies.

So now you're thinking clearly and able to choose your political affiliation without undue influence—right? Well, maybe not too much. Maybe you're being influenced by something you never considered possible.

In this chapter, we'll explore a better understanding of how vulnerable we are—all of us—to the dynamics of polarization. Most critical, this chapter will give you the tools—thoroughly tested over time—that you can use to persuade QAnon conspiracy theory believers to return to a more objective form of trust by going through a personally intimate interaction.

You're Determined—Genetically—to Choose Your Politics

Let's shift focus at this point for a moment and put on our white coats now and enter the biology lab for this next segment. What if I were to say that your political affiliation is hard-wired in your genes and contributes significantly to your choice? I would find it hard to agree if I were told that and I had not yet seen the data myself. But I have seen the data and now I'd like to share that with you.

Let me introduce you to Dr. James Fowler and his colleagues. Dr. Fowler has been experimenting with the gene known as DRD4, or dopamine receptor, D_4. According to the doctor and his team, what they refer to as "the 7R variant of the dopamine receptor D4 gene (DRD4) . . . highlights the importance of incorporating both nature and nurture into the study of political preferences."[2]

This interesting association was first revealed by Dr. Alford and his colleagues in a study of twins. What they discovered was somewhat astounding—that genetic variation helps explain both the direction and strength of political affiliation.[3] A review of the literature reveals the "mutual co-dependence between genes and environment in forming political behaviors."[4] In other words your choice to be a Democrat or Republican is, in part, due to your genetic makeup, the other part being your environment and experience of course. Now, in the next section, we'll focus on one aspect of those with the DRD4-7R gene variant, producing more dopamine, associated with impulsive, exploratory, fickle, excitable, quick-tempered, and extravagant behaviors.[5]

What Explains the Growing Power of Such Groups as QAnon?

How do people react politically when under threat?

> Those who are more impulsive, exploratory, and excitable (characteristic of those with the DRD4-7R gene) may choose affiliation with those who offer dramatic yet quick solutions. Research indicates that such individuals will move toward "right-wing authoritarianism."[6,7]

A review of the literature reveals three reasons motivating people to join outlying, conspiracy-sharing groups, including those such as QAnon:

- To enhance self-esteem, confirmed by social identity theory or sociometer theory,[8] according to which one's social circle, or conspiracy group, is the source of either self-esteem or, in the alternative, threat by rejection, leading to feelings of abandonment. Joining the group makes them feel more secure.

- Desire to manage their fear through group affiliation, which offers comfort and security through a sense of protection, validating individual world views including, for example, conspiracy theories. This is confirmed by terror management theory,[9,10] in which awareness of mortality can create paralyzing anxiety. For those who are dissatisfied or disappointed with their sunset years, this would be especially true.

- Need to reduce anxiety about uncertainty through the security offered by groups, which help define attitudes, norms, and roles. This validation through group identity by promising to predict what people will do is confirmed by the uncertainty-identity model[11,12] in which we identify with certain social groups to reduce uncertainty about our own identity. Uncertainty about important issues leads to anxiety, especially in terms of what our life purpose is all about. That is a deep, existential issue. If such individuals can identify strongly with a group with strong purpose, such as QAnon, then they assume the group's purpose as their own and they no longer feel anxious about confusion in their own life purpose.

Though this may be a bit oversimplified, it's all about transforming anxiety and depressive emotions about feeling like a "second-class citizen" because they lack the education and influence of those who went to college. Then the influential people end up managing them, becoming their bosses. And it seems as if all the politicians are talking to the educated group and not them, until a man like Trump comes along. Now here's a man who makes them feel important and appreciated. He fights for their rights,[13] fights for the coal industry,[14] tells other countries where to get off,[15] upsetting the applecart of conventional politics that have ignored them for so long.

Of course, there are also well-educated people of influence who are anti-authoritarian, and drawn to conspiracy theories, possibly for reasons having to do with their own upbringing and experience.

The conspiracy theories floated by QAnon make believers feel that they know more than the others do, and that the others are morally on the wrong side, not them.[16] Instead of feeling insecure and out of the loop, they're now in the loop with all the other QAnoners, supporting one another with a strong grasp of "the truth" that the others don't have. They're no longer second-class; they're now smarter than the others are, and more in control of the real version of truth, even superior to the others, a feeling for which they've always yearned.

In sum, if you wonder why QAnon has grown so rapidly, and has become such a powerful political force, the answer is that it provides enhanced self-esteem,[17] reduces feelings of loneliness and vulnerability, and makes for a greater sense of power and even superiority (almost like a narcotic).[18] Does that mean that it appeals to all those who lack self-esteem, need external validation, and prefer feeling superior rather than the opposite? Well, that would be a logical conclusion, except that many of us have those needs. But these individuals appear to need it quite a bit more than most, or, at a minimum, have found the answers in the conspiracies they choose to believe.

As we're learning throughout this book, social media plays a seminal role in the growth and development of conspiracy theory groups.[19] We're learning that we get our information about our social and political values from such media, which outperforms all other sources of information, including religious, civic, and entertainment sources.[20]

Never have so many been influenced by false information delivered digitally, and this "education" creates what we're recognizing as alternate realities. QAnon's system of conspiracy narratives has already taken an incredible hold on the members of this group. Most of them believed that Trump won the 2020 election, based on the large number of false narratives told over and over with a winning sense of certainty.[21]

And then there was the attack on the Capitol, egged on by White supremacists, as details revealed. "There is no question," according to *Times* columnist, Thomas Edsall, "that out-and-out racism and a longing to return to the days of White supremacy were high on the list of motivations of the pro-Trump mob that ransacked the Capitol on Jan. 6."[22] QAnon owes its dramatic growth to a number of factors, White supremacy being a major driving factor, one that Trump fell into that hit a vein of popularity and helped him win the 2016 election.

How Trump Bullied His Way to the Top

Many ask how the former president was able to appeal to so many voters despite his malfeasance and grossly disturbing behaviors. The answer is simple: he appealed to our primal response to a physically— and emotionally—domineering personality, which takes us back to our evolutionary stages.

During the primaries, the former president took everyone by surprise with his bullying of the other candidates. He called them names and insulted them—"Lyin' Ted" Cruz, "Mini Mike" Bloomberg, "Little Marco" Rubio. Even during the presidential debates, he referred to his rival as "Crooked Hillary." Yet, *despite* this, or maybe because of it, he won the primary and the election. Pundits had largely predicted the contrary. According to some social scientists, this was not surprising. As a matter of fact, it was precisely due to Trump's *primal dominance*.

"Like the alpha male of a chimpanzee colony, Trump led (and inspired) through intimidation, bluster, and threat."[23]

Well, that got Trump the presidency, where he continued his abusive name calling, this time of international leaders—"Britain Trump" for Prime Minister Boris Johnson,[24] "Rocket Man" for Kim Jong-un,[25] and "Juan Trump" for President Obrador of Mexico.[26] Trump had a way of finding some vulnerability in people's makeup, whether something physical, like short stature, or some other personality quirk, and then exaggerating it to make his opponents suffer the slings and arrows of this political bully.

Even journalists were not immune to such abuse: "The Chin" for Tom Friedman,[27] "Crazy" Jim Acosta,[28] "Fredo" for Chris Cuomo[29] and "Sour Lemon" for Don Lemon.[30] Not even his staunch supporter Steve Bannon escaped, referred to as "Sloppy Steve."[31]

Once in the White House, Trump was accused by psychotherapists, who had not examined him and who typically do not diagnose those they have not examined, of being a narcissistic liar who bent the truth to satisfy his own means to enrich his estate and milk the bully pulpit for all the attention he craved, as well as being a sociopath and suffering from cognitive impairment.[32] One psychologist came up with the term, "Trump Anxiety Disorder," affecting half the nation and special populations.[33] Yet he came fairly close to winning the 2020 elections, getting over seventy four million votes. How did that happen? Again, the primal effect of his personality—his dominance over everyone else. Such dominance, according to social scientists, "is positively associated with traits such as narcissism, aggression, and disagreeableness,"[34] all which Trump revealed.

After the 2020 election, Trump was determined to convince the country that he had won the election and that it was stolen from him, increasing the temperature of the soup in which the Big Split began boiling. And he went to court to prove it. As we know, he lost in almost every case, but not for the lack of trying. Prior to his loss, he fired many in his government who did not support him unconditionally and replaced them with loyalists to his cause,[35] hoping to create a supportive infrastructure along with the three new Supreme Court justices sworn in during his administration. Liberal democrats complained that he was doing his best to destroy our democracy so that he wouldn't have to step down and, for a while, some feared he might really get away with it.[36]

Faithful members of QAnon were expecting a revolution in which Trump's presidency would be reinstated before Biden could be inaugurated. They were religiously following the conspiracy theories that, when fit together, resulted in a much-anticipated outcome. This is a psychological process called *apophenia*, the tendency to perceive a connection or meaningful pattern among unrelated or random ideas, just as amorphous cloud shapes can be visualized as familiar images. This process of apophenia contributes significantly to the process of polarization.[37]

The Secret Strategy of Q, aka Ron Watkins, the "Master" of QAnon

The precursor of QAnon was the Anonymous movement, with its Guy Fawkes masks to maintain anonymity, which Jerome Corsi, a *New York Times* best-selling author, spent much of his time supporting along with the conspiracy theories they heralded.[38] The search for the person who personified Q revealed no clear entity, though Steve Bannon was one of the "suspects."[39] A series of documentary films by Cullen Hoback, *Into the Storm*, revealed three interactive characters who promulgated QAnon over the years.[40]

According to Hoback, one of them was Fred Brennan, who built the concept of Q, possibly inadvertently, when someone delivered a large figure of the letter Q to his dwelling. The other two are Ron Watkins, going by the moniker, CodemonkeyZ, along with his father, Jim Watkins, who lived in the Philippines. They ran 8chan, the online message board on which QAnon prevailed. This was later shifted to 4kun. When both of those boards became problematic, they relaunched on Parler.

After relentless detective work, Hoback became convinced that the sole character that could have been the mythical Q was none other than Ron Watkins, though Ron did his best to deny this to the end. In his final interview with Hoback, Ron ultimately slipped up in one of the details of his denial and the two grinned uncomfortably and uncontrollably on screen as the secret was finally, though inadvertently, revealed.[40]

The Secrets to the Vast Popularity of the QAnon Conspiracy

According to game designer, Reed Berkowitz, there are certain characteristics that make conspiracy theories successful in gaining adherents, feeding tribal thinking:[41]

1. **Follow the Breadcrumbs**
    Rather than telling people what to do and consequently create resistance and pushback to being told what to think, QAnon offered hints that led to details that needed to be put together. That way, the members were forming their own theories out of the "breadcrumbs," creating a sense of allegiance to "their own" ideas.

2. **The Eureka Effect**
    "Aha" moments, as in solving a challenging puzzle, come with a hit of dopamine, the pleasure hormone. So, when the breadcrumbs are fit together to create a new idea, it tends to gel and become part of the believer's ego, strengthening any particular theory "discovered" in that way. And that is experienced as an emotional reward.

3. **Lamestream Media**

The mainstream media are not to be trusted, according to QAnoners, because the very essence of a conspiracy theory is its clandestine nature. The idea of a shared secret amongst a select few makes it quite personal and engaging in a community of likeminded members. Now the power is within the community and not available to the general population, deprived of this "special" information. This creates a feeling of superior group power, driving the adopted beliefs, expected to be scorned by mainstream media, giving meaning to the term fake news while, at the same time, creating a stronger tribal sense of belonging.

4. **Community**

The reason corporations involve their employees in team-building exercises is to build morale and facilitate bonding, so they function more effectively. This very same thinking goes into conspiracy-theory building. QAnoners solve the "puzzles" mentioned above as a team effort with clues being tossed back and forth among its members as the "solutions" are figured out, creating the "aha" experience of success.

Could all this QAnon dynamic ever have such an influence as to affect the national political scene—even to destroy our democracy? Let's look at one possible scenario.

A Case in History When Democracy was Actually Destroyed by Another Narcissist's Alternate Reality

Though most of us are convinced that it couldn't happen in the good ol' US of A, let's look at an historical account of when and how it did happen in a liberal democracy, so we don't get overly complacent.

Many countries have suffered transitions from democracy to virtual dictatorship with the help of powerful tribal thinking, the best-known being that by Adolf Hitler. Here are the details, if you need convincing, as to how this could happen within a few short months.

For this segment, imagine yourself a Ken Burns-type reporter, focusing on authentic events from various individuals' personal perspectives, leaving no interesting detail unexplored.

Let's pull the camera back and point it in the direction of history—about ninety years ago—so that we can see what happens when a narcissistic bully pulls the strings of government to further his own power and, in the process, transforms a democracy into a dictatorship, as many feared Trump might do in very recent history. The purpose of this somewhat detailed story is to offer a vision of what might have happened had Trump been successful in getting Mike Pence to change the electoral vote to allow Trump to manipulate a new government under his control, thereby creating a Constitutional crisis, making it possible to move toward a dictatorship.

To transform a well-working democracy into his own dictatorship, a narcissistic bully must first get the support of a major political party. Here's the story of how that happened in Germany almost a century ago.

In 1931, General Kurt von Schleicher was probably the most powerful figure in the German Weimar, the constitutional republic formed after surrender in World War I in the city of Weimar. He was a confidant of the eighty-two-year-old aristocratic President Paul von Hindenburg, who was the only one who had the power to hire or fire the chancellor.

In September of that year, the two of them were planning on using Adolf Hitler, the "Austrian corporal" as they called him, to act as a junior partner in overcoming the confused situation in the Reichstag, Germany's parliament. They supported his forming a right-wing coalition to offset the growing power of the communists in the Reichstag.

Because the conservatives of Germany in 1931, including Schleicher and Hindenburg, were more open to the extremist fringe rather than to democratic norms, Hitler was able to make his way into higher levels of power over a short period of time.

We now know that Hitler was likely a sociopathic paranoid personality with a persecution complex and addicted to power. But that was clearly not how he was being recognized at this point in our story. His confidence and charisma grew, and he eventually insisted on being named as chancellor so that his newly founded "Protection Squadron" or SS (for *Schutzstaffel* in German) could create a sense of power to quell the communists and democrats that threatened the aristocratic right wing in the government.

This is what Schleicher and Hindenburg wanted. They realized that the left wing and the strong unions could only be beaten by brute force, which the SS could easily accomplish, given enough elbow room by the local police to do so. They had their own little conspiracy. They believed strongly that they could get rid of Hitler when the uneasiness between right and left was settled by his SS forces.

Now here's where things get interesting. This is where the American insurrection of 2021 and dangerous dance with the failure of democracy find a parallel with what happened in Germany:

- **The narcissistic bully emerges as a strong leader and forms a coalition.** On January 30, 1933, Hindenburg agreed to allow Hitler, after his surprise win of 37 percent of the votes in the Reichstag, to become chancellor of Germany, then a democratic republic. Hitler now led the Reichstag, which contained the largest communist party outside of Russia.

- **The narcissistic bully then targets his enemies and instills public distrust.** Within weeks of that political victory, Hitler was able to maneuver President Hindenburg to sign off on allowing him free rein to make arrests of "enemies of the people," including communists and Jews. That one step was the end of democracy and the beginning of the reign of the National Socialist German Workers' Party—the Nazis. Hitler could now follow through on his claim to make Germany great again.

- **The narcissistic bully instigates an insurrection.** Now Hitler had his own bigger conspiracy in the making. On the twenty-seventh of February, the Reichstag itself was burned down and the communists were made to appear guilty of the act. Within a week, four thousand communists and social democrats were arrested by Hitler's militia and taken into "protective police custody" without legal recourse. All this was permitted by the March 23 Reichstag Decree called the Enabling Act, giving Hitler the right to enact his own laws independently of the Reichstag, overriding the Weimar Constitution and basically putting him above the law.

- **The narcissistic bully now becomes the dictator.** Hitler's SS, now headed by Heinrich Himmler, took over as his political police arm to enforce these arrests and oversee the transformation. Soon Himmler announced that a camp would be constructed in Dachau to "re-educate" those now in police custody.

It took less than a couple short months for Hitler to transform a democratic republic into what was becoming the most powerful dictatorship in modern history.

But Hitler's conspiracy was running into complications. Two problems remained: First, a battle of power between Hitler's own SS and the brown-shirted storm troopers (*Sturmabteilung* or "Storm Detachment"), made up largely of disgruntled former soldiers of the German army. They were headed by Ernst Rohm, one of Hitler's oldest friends, who refused to yield totally to Hitler's power. Second, demands on Hitler to satisfy two groups—the aristocratic government, primarily General Schleicher and the aging President Hindenburg on the one hand, and the masses of the working class wanting more power, on the other.

For this, Hitler did his best to take on the mantle of a solid statesman, leaving it to the storm troopers and SS to do the dirty work of keeping troublemakers under control. He also persuaded the legislature to allow him to acquire the role of president upon Hindenburg's passing, so he would then have complete control over Germany, combining the roles of president and chancellor.

In April of 1933, the Gestapo (abbreviation of *Geheime Staatspolizei* or Secret State Police) was formed by Hermann Goering as a secret police force to investigate anyone threatening the Nazi party, whether politically or in any other form.[42] They were soon allowed to operate without judicial review, putting them above the law to do whatever they wanted. If the press were to complain about this shocking event, the Nazis had their own term for "fake news," calling it *Lugenpresse, or* "lying press." But there was more to do to create the level of tribal thinking that Hitler was pursuing.

The other problem on Hitler's desk was satisfying the aristocratic faction that still saw him as a puppet to their claim to power, so he had to tackle the conspiracy of Hindenburg and von Schleicher. This was finally dramatically resolved at six thirty on the morning of June 30 when fifty-five victims, seen as antagonistic to Hitler's rise to power, were arrested by the SS, while Himmler distributed a list of storm troopers and others to be arrested and/or shot. In what is known as the Night of the Long Knives, many on that list lost their lives, including General von Schleicher. The conspiracy of power that Hitler had intricately fostered in a couple months was now a total fait accompli.[43]

Germany's constitution was gone, a thing of the past. Hitler proved it can be done. The rest is history—the dreadful and evil tribal mindset of an entire nation.

Never Again

That's how simple it was to transform a democratic republic into a dictatorship within a few short months. Of course, that could never happen in the United States of America . . . or could it? Trump caused many a concerned citizen to wonder and, when it was first brought to my attention, made this author (and likely many other Americans who trusted the power of our Constitution) to lose a few nights' sleep.

We do have the advantage of our presidential elections being run by the various states rather than by the Federal government. That makes it much more difficult to control the election process. Our Constitution attempts to protect the election process without too much constraint. The German constitution, under President von Hindenburg, was not as strong in protecting the electoral process.

Hopefully, never again will the traditions around our Constitution be so directly challenged, in spirit if not in fact, by an outgoing president with all the power allocated to that role. Trump taught us how fragile our Constitution can be as he tried his best to remain president as long as he could[44] by filing so many claims in the courts with questionable arguments, hoping that some would stick, and by subverting trust as the social currency of democratic politics. Fortunately for this institution of democracy, that did not work.

As far back as 1920, the legendary reporter H.L. Mencken predicted: "As democracy is perfected, the office of the president represents, more and more closely, the inner soul of the people. On some great and glorious day, the plain folks of the land will reach their heart's desire at last, and the White House will be occupied by a downright fool and a complete narcissistic moron."[45] It seems our Trumpian adventure was preordained.

The End of QAnon?

Trump's parting shot of inciting his followers to attack the Capitol on January 6, 2021 was almost his swan song. He took the chance of losing all that power in one fell swoop, leading to his second impeachment.[46] His tribe followed his commands, as those who were subsequently arrested insisted,[47] but the evidence was too overwhelming to allow the tribe to remain guilt-free—at least the most insidious group of perpetrators, some of them uncovered by the investigation of the January 6 Select Committee.

The larger picture is much more fearful and will not disappear any time soon. Congresswoman Marjorie Taylor Greene, with a strong history of supporting QAnon conspiracy theories, was at the center of controversy when she was appointed to two congressional committees,[48] but was soon relieved of those assignments by the Democrats.[49] After the Republicans took over the House following the midterm elections, and with the new speaker of the House needing all the votes he could muster, she was back to her former position of power.

The Storm is an assortment of conspiracy-theory elements that involve Satanic rituals on the part of Democratic leaders expected by QAnoners to come to judgment by a special date. Following Trump's defeat in the 2020 election and the subsequent disappointment on the part of his followers when they expected the Storm to bring Trump back to power on the following fourth of March (marked by QAnon as historically significant), there was the newly rejuvenated site, QAnonCasualties. Here, the disappointed could find some solace in community, one where former QAnoners could commiserate about the fall from grace of their former savior.

Starting in January 2021, this site went from a membership of about 10,000 to 130,000 following Biden's well-defended inauguration. While the mythical Q could explain in conspiracy terms how to understand what was going on,[50] this new site offered respite from the great disappointment when reality overshadowed expectations.

We need to look closely at the growing politics of demographics, in which many White supremacists and their ilk fear losing their power to a growing diversity. A government report in 2021 indicated that White supremacy attacks are expected to be on the rise.[51] So much uncertainty arose about the health of our democracy.

And why not? In this age of the Big Split, so many feel free to choose their own values, then feel lost and join groups that give them some sense of validation, whether supremacists, QAnoners, and even antifa (left-wing anti-fascists). Any sense of social trust in the larger society has all but vanished. So, conspiracies of trust abound. Each group has its own set of values based on its own mythology, its own unique needs, its hopes based on fantasies of overcompensation.

Some believe there are now four demographic groups that have their own separate values: [52]

1. **Free Americans** who are conservative and want less dependency on government handouts.

2. **Smart Americans**, the liberal, educated elite who enjoy success based on their own merits.

3. **Real Americans**, blue collar workers from the Christian heartland who are most prone to conspiracy theories.

4. **Just Americans**, largely made up of woke millennials who feel marginalized and are easily found at protest rallies.

Each of these groups has its own "alternate reality" in terms of a history of shared values, purpose in, and meaning of, life as well as moral identity. In very rough terms, Free Americans could be seen, in my opinion, as the non-aligned voters who tend toward Trump's Republicans because they share his conservative values; Smart Americans as dedicated Democrats; Real Americans as Trump's base; and Just Americans as younger individuals who, if they feel strongly enough about a cause, end up coming to protests.

Another group that feared losing its power is exemplified by the senators who voted against Trump's conviction in his second impeachment trial despite vocally admonishing him the day of the insurrection. Many wondered how the tribal mindset accounted for those decisions despite the clear connection between Trump's incitement and the horrendous attack against the Capitol. The answer is simple. It wasn't fear of Trump's ire that concerned the senators but rather the loss of power in their political future should they disappoint their constituents and lose their favor in the then forthcoming elections.[53]

Getting into the Senate is a life-long aspiration and political conquest. Giving up that power is not easily done, even if it means making a choice that many considered immoral. One other tribal factor, should they turn away from Trump's protection, was the potential for emotional and physical harassment by dedicated followers of Trump, primarily members of QAnon—that was indeed a scary proposition.

Would it be possible to hasten the end of The Big Split and aspire to what we can call The Return to Trust?

The challenge, of course, is to get QAnoners and others to approach this logical thought process when most of them are so emotional and passionate about their beliefs. So, let's turn from senators and their issues to the challenging role of finding trust in an alternate reality, using an emotionally oriented solution to this logically based challenge.

A Conversation about Truth Over Lies

What if you were to know someone about whom you feel very good, maybe a close friend or even a relative, who is a staunch believer in conspiracy theories? You don't want to lose the relationship, yet you can't really hide your feelings about being staunchly opposed to those false beliefs. How can you save that relationship and still be honest about the differences between you?

Sounds like a familiar dilemma, doesn't it? You're hoping your honesty doesn't cause a break of some kind.

So, what should you do?

Well, you're in a quandary. You feel more than torn, like you want to teach this person your version of the truth, because theirs just doesn't make sense to you. So, you're frustrated. You're wondering if there's a way to convince them that they're wrong without alienating them.

But you really want to be fair-minded about this. Open-minded might be a better term. So, one solution is to really listen to them, even though you're not really interested in listening to them. You really want to change their mind, their way of thinking, like they're wrong and you're right.

You try to listen more, and not be so sold on your own ideas to be right for them even though it's a bit of a struggle for you.

So, if you're planning on being open-minded, then, yes, you need to listen with more of an open mind. But that's not what you really wanted to do. You really want to set them straight, so to speak.

That's not easy to do. It may be hard for you to hide that. You're caught between almost trying to get them to change their mind on the one hand, and really listening without judgment on the other.

You finally get to the point, without wasting much time, that to really communicate with someone with whom you disagree, it's better to listen than to prove yourself the right one. But you *are* right, you feel. Otherwise, why would you bother?

What's becoming clear is that if you're really going to make any progress in changing someone's mind, you need to

> allow yourself to be receptive to change as well.

But that's a bit concerning. Why would you consider changing your mind? Now you begin to realize what it takes.

> True listening means entering the verbal exchange with as much openness as you hope the other person entertains.

You can hope to change the other's mind only if you allow yourself to be truly open to change as well. It's like a gunslinger dropping his holster before entering a confrontation with another gunslinger who does the same. It's not fair if one of them has a gun but not the other. So, to be effective in this verbal exchange, you need to entertain as much change as the other.

The point that is so powerful here is that this will not be a brief chat. If there's any hope of success, it involves a deep dive into one another's points of view. You can be open about where you're coming from rather than being manipulative. Part of why so much rancor occurs is because people make wild assumptions on both sides, but there is truly common ground only if people are open to it.

> Exploring your belief in the truth in one of two alternate realities involves openness to the other's belief in his version of what he may consider the truth.

It's the sharing of viewpoints and values and life circumstances that might lead to change—*for either of you*! At the end of your talk, hopefully, the actual truth will prevail—for both of you.

It comes down to my Principle of Trust:

> Acknowledging the other's Point of View →
> Understanding → Empathy → Trust

Truth Conquers Lies: How to Talk Someone Out of Conspiracy Theory

So, now imagine you're sitting across from someone who is clearly a passionate believer in QAnon. You've made the decision to do what you can to persuade this individual from such wrong and erroneous beliefs and return them to normalcy. Their expression is not threatening yet slightly antagonistic, because they might feel a bit defensive about you trying to change their mind about something very important to them. You don't want to antagonize them unnecessarily, but you do want to focus clearly on heading them on the "right" path. You've got a warm cup of coffee to spur you on; they've got a cool beer at hand.

If, after hearing all this, you're still open to the position to do your best to talk them out of conspiracy theory beliefs, then you might try the following:

1. **Keep an Open Mind**: Don't be dismissive of your friend's system of beliefs. Be there. Approach them with an open mind, ask questions, and do that as sincerely as you can. That means making yourself vulnerable, of course, and that's the point. You're not coming to beat down the other's belief system; you're coming to explore possibilities. Otherwise, you're wasting your time.

2. **Explore Together:** Discuss the existence of true conspiracies. You can start with the covering up of such well-known sexual predators as Jeffrey Epstein and Harvey Weinstein; and the real possibility that JFK was shot—accidentally—by a Secret Service agent as depicted in the well-documented book, *Mortal Error*;[54] the cover-ups in the Catholic Church; how Big Tobacco hid data on cancer due to smoking, etc. That'll give you some common ground to tread on together as a beginning.

3. **Talk about the Technology**: Ask them what they know about the technology of social media and about algorithms. If you can get them to understand the process of information dispersal and the selection of information via algorithms, at least they'll have a working knowledge of what is possible in terms of "fake news."

4. **Examine the Facts:** Then, together, look for the data in real life. If there were any truth to the Pizzagate theory, to use a very well-known one, where are the reports of the

mothers of these abducted children? Why are they staying so silent from the press? Most children reported missing, in truth, return home after a few days (about 99 percent). And others involve custody disputes in which one parent takes the child for a long weekend. So where are the data? According to an estimate from the federal Office of Juvenile Justice and Delinquency Prevention, there were only 165 kidnappings between late 2010 and late 2011, and only sixty-five were by strangers.[55] These aren't the data believed true by QAnoners—they believe something like 800,000.

5. **Take Your Time:** No one is going to change a belief system in one day, just because they talked with you for an hour or two. It'll take time, for both of you, to let things gel, be digested, thought about and mulled over. In our media-saturated world where we want things so fast, few people can sit with their thoughts and reflect. For the conspiracy theorist, I'd say that time is the enemy—any sustained thinking on x or y or z will pose a threat to them, so they refuse and just go with dramatic and quick solutions. So, slow down with all this.

6. **Take the Initiative in Hearing the Other's Story Deeply:** Here's the toughest part. If you want the other to be receptive to changing beliefs, you've got to be coming from the same place. Can you, for the moment, enter your friend's point of view and understand the conspiracy theory they hold so dearly to fortify their world of beliefs? There's a whole structure there that fits in with their personality needs for control, security, and freedom from the uncertainty that keeps people awake at night. There's a lot to be gained from a group that identifies membership with solidarity in a mixed-up, complex world. Who knows—you might even understand more deeply why they considered believing in conspiracy theories to start with. They might then switch

to your point of view. But at least you're in this exploration together, not one-sided, and that's how change begins.

7. **Tell the Stories of Your Life:** Finally, here's a possible magic bullet that will make things happen when you're down to your last-ditch effort. Tell the stories of your life that help the other really feel where you're coming from and invite them to do the same. Tell the stories that reveal your deepest self, what gave birth to your values and beliefs, possibly from the perspective of a young coming of age. Now encourage them to do the same so you can get a sense of why they chose the path they took, including their allegiance to the conspiracy theories by which they live. Once these stories are shared, you are as close to one another as you can be and here's where the shift to fact-based reality is most likely. But, beware, whatever the ending, you will likely feel like friends for life.

If all this sounds like too much work, let me ask you this: what would it take to change your mind to cross over the chasm of difference and be persuaded to become a QAnoner? It's not about talking anyone out of anything; it's rather about stepping into one another's shoes. That's how change can take place. Neither easily nor quickly, but it is clearly possible to achieve this, if you are open to putting in the energy.

So, if you are brave enough to enter this very personal dialogue with a "believer," go through each of the seven points to reach an end point where both of you have shared very personal experiences, values, and aspirations, then you earn the title of open-hearted communicator. Whether you succeed or not, you've done your part in maintaining a relationship with someone who is important to you despite the philosophical differences. And the skills you gained in trying this out will last you for the rest of your life. It *is* a life-changing exercise.

In this chapter, we began by outlining why QAnon has been so successful in growing over the years, what psychological factors draw its members. We saw how Trump's bullying approach got him to the top. We saw how powerful conspiracy theories can work, influencing a nation's government sufficiently to warrant concerns about a coup, as almost happened in our nation, or create circumstances for taking over a nation, as Hitler was able to do following the burning of the Reichstag in 1933.

Finally, we offered a seven-step approach to bridging the gap between you and a close friend or relative by taking the time to explore the differences that keep you apart politically, and perhaps emotionally.

In the next chapter, we'll start with the question, where is the real truth in politics? We'll take a final overview of the split in American politics and see how Trump went wrong, lying to the nation and, at the same time, labeling mainstream media as fake news. We'll also take a look at threats against reporters and a birds-eye view of the growth of conspiracy theories, particularly the original Pizzagate conspiracy theory, and the essential role played by TV huckster, Alex Jones, in building Trump's image (just as Trump was simultaneously building Jones' image).

CHAPTER SEVEN

More Bias, Less Accuracy: The Growth of Nastiness

*I've sat in the Oval Office with both people. Just in case
you couldn't tell, they're very different people.*

—Barack Obama, about Trump and Biden, in a talk in
Florida on Oct. 27, 2020

*It's all one big conspiracy. Just there's naebody [sic]
pulling all the strings.*

—James Oswald

*Conspiracy theory is the ultimate refuge of the
powerless. If you cannot change your own life, it must
be that some greater force controls the world.*

—Roger Cohen

What is political truth these days of the Big Split? How do we separate the *actual* truth from the embellished, alternate truth? How do we learn to trust what is real from what is fed to us by political pundits, on one side or the other?

I once asked an attorney how best to make a point in court, and she said, "Repeat it often." At another time, I asked a highly successful social scientist how to make your new discoveries heard, and he said, "Share them often and loudly."

Two Political Realities

Truth is not absolute, though we tend to think it is.

We think of truth as irrevocable, like the Earth traveling about the Sun. But at one time in our history, it was considered true that the Sun revolved around the Earth. And, at that time, it was an incontrovertible consensus of truth. Science, as well as other institutions, continues to adapt to new findings, just as the laws of our nation keep changing, depending, in part, on the decisions of the higher courts.

Some years ago, we had a well-balanced Supreme Court. Recently, it became more conservative. Then, as we were in the process of exchanging one Democrat nominee for retiring Stephen Bryer, look at the haranguing that Judge Ketanji Brown Jackson suffered during her interrogation by the Senate Republicans. There appeared to be two distinct versions of the truth behind the questioning by the respective parties—two alternate realities.

One line of questioning, on the part of the Democrats, was cordial and respectful, as it should be. That reflected one reality. The other, by the Republicans, was quite the opposite—aggressive, demeaning, and coming from a totally different sense of reality. This hardworking judge with an impeccable record, was treated like an evil villain, with leanings toward pedophilia and softness on crime.

"But Republicans could not help themselves," reported journalist Carl Hulse. "In long days of questioning, many of them tried to destroy Judge Jackson, or at least drag her through the muck on her way to a confirmation they knew was certain if Democrats remained united behind her."[1] Two separate realities in one legislative body—two versions of truth. What was true in characterizing the nature of the Supreme Court in years past will not be true in the coming years. Indeed, the court in which Ruth Ginsberg thrived some short years ago will not be the same, just as the legal arguments from the

Supreme Court will change reality as cases are decided in a much more conservative fashion. Institutions and their values change, in this case transforming the truth of what is legal and what is not.

So, what is true today is true for today, but not necessarily for next year. And, as institutions change, whether science or law or religion, our values change as well, sometimes quickly, as in these two examples, other times in such subtle manner that we hardly notice it, just like the proverbial frog sitting in a pot of water being heated to the boiling point ever so slowly. We are more vulnerable to changing attitudes than we realize, whether that's in shifting musical tastes or the acceptance of same-sex marriage.

When we hear inaccuracies offered as truth, we can clearly discern the departure from reality—but only if we oppose the values of the speaker.

We create our own versions of the truth

as we develop our understanding of the world with all its complexities. That's why we have two parties that struggle with two version of political reality. In our democracy, we allow for varying versions of political reality and attempt to resolve these differences through elections, debate in Congress, and the courts. The interrogations of Ketanji Brown Jackson as nominee for the Supreme Court revealed that clearly.

Your version of the truth depends on your outlook and values, as well as the information you prefer to access. The current political discussion has become so heated that two so-called truths often clash. That's what's happened to trust as seen in the recent years of American politics. Many of us just don't know whom, or what, to trust in this Big Split.

For example, is there a "deep state" working as a countermeasure to the Republican influence? Absolutely, for some Republicans; and laughable for many a Democrat. Both groups trust their sources of information equally.

Some governments, like those of France and Malaysia, punish those who dissemble false news. France, as it turns out, does have a law against publishing material that is too inflammatory on racial or ethnic issues.[2] Now the question becomes, who will check on the accuracy?

Bias Overrides Accuracy: We Learn from Those We Trust

Having two sides to a story is hardly new. Until it was revoked by the courts in 1987, a Fairness Doctrine was enforced by the Federal Communications Commission, giving equal time to opposing factions on the air, especially on controversial topics. It was after the revocation of that law that the flush of right-wing pundits became so popular on the radio waves.[3]

The standard television networks, on the other hand, seem more liberal, Fox News and a collection of MAGA-leaning networks being the exceptions. Why is this so, I've wondered over the years. Could it be because radio pundits talk with less restraint while TV reporters have producers behind the scenes, reminding them of what to focus on through their earpiece? Radio may have a different audience, drivers to and from work whose attention must be maintained through emotional engagement, while the TV audiences are seated and prepared to spend time with the screen in front of them.

Would such forcefully mandated equal time in dialogue by the FCC merit more trust in the accuracy of information? Hardly so, according to research by Brendan Nyhan of Dartmouth College and Jason Reifler of the University of Exeter.[4] People trust whatever reinforces their existing value system. The research found that even when fact-checkers corrected errors, those who disagreed with the correction trusted the initial message (in error) even more. Fact-correction is not a cure for fake news because of the underlying bias held by those viewing the news.

White supremacists, for example, will not be persuaded to give up their intensely held values by the facts supporting human diversity.

> Bias overrides accuracy.[5]

Such bias and the resultant trust issue are strongly reinforced by group learning from friends, relatives, and colleagues. This social process sometimes overwhelms learning from more reliable sources.

According to Theunis Bates, editor of *The Week* magazine,

> For decades, Americans have been steadily segregating themselves into likeminded communities: Liberals live near and socialize with fellow liberals, gun owners with gun owners, evangelicals with evangelicals. This clustering is echoed online. The algorithms that power Facebook, where 44 percent of Americans get their news, ensure that we're only presented with stories and opinions from friends, family, and news outlets that confirm our pre-existing biases—including fake news.[6]

The Growth of Nastiness

> Not only do those who think alike tend to live near one another, they also dislike the other side more than they support their own.

So, trusting others has decreased not only in terms of proximity but also in terms of choosing animosity rather than cohesiveness. The Big Split is sometimes based on dislike rather than togetherness and on an "us versus them" basis. It takes time to become well informed and base one's trust on facts. It's much easier to scan what the friends around you think and say and to create a simplistic enemy out of those who are different and difficult to understand.

In his book, *The Great Alignment*, Professor Alan Abramowitz of Emory University writes:

> Over the past two decades, the proportion of party supporters . . . who have strongly negative feelings toward the opposite party has risen sharply. A growing number of Americans have been voting against the opposing party rather than for their own.[7]

According to Abramowitz, this has to do with factors that have arisen since the end of World War II: issues of immigration, globalization, technological change, growing ethnic and racial diversity, and changes in family roles and structure.

Like-minded friends affirm one another, sharpening the divide. And with social media readily available, we can choose to reinforce our bias in so many ways and contexts. Fox News, for example, pushes its viewers to the right and, in response to the viewing public, broadcasts material even further to the right to maintain its hold on this audience. According to Gregory Martin of Emory University and Ali Yurukoglu of Stanford University, removing Fox News from the media would have reduced the Republican vote by about 0.46 percent in 2000 but, in 2008, that same removal would have reduced the Republican vote by 6.34 percent.[8] Apparently, in the interim between these elections, news media have become more influential, creating more partisan-based trust. Might this dynamic be true for CNN as well?

This bias works both ways. According to Alan Abramowitz, on a 100-degree "feeling thermometer," each of the two parties gave their own group 71 degrees in 1978 and 70 degrees in 2012. But, over that same time span, the scores they gave opposing parties slid from 47 degrees to 30 degrees. Nastiness has grown over the years, and trust in the other side declined significantly. Even independent centrists are now more likely to lean into one side or the other, "voting more along party lines than at any time in the past century," according to Abramowitz.[9] There's no denying that any openness to the other side has significantly diminished.

Draining the Swamp

Part of the falling level of trust has to do with promises made by the past administration and not ever fulfilled, such as:

- Keeping immigrants out by building *the wall*.[10]
- Returning coal mines to their decades-earlier prominence.[11]
- Fixing the infrastructure.[12]
- Offering better, cheaper, and more available health care.[13]
- Draining the swamp, instead of recruiting individuals who were forced to leave the White House because the "swamp" just got worse, like former EPA chief Scott Pruitt and many others.[14]

As a specific example of not "draining the swamp," Pruitt was suspected of using federal money for personal travel and living arrangements and having a shady role in getting a business for his wife. He had to battle eleven federal investigations. Here are some of his extravagances: a $43,000 phone booth with soundproof enhancement, flying first class at government expense amounting to $160,000, round-the-clock guards amounting to $3 million, biometric locks on his office doors, and a custom SUV, all at our expense. And then there's the rental of part of a Washington, DC condo for $50 a night from a fossil fuel lobbyist.[15]

And his approach to environmental issues? Allowing manufacturers to dump more toxins into our rivers, persuading President Trump to pull out of the Paris climate accord, and basically tearing down everything that President Obama had worked hard to make the EPA a more effective agency.[16] Why did Trump get rid of Pruitt? Not because of all the transgressions themselves, according to *The New York Time*'s Frank Bruni, but because Trump felt it was generating too much negative press.[17]

So, what did Trump have to say at Pruitt's departure under the shadow of such disgrace? "Scott has done an outstanding job, and I will always be thankful for this," according to the *Wall Street Journal*.[18] With Pruitt's departure, according to John Fund in FoxNews.com, "Trump has unburdened himself from a political liability."[19]

Are you still wondering what ever happened to the level of your willingness to trust politicians?

Fake News or Fox News?

In his book, *Standoff*, Bill Schneider maintains that, although this mutual decline in trust did not begin with Trump, he "uses every issue, every policy, every tweet to set one group ... against another,"[20] whether in the context of race, immigration, our response to the Covid-19 pandemic, or other prominent public issues whatsoever.

According to *The Washington Post*, during his entire term in office, Trump made 30,573 false or misleading claims. Almost half came in his final year, as tallied by The Fact Checker. As a result of Trump's constant lying through the presidential megaphone, claimed presidential historian Michael Beschloss, "more Americans are skeptical of genuine facts than ever before." [21] Some may seem like paltry mistakes, but they set a tone for the difference between such lies or inaccuracies and what Trump referred to as fake news, what the mainstream news reports after the due diligence of professional journalists. Since 39 percent of political viewers get their news from Fox broadcasts, it's not surprising that all these errors were accepted by so many.[22]

Threats to Reporters

Tony Schwartz, co-author of Trump's 1987 book, *The Art of the Deal*, commented on a CNN broadcast on July 15, 2018, that "we are in a true emergency" of Trump's "decompensating." After the showing of a clip in which Trump declared, "I'm a very stable genius," Schwartz went on to opine that this conveyed "a deep insecurity" on Trump's part, explaining that he had been trying to understand Trump's behavior by consulting with psychiatrists for over thirty years. "Journalists are in a challenging position" these days because Trump was so hard to understand, he said. "I'm relieved not to be a journalist right now." [23]

So, when does trust stop depending on accurate information and start leaning toward partisan values? In so many words, what ever happened to trust? Part of the answer may be the past administration's attitude toward the mainstream press. Trump's characterization of the mainstream press as *fake* had deep ramifications. Kathleen Parker of *The Washington Post* reported on the 2018 murder of journalists at the *Capital Gazette* in Annapolis, Maryland. She quoted one of her regular readers, a Vietnam Marine veteran, from a message he sent to her: "I'm concerned for your safety. Trump's demonizing of the press has led us down a dark path." She goes on to speak for herself:

> Rhetoric matters, and Trump's has been toxic toward the media. "Fake news" has become the Trump base's second-favorite mantra, following "Make America Great Again." What's clear is that Trump has made it a verbal open season on journalists. For all of us ink-stained wretches, the hate mail is more vicious. The death threats more frequent.[24]

Before the November 2020 elections came up, what were former Trump administration members saying about him? John Bolton came out with his highly critical book, *The Room Where It Happened*,[25] where he describes how totally uninformed and impulsive were Trump's decisions. Retired Marine General Jim Mattis accused Trump of making a "mockery of our Constitution." General Mark Milley, a former top military advisor, apologized for being part of the photo op that Trump engineered after clearing Lafayette Square of peaceful protestors with force so he could be seen holding a Bible at Ashburton House at St. John's Church across from the White House. NFL Commissioner, Roger Goodell, reversed his position on the players kneeling as protest, causing Trump to refer to the protesting players as "super-left liberals." Even those who were originally supportive of the Trump administration had lost their trust in him. And then we had Trump's niece, Mary Trump, reveal her story about her childhood experience with a man she learned to mistrust completely.[26]

The Trump-Putin Intrigue

What about trust between Donald Trump and Vladmir Putin? Russia and other political players shared destructive statements that did not connect with the standard media's version of truth. Their hacking into the voters' realm of influence fed into this convoluted issue of trust. When Trump visited with Vladimir Putin in Helsinki in July of 2018, Trump delivered the message during the subsequent press conference that Putin's denial of influencing the presidential election settled the case. And that would be the end of it. A day later, Trump attempted to change his story. On the *Anderson Cooper 360* TV show, Tom Friedman, author of *Thank You for Being Late* and other seminal books, referred to Trump's comments on this as an "ex-post-facto Scrabble game" tinged with "dictatorship envy."[27]

Others, trying to understand Trump's patronizing attitude toward Putin, wondered if Trump had been compromised somehow by Putin. Leon Panetta, former CIA Director, wondered out loud whether Trump's actions at Helsinki were disloyal to America.[28] Others wondered if Trump could be accused of giving comfort to the enemy. Trump's response to all this was to turn it around, his usual modus operandi. "The level of dishonesty in your profession," he told reporters, "is extremely high."[29] He began using the term *fake news media*, rather than merely *fake news*, characterizing this as the real enemy of the people. A former *New York Times* journalist quit her profession because she was tired of dealing with the hall of mirrors that journalism had become. "He makes us the story," she claimed.[30]

In the last week of July 2020, reports indicated that Putin was paying a bounty for American troops killed by the Afghans. At the same time, Trump shared with the public that he had had one of his phone calls with Putin that week. When asked by the press whether Trump had confronted Putin with this issue, Trump claimed that the news had "never reached my desk," but that he would "take it under consideration" since the reporter had now informed him of this. The press later learned that he had been informed of this in his daily briefing nearly six months earlier, on February 27. Then, in his interview with *Axios'* Jonathan Swan, Trump defended himself by saying, "Well, we supplied weapons when they [the Taliban] were fighting Russia too."[31]

Though tough on other top nations such as China and Iran, Trump seemed to have had a special "sweetheart" relationship with Putin. American pundits couldn't figure that one out. What was Trump's motivation? Could it be that Trump so much appreciated Putin's contribution to social media during the presidential elections to help him get elected? And that he hoped for more of such support?

What more is there to add? You, as a reader, can draw your own conclusions about how Trump was continuing to erode any trust in his word.

Pizzagate and Other Conspiracy Theories

In October of 2016, a conspiracy theory involving a pizza joint called Comet Ping Pong came into being. This is where Hillary Clinton was reported by Reddit to have a child pornography ring going on and that she was kidnapping children for this purpose.[32] The conspiracy took on momentum as the election date approached.

The term "Pizzagate" was coined, and this conspiracy theory was off to the races. With 24,000 followers, it was getting too dangerous. "We were all in fear—serious fear," claimed James Alefantis, the owner of Comet.[33]

There was a following of conspiracy believers and one of them, carrying an AR-15 assault rifle, came "to the rescue," making his way through the building and, of course, finding nothing. Fortunately, the police were called in time, the man was arrested, and no physical harm was done. But the possibility certainly was there.[34]

Conspiracy theories have been with us for a long time, dating as far back as the beginning of our nation's battling the American Indian as we strove westward to fulfill what we believed was our Manifest Destiny. According to historian Jeffrey Pasley, every resistance of American natives protecting their home turf, according to the theory, was under the control of an Indian mastermind, possibly the Devil himself, controlling tens of thousands of warriors. Known as the *myth of the super chief*, this was one of the first historically recorded incidents of conspiracy theories.[35]

In modern times, there were conspiracy theories about Kennedy's assassination and faking the trip to the Moon, and always stories about the Clintons. In the 1950s, Senator Joseph McCarthy made a successful political career with the theory that Hollywood was awash with communists.

> The fact is that uninformed people want simple answers to complex questions but garnished with creative imagination and drama.

When Trump started using the term *fake news* in 2017, aimed at all stories critical of him, it became so broadly used that, at one point, Sean Hannity, Trump's main man at Fox News, reinforced the term by pointing to the back of the room and calling out to the TV camera, "All those people in the back of the room are fake news."[36]

Conspiracy theories work well for their makers some of the time but not always. Jack Burkman tried to make a career of using them. In one attempt he promised to bring a woman to the public who would claim that she was sexually assaulted by Robert Mueller, principal of the impeachment investigation against Trump. In a very awkward press conference he called, the skepticism among the reporters attending was highly evident. There was no woman, no name, just promises, which the more veteran reporters recognized as empty.[37]

Other conspiracy theories reported by Burkman involved Chief Justice John Roberts being accused of having an addiction to opioids and one account accusing the government of killing former Democratic National Committee staffer, Seth Rich, who actually died in a botched robbery attempt on him two years prior.[38]

From Jones's Mouth to Trump's Ears

Alex Jones, a professional conspiracy entrepreneur, has a radio show called *InfoWars*, in which he initiates stories that are strange, imaginative, highly dramatic, and totally unfounded in fact. Trump was one of his guests and said on the air to Jones, "I will not let you down." As a matter of fact, many of Trump's strange falsehoods were almost direct quotes from Jones, from whom Trump was apparently getting his cues to attack Hillary Clinton during the 2016 elections.[39]

Some of Jones' theories: that the 1995 Oklahoma City bombing was fake;[40] that the yogurt company, Chobani, was importing "migrant rapists" to their plant in Idaho;[41] and that Hillary Clinton was enabling others in the raping and murdering of little children.[42]

In her book, *Republic of Lies*, Anna Merlan writes:

Jones and Trump were in fact longtime mutual fans. After announcing his run, candidate Trump made one of his first media appearances on Jones's show, appearing via Skype from Trump Tower. Jones endorsed him early and often and, in turn, many of the radio host's favorite talking points started turning up in Trump's speeches. Jones began darkly predicting that the elections would be "rigged" in Clinton's favor, a claim that Trump quickly made a central tenet of the latter days of his campaign.[43]

So, conspiracy theories live on, and they show no signs of dying off. As Sally Buzbee, executive editor of the Associated Press, put it in 2020, "Conspiratorial thinking is the future of this presidency."[44]

QAnon: From Conspiracy Theory to Political Movement

As a matter of fact, Trump had been questioned by the press about his support of QAnon, a group dedicated to revitalizing conspiracy theories like Pizzagate and several other theories that revolve around the so-called deep state and other plots to take down opponents of the government. Trump's response was that the theory was "something worth listening to and paying attention to," and referred to Q as a "patriot."[45]

Supposedly, Q was a military officer who began posting messages on the internet anonymously. This grew to include millions of followers, enough for the FBI to consider the group a domestic-terror threat.[46]

How many believe conspiracy theories? Up to one fourth of the American population, according to the Pew Research Center.[47] The main explanation for that is the need for people, especially those who feel disempowered, such as the less educated and the poor, to feel that they belong to a group that claims power, as was thoroughly discussed in the last chapter. This need for belonging is clearly manifested in their motto: "Where we go one, we go all."⁴⁸

Left out of the mainstream of Washington politics, they create their own center of power and follow the conspiracy theories, as opposed to "fake news," like a religion. Their hope is to "take this global cabal of Satan-worshiping pedophiles [referring to Pizzagate] out," as Georgia Republican Marjorie Taylor Greene put it. "Together, we can save our republic," added QAnon supporter Republican Jo Rae Perkins of Oregon. According to Secretary of Transportation Pete Buttigieg, the followers of this extremist ideology are needing "a sense of belonging that people are looking for any place that they can find it.⁴⁹

QAnon started on October 28, 2017, when the anonymous Q predicted the arrest of Hillary Clinton, and that Trump, whom believers saw as a messianic hope, would send thousands of Democratic elites to Guantanamo Bay. This would be known as The Storm. It was suspected that the size of QAnon was somewhat over three million members spread over 175 groups, many of them believing that Trump himself might very well be Q. According to University of North Carolina researcher Alice Marwick, QAnon has "a different way to interpret the world, which colors everything they see."⁵⁰

The influence of QAnon just continued to grow months before the 2020 election. *The New York Times* revealed how much:

A small but growing number of Republicans—including a heavily favored Republican congressional candidate in Georgia—are donning the QAnon mantle, ushering its adherents in from the troll-infested fringes of the internet and potentially transforming the wild conspiracy theory into an offline political movement, with supporters running for Congress and flexing their political muscle at the state and local levels.⁵¹

In that same article, one well-known Republican did not hide her love for Q. Marjorie Taylor Greene was quoted by the *Times* as saying that she looked forward to "a once-in-a-lifetime opportunity to take this global cabal of Satan-worshiping pedophiles [the Democrats] out."

Collusion? What Collusion? Oh, That Collusion!

But sometimes the truth, in a somewhat rare outcome, is finally revealed, a truth determined by both parties in the Senate, about an issue that had been heavily debated over time: the question as to whether the Russians interfered with the 2016 elections. After three years of investigation, the Senate Intelligence Committee released their report of almost one thousand pages revealing the following:

- "Russian intelligence services viewed members of the Trump campaign as easily manipulated.
- "The report portrayed a Trump campaign that was stocked with businessmen with no government experience, advisers working at the fringes of the foreign policy establishment and other friends and associates Mr. Trump had accumulated over the years."
- Even though there was no direct agreement between Trump's campaign and the Russians, and therefore no evidence of collusion as such, "The report showed extensive evidence of contacts between Trump campaign advisers and people tied to the Kremlin."[52]

What a breath of fresh air, to see both sides of the aisle come together to spend enough time to determine a truth that no one, except perhaps Trump himself, could deny! So, the good news is that fake news, given enough time and bipartisan attention, can ultimately prevail as not fake at all. But this is only a single truth that must fight against the multitude of conspiracy theories.

Trust During the Pandemic

In the final analysis, trust is essential for cooperation in the world of politics. The pandemic raged in one country after another and governments attempted to mitigate the illness by having their populace tighten up with their discipline of the Three Ws: Wear your mask, wash your hands, and watch your distance. But then there's the case of Iran, where lack of trust was clearly a barrier to controlling the virus. According to Jonathan Wolfe of *The New York Times,*

> This is a government [Iran] that for forty years has told people what to do, how to dress, how to behave—and many people's mindset is to always defy what the government says. So now, when there's a pandemic, and the government tells them, "Stay home, wear a mask," they're like: "No. We don't trust you."[53]

Trust is a primary issue, especially when it comes to leading a nation through the threat of Covid-19. An even greater cause for fearing loss of trust came closer to home when Trump threatened to create chaos during the past election, referring to the balloting process as "a fraud and a sham and proof of a rigged election."[54]

This attack on Biden's win continued for months and months. By the fall of 2021, there were three Republicans who had backed the Stop the Steal movement who were now running for chief election officials in Georgia, Arizona, and Nevada.[55]

How Trump's Win Was "Called Off"

Election denialism was becoming a stock phrase in the news, referring to the boiler plate attack on any Democratic wins, fostered by such Fox News commentators as Tucker Carlson and Tomi Lahren. "This whole notion of fraud and elections," according to lieutenant governor of Georgia, Geoff Duncan, "it's a shiny object that quite honestly is about trying to save face and not own reality."[56]

In order to keep the election denialism alive after Trump's loss to Biden in 2020, Fox News competitors like One America News and Newsmax just ignored the loss and insisted that Trump had won, or at least that the election was rigged. Fox was losing eyes on the screen, so its owner, Rupert Murdoch, decided to move even further to the right, giving his viewers what they wanted: their own version of the election, supporting the Stop the Steal movement.[57]

One of the reasons Trump and his followers were so chagrined at losing the election was because the early votes looked very good for him—what pollsters called *the red mirage*—only to be followed by late Democrat mail-in votes—creating *the blue wave*. Trump chose to call this "an embarrassment to our country . . . We were winning everything and, all of a sudden, it was called off."[58]

Not Social Media But Trump Media

Trump began spreading mistrust of the election process, starting the Stop the Steal movement, despite the lack of any evidence of fraud when those claims were investigated. Bill Gates, on the Board of Supervisors in Maricopa County, Arizona, reported, "This has been the most scrutinized election we've ever run."[59]

Trump's next tactic was to change the Electoral College votes that took place on December 14. He even attempted to coerce the states to send separate electors to change those results.

On January 2, 2021, Trump called Georgia Secretary of State Brad Raffensperger and demanded the votes be recounted to get an extra "essentially eleven thousand votes . . . and there's nothing wrong with, you know, um, that you've recalculated."

When Raffensperger told Trump that social media was not always accurate, Trump replied, "Oh, this isn't social media. This is Trump media."[60]

With Trump questioning the election in the State of Georgia, attempting to disenfranchise the votes there, Raffensperger ordered a hand count to verify the original results, which was verified as accurate.

Geoff Duncan, lieutenant governor of Georgia, was the most outspoken Republican, characterizing the Stop the Steal movement as "hate growing . . . over a mirage." In his book, *GOP 2.0*, he points to the possibility of a new Republican Party, with empathy and engagement rather than conspiracy theories and personal threats.[61]

A Political Calculation of Faking Mob Mentality

According to Bob Woodward and Robert Costa, co-authors of the book *Peril*, Trump demanded that his vice president, Mike Pence, force a change in the Electoral College vote when the votes were to be officially declared on January 6, 2021. Pence was in a quandary. He conferred with former VP Dan Quayle, who told him that Pence didn't have any legal power to do so, and Pence accepted that advice.[62]

But, on that very infamous day, at the Stop the Steal gathering near the Capitol, Trump declared to the eager crowd that cold morning, "We're taking this country back!" and then added, "We'll never take back our country with weakness."[63]

The violence that followed was predicted by several people. Republican representative Adam Kinzinger predicted, "You have to understand, there will be violence."[64] In the book, *Peril*, Steve Bannon is described as happily announcing the day before on his War Room broadcast that "It's going to be quite extraordinarily different."[65]

US Representative Anthony Gonzalez was concerned. "The country can't survive torching the Constitution," he said.[66]

When the vote came for impeaching Trump for all these activities, only ten Republicans voted for impeachment. Those who talked with the Trump supporters in person and in private, such as Liz Cheney, revealed that most of them did not really believe the election was stolen, but were going along with the mob mentality to maintain their status in the party and because of the pressure put on them, particularly threats to the families of those who spoke out against Trump. "Very few," she revealed, believed the election was stolen. It was more of "a political calculation."[67]

Cheney, then the third most powerful person in her party, was replaced by lesser-known New York representative, thirty-seven-year-old Elise Stefanik, who was much more receptive to Trump's issues.[68]

From Civil Strife to Civil War?

Those who invaded the Capitol appeared convinced that Trump was still legally the president. Their passion and anger were clearly seen. "We're taking this country back," seemed the overall sentiment.

Republican Anthony Gonzalez of Ohio shared his concern about what might happen if Trump were to win the next election. Would Trump try to get rid of any who didn't clearly support him?[69]

In his book, *The Next Civil War*, Stephen Marche warns us of scenarios—successful assassination attempts on our president, a financial crash followed by debilitating droughts, a New York City hurricane plunging neighborhoods under water—that just might result in a real conflict between the opposing factions in our nation. "It's so easy to pretend it's all going to work out," he writes but, he continues, the US "is already in a state of civil strife, on the threshold of civil war."[70]

After the FBI's search at Mar-a-Lago,[71] there were threats of civil war once again, as pro-Trump agitator Tyler Welsh Slaeker encouraged his many followers to "lock and load."[72] There were even some Congressmen who argued against the rule of law in following up on Trump's alleged criminal actions regarding the secret documents he took home illegally.[73]

Tucker Carlson, then the most-watched Fox News commentator, reported that the Capitol insurrection was engineered by antifa groups and the FBI, not fans of Trump.[74] "Fake" news or Fox News—which reality do you choose?

A Lackluster End to the Trump Era?

Nastiness in politics has grown over the past years, thanks to some Republicans hammering away at Democrats without recourse. Those who had left Trump's administration seem to agree that there were problems that sorely needed correction. Books written by them and by those close to Trump seem to agree. The connection between Trump and conspiracy theorists like Alex Jones and QAnon is hard to ignore.[75]

There are remedies to avoid being taken in by all this, and we describe them. We end the chapter with the election denialism focus of right-wing news sources. The growth of nastiness continues, sometimes with more bias and less accuracy.

But, with the midterm elections of 2022, it seemed as if the Trump craze might be coming to an end. According to an NBC News report, while 32 percent of the national electorate voted "to oppose Joe Biden," 28 percent voted "to oppose Donald Trump" even though he wasn't running at the time. In any case, the Democrats did much better than pollsters had predicted, and some Republicans blamed Trump. One Republican operative claimed, "Independents didn't vote for candidates they viewed as extreme and too closely linked with Donald J. Trump."[76]

But there were still those who weren't giving up. There was more distrust about elections among GOP voters, 56 percent of them, after the 2022 midterm elections, according to the Pew Research Center, than in 2020.[77]

However, when Trump announced his run for the presidency at Mar-a-Lago right after the midterm elections, it seemed very lackluster. His base was much weaker.[78] And then there was Ron DeSantis waiting eagerly in the wings, along with Ted Cruz and others.[79] Legislators in the State of Florida even considered changing the law so that De Santis could run for president without having to resign from his role as governor.[80] Was it possible that Trump had finally lost his mojo?

As columnist and best-selling author Tom Friedman put it so eloquently, "given the unprecedented degree to which election denialism was elevated in this midterm and the way several big-name Trump-imitating knuckleheads who made denialism central to their campaigns got their clocks cleaned—we may have just dodged one of the biggest arrows ever aimed at the heart of our democracy."[81]

In this chapter, we began by inquiring about the nature of truth in politics, and we learned that sometimes different "truths" can clash. It seems that, at this period in the Big Split, the two competing truths are very far apart. There is a crisis of trust in the political realm. Each side is well fortified in its value system, getting validation from members on its own side and fully distrusting any information coming from the other. About 44 percent of us were getting our news from Facebook, from those who already take our side. It's CNN or MSNBC versus Fox News and MAGA outlets. Many people saw these channels as the basis of their truths rather than the purveyors of more objective facts that come from other sources.

We looked at how difficult it is to change people's perspective on the truth once they've alighted on one side or the other of the Big Split. As time goes on, we see how the divide between Democrats and Republicans increases as each party feeds on the media with which they originally identified, whether journalism or social media. We saw how some individuals in government abused the system, either by mischaracterizing the news or by using the system to aggrandize their own interests.[82]

We then looked at the increase in conspiracy theories that have been supported by some individuals in our government in the former administration, and how this may be a growing phenomenon. We need to ask whether QAnon will grow or fall into disrepute over time. And we ended with why these theories may continue to increase.

Trust can be a daunting challenge, nowhere more so than in the realm of social dynamics. In the next chapter, we'll take a deep dive into the world of social psychology, including how it goes beyond politics into the realms of self-awareness and the issue of control. We begin with answering the question of why we don't trust science or the power of Big Data, even when our lives depend on it. A brief dip into the history of the growth of political mistrust, aided in no small part by the renegade Newt Gingrich, will help us understand how we got to where we are. We'll end up exploring how such factors as the need for control and the existential issues of vulnerability, loneliness, and meaninglessness affect our ability to trust.

CHAPTER EIGHT

Trust This but Not That

Learning to trust is one of life's most difficult tasks.

—Isaac Watts

I doubt I'd be here if it weren't for social media.

—Donald J. Trump

It takes trust to get things done in a divided government.

—Joe Biden, at the Democratic Convention on
Aug.18, 2020

Earlier in this book, I asked you the question, whom do you trust? In your family, your work relationships, your professional providers, your government leaders—both local and federal?

One of the purposes of this book is to examine the experience of trust and its troubling shadow, mistrust, both at the personal level as well as at the social and political level.

Hopefully, we're discovering how to regain trust in our lives by taking responsibility for our choices, understanding the psychology of trust, and applying this learning to our work settings, and even our loved ones at home.

Mistrust: The Shadow of Trust

Trust is learned in our earliest years—before our ability to use language or conceptualize anything about it[1]. Yet it forms our personality and shapes how we interact with others for the rest of our lives.

Those of us who are lucky enough to have had loving family members enjoy the benefits of trust: helpful siblings, long-term friendships, supportive associates at work, dependable neighbors in times of need. The beauty of trust is precious. It helps make life more fully meaningful and enjoyable.

In the beginning, our basic needs, if we are fortunate, are met by our parents and caretakers. Even after we start school, we depend on returning to the safe haven of family. We rely on that for our day-to-day fundamental emotional and physical survival. But most of us are likely to experience a betrayal of trust. It can be a parent with a short temper, or lack of empathy, or some other shortcoming. Or it can happen when we are confronted by that first rejection in a dating relationship. It can also come from loss of trust in a leader, even a president. At each of these levels of broken trust, it feels like a personal loss if not a tragedy.

Understanding the Other Side

The first few chapters were in part about how to escape the crisis of trust by looking more closely at those in power, whose intent and methods prevail within the context of social media and the dynamics of the Big Split. We started by exploring how we could better understand the tragedies of misplaced trust through acceptance of what's really happening in terms of the two separate realities of our two major political parties as we gain more awareness about the world's urgent identity crisis.

We have networks like MSNBC and CNN on the one hand and Fox

News on the other, broadcasting separate realities. The Big Lie about the stolen election of 2020 gave way to the Great Replacement Theory, where Fox News inspires its over three million viewers to believe one of the greater conspiracy theories, that there is a "White genocide" by colored minorities going on, aiming to overtake the White race.[2]

The High Cost of Low Trust

Sadly, some Americans can be highly suspicious of scientific methods and findings. Take, for example, the remarkable belief that the world is flat.[3] Of course, we trust what we see, and looking out over a level plane reveals a seemingly flat horizon far into the distance, promising an abrupt drop off. We all know that seeing is believing. There are even some people who doubt that we walked on the moon. They'd say it was simply a film made in a western desert. The purpose, they'd say, was perhaps to assert claims beyond what was possible, and that was manufactured for political gain.

A more widely held belief is that autism is caused by childhood vaccines.[4] For some it makes perfect sense: autism begins to be noticed around the age when children receive vaccinations. The cause of autism is not clearly determined, but it is known that more boys than girls are autistic, that children with autistic siblings are more likely to be affected, and that genetic factors are likely involved. But this scientifically obtained information does not tell us how to prevent children from becoming autistic. Therefore, why should we trust science?

Suspicions are strengthened when scientific methods are not understood.[5] Scientists begin their research with a theory that they try to confirm through their experimental studies. Though a theory is just a starting foundation, it is likely based on a great deal of information. The word *theory*, to some, means a guess or a wild idea put forward as factual but without sufficient basis until proven.

Why this lack of trust in science? First, good science is difficult and time consuming to conduct. It is slow to come to clear-cut conclusions. So why does it take so long, anyway, some may ask. Many people are not well educated in science, so they just don't understand how it's done, or the ethical principles that good scientists adhere to. Or it's too hard to study about in school, or doesn't seem relevant to their real life, or is done by strange people. If they're conspiracy theorists, they may believe that it may be used to trick people into believing things that are not true so that some group can take advantage of them.

In the years 2020 through 2022, the world was barely coping with the Covid-19 virus that was sickening and killing millions around the world despite the newly arrived vaccines. At the same time, many failed to take simple steps recommended by medical research to protect themselves. In the United States, the issue had been politicized as one group tried to control another for political gain.[6] To some extent, this tragedy was unfolding because of lack of trust in what is scientifically known, and suspicion due to the lack of information about the causes and progression of the disease, and how it should be treated.[7]

Many people were afraid and didn't know whom to trust. At the same time, they were exhausted by restrictions on everyday life, and were willing to risk being infected in order to get back to normal. And the so-called smart scientists were coming up with contradictory answers, or no answers at all. At the start, to some extent, the global cure for Covid-19 was impacted by lack of trust in science.[8]

Even beyond the realm of Covid-19, there was little trust in science and the Big Data enterprise on what we could learn about the world at large.[9]

Little Trust in Big Data

As Covid-19 spread, the internet was awash with a confusion of legitimate information and lies and condemnation. Many people were wanting to demand their rights as they saw them. They wanted to overcome the central powers and refuse to be overlooked and be taken for granted, especially so among the less educated and marginally employed.[10] So, the liberal press, more focused on principle and ethics, was seen by this segment of society as out of touch with the real issues of unemployment and scarcity. The term *fake news* made sense to them, especially as the internet gave so much exposure to the propagandists and loudmouths that yearned to shout out their claims.[11]

In a commencement address at the University of Maryland a few summers ago, former New York City mayor Michael Bloomberg warned his audience of lack of trust in the federal government, referring to it as a "group so risk-averse that they are embarrassing themselves daily," and "just too afraid of losing their next election to do what their job requires."[12] Yet political commentators encourage our national leaders to be honest and to treat us fairly but end up frustrated when this isn't always the case. So, guess what happens to trust if this trend continues?

Rule of Trump: Loss is Not as Option

The crisis of trust, simply put, is a result of the misplacement of trust in any entity that uses that trust for its own purposes to the detriment of those who trust it.[13] Its importance these days is of great political significance.

The crisis of trust is exemplified by recent events such as the insurrection on the Capitol triggered by Trump and his Big Lie about the rigged election.

Donald Trump acquired the trust of his following not only because of his charismatic, demagogic approach, but also because of timing. The turning point was the Big Lie, that Biden's victory was rigged. That purported loss could not be tolerated by Trump, and he did all he could to reverse the choice on the part of the American electorate.[14]

On the very day that Biden's victory was to be certified by the vice president, Trump took to the stump and declared to the most avid of his followers, who were carrying banners indicating that Trump won in a landslide, "We're gonna' walk down to the Capitol." He incited the mob, as we now know, with many aggressive comments, including "Take the Capitol right now!"[15]

With Senator Ted Cruz's statement to his Congressional colleagues that half the population was concerned about the election being rigged, the attack was on.[16] The sentiment at the time was that more than half of all Republicans believed in the stealing of the election.[17]

All this did not happen just because of Trump's inability to admit to loss—of anything, much less the power of the presidency. Trump had fallen into a time and place in American history where his personality fit like a newly found key in an old lock. Let's take a step or two back in history. As before, let's take a Ken Burns approach to history, focusing on some interesting details.

Setting the Stage

At the end of World War II, there was a period of prosperity as GI's returned from war and settled down to raise families. The 1950s and early '60s saw the US at the top of its game—rating a high in economic, social, industrial, and political trends, as the citizens morphed from an *I* mentality to a *we* community.

"America got increasingly fair, with more social cohesion, and the sense that the great majority of people thought the country was headed in the right direction," according to author Robert Putnam.[18]

Of course, the GI's needed housing, along with all the accoutrements of living the good life in the American dream. Conformity was the trend of the times, politically as well as culturally. Behind this façade of common values was the pervasive, irrepressible conflict between progressive liberals who welcomed diversity and those conservatives who feared it, but this was not out in the open until civil rights became a focus in the mid-1950s.

At this point, it became clear that there were opposing forces forming coalitions. The Alabama Democrats (called Dixiecrats) were for segregation. Following his election in 1963, Governor George Wallace exclaimed to the nation his infamous but well popularized declaration: "I draw the line in the dust and toss the gauntlet before the feet of tyranny, and I say segregation now, segregation tomorrow, and segregation forever!"[19]

How We Got to Where We Are: From Newt Gingrich to Donald Trump

At this point, I was at West Georgia College and one of the more loquacious members on the faculty was Newt Gingrich, a professor of history and geography. I'd often see him walking the campus, lost in thought, but then very gregarious once he had an audience for his intellectual take on the politics of the day. In fact, he seemed more like a student than a professor. With an ambitious streak, Newt took advantage of the college president's open-door policy and went to his office to share his thoughts. Newt was a very practical, focused individual, his ambition readily visible, ready to take on all comers in debate or to gain support. He was nimble enough to combine his studies of history with current politics and get to the point of his own aspirations in government dynamics.

With encouragement from his colleagues, Newt ran for Congress but lost twice. The third try was the charm he needed. He won a seat in Congress in 1978 and, by 1995, had become Speaker of the House.[20]

At the time, the Republicans were headed by Bob Michel, known as Mr. Nice Guy for his friendly and non-confrontive character, serving since 1981. He and Newt did not see eye to eye.[21] Newt wanted to wage war against the Democrats in a manner not popular at the time. He lectured widely about how to be nasty and mean in order to win the next election over the Democrats who had been successful too long, in his opinion. He was able to talk freely about his ideas on CSPAN, even though it wasn't known by the TV audience that he was lecturing to an empty Congressional Hall about "the loony left" until he was confronted on this by former Speaker Tip O'Neill.[22]

In these televised talks, Newt was explosive in his rhetoric and highly confrontational toward the Democrats, an aggressive style that was highly innovative at the time. He was one of the first to work the media by engaging viewers with conflict and bluster, even ferocity, with his highly charged rhetoric.[23]

Despite this, Newt was able to get support for his aggressive approach and took control of GOPAC (Global Organization of Parliamentarians against Corruption), a training organization for Republican candidates.[24]

Not surprisingly, the contrast between liberals and conservatives soon began to transform. In 1996, media mogul Rupert Murdoch wanted a TV enterprise that would make money by targeting the right wing. He hired political consultant Roger Ailes to head it, along with the statement, "Our job is to be objective." With the motto, "We report. You decide," Fox News won high ratings and a growing following. Murdoch's approach was to stir people up and keep them watching, the beginning of tailoring reporting with the aim of focusing on "the return audience."[25]

Then came Facebook with a similar philosophy, but now with the aid of increasingly efficient algorithms to do the heavy lifting. When fear and anger became the fuel for return audiences, Facebook just looked the other way when victimized groups were targeted with hate pieces.[26]

After Obama won his presidency in November 2008, the division between the parties began to grow substantially, especially with the arrival of the Tea Party in February 2009.[27] Issues of race and immigration came increasingly to the forefront, aggravated by the fact that the proportion of Whites to non-Whites was decreasing dramatically. In the 1950s, 90 percent of Americans were White. Now the proportion was approaching 58 percent.[28]

Newt Gingrich transformed the Republican Party from "Mr. Nice Guy" Bob Michel's soft approach to his own hard-hitting but successful style.[29] This was exactly the working plan that Trump could use when he ran for president decades later. By this time, the bifurcation of American politics was etched in stone. There was a clear divide between the less educated farmers, factory, and other hourly workers in the heartland and the more sophisticated professional types on both coasts.[30]

It was all about class and social status, about an existential fear of losing what little esteem the less educated workers had as they saw themselves left out of the body politic, a group President Nixon had earlier referred to as the silent majority.[31] It had transformed into an issue of class and personal identity—between the college-educated, elite professional component *haves* on the one hand and the less-educated *have-nots*, on the other, inhabiting smaller cities and towns across the heartland.

Even before Trump's arrival on the political scene, a permanent state of war was developing, based on geography, class, and culture. The Oklahoma City bombing in April 1995—when a Ryder truck filled with almost 5,000 pounds of explosives killed 168—was a most serious, destructive incident.[32]

And then came the most infamous physical battle, waged at the Capitol on January 6, 2021. Those who had based their trust on Trump came as patriots to reclaim their country and win back the election, motivated by emotions related to the great class divide, only to slowly realize the possibility that all this was the Big Lie, perpetrated by their "savior."[33]

That's the short version of how we got from the innovative rhetoric of Newt Gingrich to the narcissistic bullying of Donald Trump that accounts for whatever successes the Republicans have mustered over the past few decades.

The Big Lie Lives On

Of course, history promised a beginning of change when Trump lost the 2020 election. Many of the members of QAnon were now in doubt. Had they misplaced their trust? In their minds, they were clearly the victims of fraud.[34]

But only for a while. The devotion to their "savior" lived on, and even grew, fomenting more and more conspiracy theories to further their cause. Instead of waning, the fervor grew.[35]

Most Republicans fought the Stop the Loss battle, even though they were privately known by their more objective colleagues to know that Biden was the true winner. But the pressure to insist that the emperor still had clothes on was too much for most Republicans to deny. Those who told the truth as they knew it paid the price of loss of power, the most blatant example being Liz Cheney.[36]

It soon became apparent that Trump had done whatever he could to hold on to power, even trying to manipulate and cajole the Department of Justice to intervene on his behalf in the search for election fraud.[37] But in the end, Trump could not succeed in getting others to overcome the election results, as the January 6 Select Committee revealed. Trump and his followers abused social media as much as they could to try to meet their own needs. The Big Lie persisted. And so many believed it. Social media allowed for lies to resonate so strongly that they took on the cloak of reality for Trump's true believers It seemed that so many lies were accepted as truth because of the repetition and strong sense of conviction by the MAGA media. Lies became the political mode of the Far Right. Everybody there thrived on lying, contributing to the Big Split.[38]

Everybody Lies

In his book, *Everybody Lies*, Seth Stephens-Davidowitz points out how social media is changing how we see and understand society just as the microscope and telescope transformed the natural sciences. Big Data, he says, can capture new information, revealing what people really think and do rather than what they end up telling pollsters. The use of graduate students as subjects for experiments and tests is coming to an end, to be replaced by Big Data. "In their place," he writes, "the social and behavioral sciences are most definitely going to scale."[39]

So where does trust fit into this change? The problem is that the Big Data revolution allows for more manipulation of the numbers, leading to the possibility of abuse of data, and the diminution of trust in statistical analysis, and therefore less trust in science as an institution. Ideally, hopes author Stephens-Davidowitz, we will "be able to learn a lot more . . . in a lot less time."[39] But practically, for the time being, he continues, there is the danger of the risk of statistical abuse in this age of polarization.

Predictability Leads to Trust

Big Data is not something we're too often concerned about in our daily, personal lives. Our personal focus is more on the relationships with which we deal on a day-to-day basis—our spouses, family, significant others, sometimes even including our religious or spiritual leaders. That's where the rubber of trust hits the road of life. It's those closest to us that we're most concerned about trusting.

Trust is what we feel when we are somewhat assured that the individual, family, or group we're dealing with will act predictably in making us feel understood, respected, comfortable and safe.

> Trust grows between individuals when they both become more aware of one another's needs as they relate to their relationship.

By putting more energy into learning about you, becoming more aware of you with all your needs, foibles, habits, and tendencies, the more we trust our relationship. Of course, I share myself with you so you can learn about me as well. In other words, the more we reveal ourselves to one another, the greater the trust being built.

This was spelled out in detail by Irwin Altman and Dalmas Taylor in their theory of social penetration. They use the metaphor of the peeling onion: the longer you know someone, the more layers are peeled off the onion. Starting with superficial sharing of information about self and moving toward what they call the "exploratory affective stage," emotional sharing is predictable, according to the authors.[40]

Trust This but Not That

But what if my awareness of you involves the knowledge that you don't follow through on your promises and even lie when it suits you? Then I can predict that aspect of your behavior and trust you to be consistent with that as time goes by. I may not like being treated that way, but I trust that you will be consistent. If I'm getting something of value from the relationship, I will adjust to its shortcomings and appreciate what is positive.[41]

So, I trust the relationship for what it is, and my comfort comes from a sense of familiarity in knowing what to expect in my dealings with you. Granted, my trust is limited to what I get out of the relationship, keeping in mind that there are certain areas that are not trustworthy. Let's look at a couple of examples, one personal, one political.

A personal example: a good friend of mine is married to a very controlling, judgmental woman who is a very successful professional. He complains about being unfairly criticized, sometimes quite intensely, about minor infractions on his part, like using too much water when rinsing off dishes or being too messy in general. But he enjoys her attention to detail when cleaning house or cooking great meals. So, the tradeoff, at least for him, is justified. He trusts her efficiency, if not her critical judgment. But he trusts what to expect from her on both counts.

A political example: former President Trump may not have been known for his accuracy of observations, but those who supported him knew that about him, and even enjoyed the predictability of his opinions. If he had committed errors, whether involving infidelities or inaccurate statements, his followers expected that of him and still appreciated his style of creating change favorable to them despite these other shortcomings, if that's what they were. They trusted him to follow through on his campaign promises such as building the wall and getting a handle on the immigration issues and they focused on that and trusted him on that basis while overlooking the otherwise consistent foibles. They even overlooked his "report" about the election being rigged.

In one Tweet, he wrote, in all caps: "REPORT: DOMINION DELETED 2.7 MILLION TRUMP VOTES NATIONWIDE. DATA ANALYSIS FINDS 221,000 PENNSYLVANIA VOTES SWITCHED FROM PRESIDENT TRUMP TO BIDEN. 941,000 TRUMP VOTES DELETED. STATES USING DOMINION VOTING SYSTEMS SWITCHED 435,000 VOTES FROM TRUMP TO BIDEN."[42]

Those who knew better, forgave him. Others just accepted his commentary as reliable and true, fueling the fire of the attack on the Capitol. Such devotion contributed to the Big Split.[43]

But why such a great need to trust, leading to this crisis of trust?

Control, Connection and Competency

At a deeper level, trust has to do with three existential issues that may confront us all:

> First, we all have a sense of vulnerability in life, wanting more control.

Like most others, we feel more comfortable when we feel a sense of control over the important aspects of our lives—our health, our finances, our relationships, the maintenance of our homes. When we dream at night, those dreams that disturb us have to do with loss of control.

So, we go see a physician if we feel something in our body is going out of control. We consult an advisor if we need help organizing our finances. We may see a counselor if things get too out of hand in significant relationships. We look for a good handyman if the banister of our outdoor steps gets too loose. We feel better if we can control all these factors. Otherwise, that sense of helplessness is too bothersome. All these concerns make us feel less trusting in general, while increasing our need to trust those who might be of assistance.[44]

> Second, loneliness or feeling separate or isolated from others, builds our need to trust.

During the Covid-19 sheltering at home, almost everyone we spoke with expressed anxiety over the feelings of social deprivation. We need to connect with friends, family, and associates. It's human nature. One of the multiple factors that might have led to the strong wave of social protests in 2020 may have been that very need to connect with others. We were advised by professionals to stay in touch by phone and Zoom, and most of us did. But there's no comparison to being together in the flesh, eating together, confiding face-to-face, or beginning and ending with a friendly hug or handshake.

The more time we spend with others and share ourselves, according to the experts on social penetration, the more we feel comfortable and trusting of them.[45] Our need to trust is no longer stymied or suppressed and becomes fulfilled with the increase in emotional intimacy.

> Finally, we all need to feel a trust that our efforts at work and at home contribute to something meaningful to others as well as ourselves.

Freud is reputed to have said that the two important factors in meaningful living are love and work. Romantic partners and family are crucial to a sense of emotional contentment. Being recognized for being productive at work, whether that involves professional expertise, dedicated focus, leading a team, or getting a tough job completed, all contribute to our sense of meaning in life.

These three issues make trust a bigger part of our lives when they are satisfied in a positive direction. We can more easily trust others when we feel in control of the various aspects of our lives, when we feel more connected with others than isolated and socially deprived, when we feel our lives are meaningful in terms of the contribution we make to others. When these three issues of our lives are resolved in a positive manner, then we are more open to trusting others. We can more easily relate to their needs and wants since ours are well satisfied.

In general, trust comes about more easily when we are less anxious and less stressed. Otherwise, we might feel paranoid that we're doing something wrong, blaming ourselves for whatever is the problem. When that is happening, we are less inclined to trust others. But when we feel in control of our lives, we are more emotionally relaxed and optimistic—and more trusting.

A study exploring the influence of emotions on trust revealed that "negative emotions can decrease trust, but only if those negative emotions make people feel less certain about their current situation."[46] So, if we feel a lack of control in our own lives, then trust does not come as easily.

But the more mistrustful we feel in general, then something unexpected happens. We may look for a special, "secret" group to trust to make up for the lack of general trust in our lives. That helps explain the popularity of QAnon among otherwise untrusting individuals who have now intensified their trust in this special group in an otherwise untrustworthy world. Does that help us understand the intense dedication and loyalty that QAnoners feel toward their special group?

Trust Begins Within

Let's return to the healthy dynamics of trusting the world at large. At an individual level, trust begins with knowing ourselves. To experience a deep sense of trust with another, we first need to acknowledge and recognize our feelings, needs, wants, and values. Only when we know our own deeper self and our values, can we then share them with others which, in turn, makes us more trustworthy to others. For instance, you are more likely to trust me as the author of this book if you have a sense of my values about what I write. That's why I shared some of my own experiences leading to my values about trust. So, first we need to know ourselves in order to share that. Then, understanding others, and sharing our values with them, increases the bond of connection that leads to trust.[47]

Socrates said, "To know thyself is the beginning of wisdom." If you can share your self-knowledge, particularly your vulnerabilities, then trust comes more easily. According to psychologist Meg Selig, author of *Changepower,* "Your awareness of your own foibles and struggles can help you empathize with others."[48] The more we know ourselves, the more we can share that with others, the more likely is the process of trust.

So, trust begins within. We need to know who we are, deeply, before we can build trust with another. If we do not know ourselves deeply, how can the other? Sure, others can observe our behaviors but, to really become aware of us, they talk with us and we with them, about our needs, particularly from one another.

Trust Based on Mutual Awareness

The more aware we become of one another, the greater the potential for trust. This is true at a personal level between two people as well as at the international level as when antagonistic countries negotiate for peace. The tradition-breaking approach of Track II diplomacy that President Jimmy Carter brought to the bargaining table between Egypt's President Anwar Sadat and Israeli Prime Minister Begin, leading to the Camp David Peace Accords, still stands today despite growing tensions in the mid-East. The more the delegates could open up about their views, frustrations, and aspirations, the more intense the process became, at times headed for failure. But, by persisting in attempts at understanding and becoming more aware of one another's perspectives, the process ultimately succeeded.[49]

And what about former President Trump's decision to meet with Kim Jong-un on a personal basis despite the acrimony that preceded this meeting? Was there political manipulation going on? Of course, but Trump thought the tradeoff was worth it. With the possibility of personal acrimony leading to more threats and ultimately a show of power by igniting a nuclear war, the option of talking one-on-one to share personal interaction rather than threats was, most would agree, a good idea. Sure, nothing was accomplished in terms of specifics for the future, but at least a basis of trust was attempted, one that might lead to compromise and peace rather than merciless and massive nuclear damage.[50] Perhaps the two leaders were drawn together by their mutual value of power over rather than power through, i.e., tyranny (which Trump seemed to admire) versus democracy (which Trump tried to overpower).

Letting Go of Control

Here's an equation worth pondering:

$$\text{Trust} = \text{expectation} + \text{desire} - \text{control}$$

Let me explain.

Unless we're carrying a loaded gun (or nuclear bomb) aimed at someone, or some such punishment, we have no direct control over that individual (or country). We certainly have expectations, based on our former experience. We also have desires for certain behaviors that are favorable to us. But, without the gun, we have little direct control over that individual's behaviors.

So, trust depends on our expectations of behaviors and choices based on about what we've observed till the present moment. But, if I freely remain in a relationship with you, I have some desires to be fulfilled by you, whatever they may be—social attention, business opportunities, political influence, or intellectual stimulation. I accept you as you are and I don't try, in any organized fashion, to control your behaviors. That's trust. I desire something; I expect some of my needs to be met; and I agree, at least ideally, not to try to control you in any intentional manner.

Different people have different personality types, and we can trust that each type will act accordingly, so we will be less disappointed if our needs are not as fully met as we might wish. The more we trust the other to be that type, the less disappointed we will be.

Interdependence

Trust is the basis of healthy relationships. Let's face it. People have different behavioral characteristics reflecting their values, quite often different from our own. Some, for example, are predictably late. If we can't change that, can we accept it and trust its consistency of habit? Some values, including procrastination, seem impossible to change. Some are control freaks, perhaps self-centered, others manipulative. We can make them feel wrong by criticizing them or giving them our advice on doing better. But we probably can't change them. We may have to just accept them as they are.

If you are sufficiently turned off by any of these qualities, you can decide to end the relationship, unless they're family. Separation from family is possible but usually more challenging.

Then you can choose to ease the pain by deciding to trust who they are, and work around or through it, by whatever means you can create, to make it more palatable to you.

Understanding the individual, with all the faults, leads to acceptance and trust that change is not an option for now, at least not immediately. The key to trust is entering into the interdependence of the relationship. You get some of your needs met and others not so much. But you have the choice to stay . . . or leave.

Coming Together

We want to feel independent, yet still have connection with significant others. We want to feel connected to a larger group through social entities, whether work-related, religious, or other social networks. Another way of putting it is that we want to be a significant part of something larger than ourselves. That's why social media is so successful. We can find others online who make us feel affirmed and accepted. The agreement of values leads to trust in such groups[51].

At the individual level, the most physically but not emotionally intimate, sex without love, is typically unlikely to lead to mutual trust. If there is no attempt at understanding the other, no awareness of the other's needs, wants, or vulnerabilities, how can trust be established? Sex in love, however, is just the opposite. There is a deep feeling of emotional connection, and we want to know as much as possible about the other.

But the tender trap here is that falling in love involves hormones that flood our senses and block awareness of our differences. Hence the old saying: love is blind. That kind of trust is great but may not last much beyond the honeymoon phase (or hormonal blast). That's why love that begins without sexual intimacy while we build awareness of one another may last much longer and with fewer conflicts.[52]

Trust: Acceptance with Less Judgment

At a lesser emotional level, trust in words can lead to great changes in social groupings of trust. The more we share a common language with others, the more trust we share. Those who read the Bible are more likely to trust one another. Those who share a technical vocabulary, such as medical doctors, or scientists, tend to trust one another within the context of their professions. Language creates a bridge of trust for groups who gravitate to a common conceptual framework, based on words.

At the end of the day (or chapter), trust means being more comfortable and relaxed with others, whoever they are, if we choose to be interdependent with them, whether that involves family, romantic relationships, work associates, church attendees, or even QAnon groups. Life's biggest goal, after all, is to be comfortable and fulfilled—feeling safe, well, and happy. Part of that comfort is the ability to be ourselves without judgment.

Acceptance—of self and others—is paramount for our sense of comfort. Trust in others to be who they are with less judgment on our part helps create this sense of comfort.

> The path to trust consists of deeper communication and the quest for fuller awareness of one another, whether with individuals, social groups, or institutions.

In this age of polarization, we build political trust wherever we can find it, on one side or the other.

In this chapter, we began by exploring the shadow nature of trust—mistrust—and its place in the age of the Big Split, emanating most notably from the Big Lie. We took a brief look at the history of the beginning of the political bifurcation, starting in the 1950s when American democracy was at its height, and then into the '60s and '70s when the battle of civil rights took place, and then into the 1990s when Newt Gingrich introduced a belligerent approach to the Republican Party, one that continued to grow over the decades, culminating in the promulgation of the Big Lie and then the 2021 insurrection against the Capitol.

We then traveled inward to explore the personal nature of trust, and the role of predictability, control, and interdependence. We finished with the realization that trust is a complex process, involving less judgment, better communication, and more mutual awareness. The theme of this chapter was what to trust and what not to trust and, finally, the how of it.

CHAPTER NINE

Coda: Overview and Updates on the Big Split— and Some Hope

Polarization affects families and groups of friends. It's a paralyzing situation, a civil war of opinion.

—Mick Jagger

There is a computer disease that anybody who works with computers knows about. It's a very serious disease and it interferes with the work. The trouble with computers is that you "play" with them!

—Richard Feynman, Nobel Prize winner in physics

Tonight, I say this to my Republican colleagues who are defending the indefensible: There will come a day when Donald Trump is gone but your dishonor will remain.

—Liz Cheney

According to several authors, the battle between urban, secular, highly educated citizens and the rural, less college-educated counterpart who are more likely to embrace religion, has been in the process of leading to a fissure in our government that may be very difficult to bridge. But it's not just the two opposing factions with which we're so familiar and which led to the Big Split. Beyond that is the multiplicity of cultures, the *pluribus* of the *E Pluribus Unum*, if you will. The United States of America is made up of immigrants that arrived in subsequent waves, from the colonists and founders of our Constitution, rebelling against their King George III; to their British cousins in the 1840s and '50s; to the Northern Europeans in the 1880s; to the Eastern Europeans at the end of the nineteenth century; and to the Asians and Latin Americans in the past half-century.

> The fact that our democracy has lasted this long is, somewhat of a miracle, given the multiplicity of cultures among us.

Of these, social media has given more voice to one cultural group in particular—those Whites who consider themselves superior, especially a group of those who are, in fact, less educated and somewhat more communalized by religion. Freedom of expression, guaranteed by our Constitution and amplified by social media, offers opportunities for voicing cultural differences. "Democratic institutions," claims Yascha Mounk, author of *The Great Experiment* "can do as much to exacerbate as to alleviate the challenge of diversity."[1]

How Democracies Die

Anti-democratic ultranationalism, as espoused by some in the Republican Party, such as the election deniers, has a long history, going back to Mussolini and Hitler.[2] Some in that group, wanting to veer away from a common frame of reference so necessary for effective democracy, construct their own reality, including polarizing conspiracy theories, as created by groups like QAnon.[3]

Some see this movement as enhancing different realities that took place between Russia and Poland, fortified by a single event occurring in 2010, when Polish Air Force 101 inadvertently crashed on a flight to Russia while carrying Poland's president and his wife, as well as senior Polish military officers, government officials, and eighteen members of the Polish parliament. They were all on their way to commemorate the memory of 22,000 Polish victims murdered and 100,000 women raped by Russians in World War II, known as the Katyn massacre.[4]

The plane crashed, most likely, because a of a combination of factors, including poorly trained pilots, use of an abandoned airfield, and a growing fog that led to a blinding effect just at the time of the scheduled landing. But because of the tensions between the two countries, there were numerous conspiracy theories that grew to be part of the overall political scene. Russia and Poland had been struggling with a type of love-hate relationship based on a history of shared communism until a decade earlier. When Poland converted to a liberal democracy, the tension between the two countries grew.

This incident caused a socio-political clash between Poland's sense of progressive, democratic destiny—a reflective nostalgia—and Russia's sense of a history that never happened—a restorative nostalgia— including a mythology of supreme authoritarian power.[5] And so, the battle between democracy and communism was rewoven as a Big Split between two originally communist counties. Poland ceased being a communist country in 1990 and Putin became prime minister in 1999, then president the following year, presumably heading a federal democratic state, but in all practicality, a dictatorship. This became increasingly clear when Putin decided to invade Ukraine in 2014. So, this plane crash marked a point at which the two countries crossed paths almost simultaneously in overall historical timing; while one country shed communism for democracy, another shed democracy for dictatorship. Forms of government can shift dramatically, even in this age of free speech through social media. They had their own protracted version of the Big Split, but in this instance between communism and liberal democracy.

In their book, *How Democracies Die*, Steven Levitsky and Daniel Ziblatt point out how modern democracies die not at the pointing of guns but rather by election of those secretly inclined toward authoritarianism who seductively use ethnic differences to polarize their constituents. They point out that what leads to the death of democracy is the refusal of the anti-democratic leaders to acknowledge their opponents' legitimacy and the encouragement of violence to show their strength, just as Trump did.[6]

Though social media, in our time, can be blamed for the amplification of such processes of political seduction, there is no easy way to diminish such power. When many in one of our two major parties continue to deny honest election results, then there is a crisis of trust. We must deal with this in one fashion or another, or our democracy may suffer severely if this trend continues.

The Select Committee Selects Trump

We began this book with the analogy of capuchin monkeys rattling their cages because they were getting cucumbers rather than the juicy grapes that their neighbors were earning for the same work. This helped us see more clearly why the workers of America were rattling their cages because they were feeling left out of the political system, watching the rich get richer while the poor got poorer. Now, with the added factor of inflation and the prospect of recession, that difference has become even more painful, adding fuel to the Big Split.

This economic divide helped account for the dynamics of polarization. And former President Trump stepped right into position to convince the cucumber-eating populace that they could get their share of grapes. That never happened, but it did ignite a frustration that led to the insurrection of January 6. Only a portion of those participants were planning on an organized invasion of the Capitol but, as we saw in Chapter One, the rest were galvanized by the drama of the moment; we saw exactly how their brains were triggered by the intensity of the emotion. Most of those who were arrested and sent to court were able to express remorse in hopes of a merciful sentence and some were forced to face more serious charges of seditious treason.

In the end, over 978 were charged with federal crimes. About one third of the approximately 2,000 insurrectionists were affiliated with such militant groups as the Proud Boys, Oath Keepers, and Three Percenters. Of these, 465 have pled guilty, 185 were sentenced to jail, 18 to home detention, and the rest to periods of probation.[7]

We quoted one of the headlines describing the insurrection, from France's *Le Monde*: *TRUMP PROVOQUE LE CHAOS A WASHINGTON* [Trump provokes chaos in Washington], and that he certainly did. The US House Select Committee then took up the work of figuring out who was behind this seditious act and made a public statement on their decision to subpoena Trump to testify; he chose to ignore that request but then the Committee ran out of time. As a matter of fact, he was reported to have exploded at the prospect of having special counsel Jack Smith follow up on investigations against him.[8]

Several of Trump's close associates did testify and their statements revealed how central Trump was to fomenting the seditious plan. As it turned out, some of Trump's closest supporters, Vice President Mike Pence and Attorney General Bill Barr, ultimately turned against him. In his book, released right after the midterm elections, Pence reveals the detail of his break with Trump after he refused to go along with the plan to replace electors to reinstate Trump as president. Bill Barr also turned against Trump in his response to questioning by the Select Committee on January 6. In media interviews, Barr claimed that it would be a "tragedy" if Trump were to become the presidential nominee for 2024.[9]

We looked at the strong support that Trump had for his plan of extending his presidency from the group QAnon, and how Trump himself was not so subtle in acknowledging his liking for this group, which was soon characterized as a domestic terrorist threat by the FBI.[10]

Overcoming Click Addiction to Social Media

In Chapter Two, we took a close look at Facebook and its role in amplifying polarization, and how Frances Haugen revealed that with the help of the many documents taken from Facebook to prove her case in the court of public opinion. She pointed out how Facebook supported Trump with lies and conspiracy theories and how its executives were likely aware of this.

Megan Smith, former US chief technology officer, speaking at the 2022 Social Innovation Summit, claimed that Facebook did spread misinformation helping Trump in 2016, as well as continuing to spread misinformation leading up to the Capitol insurrection.[11]

Some said it was time for Meta to shape up to its moral obligations. A group of ten state attorneys general, bipartisan by design, began looking into new regulations about its use of algorithms in influencing its users.[12]

We also looked at so-called click addiction, in which individuals, but most importantly, children and young teen-agers, 45 percent of whom are online almost constantly (according to a Mayo Clinic report), become strongly addicted to social media, with substantial emotional issues as a result. It appears that the teens feel self-imposed pressure to check their updates, change their status, post photos, and engage in other activities. The most often used apps are TikTok, followed by Facebook, followed by WhatsApp, and Instagram. Exacerbated by the pandemic, children and teenagers have suffered more depression, sadness, and suicidal ideation, with suicide becoming the second leading cause of death for them. Smart phones and social media play a central role, resulting in less time spent on face-to-face contact with friends and adults, or with sports, exercising, or community activities, including religious and spiritual involvement. And the concerns for their parents about the dire forecasts of planet warming and future pandemics, not to mention acrimonious politics, are not lost on the younger set.

One scientific survey, reviewing fifty-five empirical studies, came up with a clear conclusion: addiction to social media is damaging, involving a marked decrease in self-discipline, school-related burnout, mood regulation and the habit of choosing virtual communication over personal socializing.[13]

> More recent research indicates that as more and more people are using social media (over 4.6 billion worldwide by the beginning of 2023), more and more will be affected by addiction, resulting in "mental health issues such as anxiety, depression, self-evaluation problems, eating disorders, and sleep problems," affecting 5 percent of all users.[14]

Thank goodness for the $300 million in funding that the Biden administration has earmarked for mental health services for the young.

Falling in Love with a Beautiful Bot

In contrast to this click addiction, we also mentioned the Roseto effect, in which those living in warmly nurturing Italian families had lower mortality rates than those who lived in emotionally disconnected families.

> And don't forget those socially starved users who fall in "love" with the chatbot XiaoIce, the eighteen-year-old female avatar who is engineered with the latest technology of emotional intelligence and can change topics on a dime, based on the nonverbal language (including hesitations) of the user.

Taken together, these scientific findings clearly point to the benefits of person-to-person socializing as much healthier than being glued to an iPhone, even when with family, which often happens with social media users. At the end of Chapter Two, we offer ways of overcoming click addiction. Given these newest research findings, it makes such recommendation even more valuable.

Incidentally, in case you are unfamiliar with XiaoIce, or think it's disappeared, at the end of 2022, its developers, headed by CEO Li Di, raised over $138 million in its latest funding round to accelerate the research and development of its "AI Being" technology "to understand, interpret, and perform human communication and related tasks" to create "a stronger social and interactive nature."[15]

We explored Big Social in depth, and it turns out that the issue of controlling who is disallowed on any venue is troublesome, as occurred when Elon Musk took over Twitter. Limiting members of an app can lead to dangerous "echo chambers," according to social scientists Matteo Cinelli and his associates at the Sapienza University of Rome.[16]

It also turns out that conspiracy theories have short-term benefits that are highly appealing to many. According to Dutch Professor van Prooijen, they include providing instant gratification, a sense of meaning and purpose, and sparking feelings of importance and excitement,[17] enough to entice more victims into what the scientists call the "Rabbit Hole Syndrome, in which some individuals' subscription to conspiracy beliefs is initially inadvertent, accelerates recursively, then becomes difficult to escape."[18]

Some, and they're a growing number, according to the Associated Press, are so enmeshed in the syndrome that they see the war in Ukraine as "totally scripted" and Covid-19 as "completely fake."[19]

At the End of the Day, Can We Just Get Along?

With all the belligerence and violence, not to mention conspiracy theories, that are part of the Big Split, is there any hope of reconciliation at some point? If not immediately, then what about the next generation? Fortunately, if we are to address this issue with sincerity and diligence over time, there is a great deal of hope, according to the research on this issue of intolerance. The solution lies in the young generation, our children. Can our educational system take the initiative to train its young students to transcend the bigotry and hate that their parents are now victims of in this time of the Big Split? It all begins with empathy.

At the end of the day (or book, in this case), there remains the issue of intolerance of the *them* versus the *us*. Polarization is the basis for this, with varying degrees of tolerance for the other side. One of the concerns that came to our attention was the January 6 insurrection of the Capitol, but this should not have been surprising for several reasons. One is that when there is significant intolerance, then it appears that belligerent behaviors, perhaps suppressed under normal conditions, can find surprisingly quick release under certain circumstances.[20] The neuroscience of that phenomenon was clearly spelled out in the first chapter of this book.

Research reveals that prejudice or intolerance begins in childhood and becomes ingrained by adulthood.[21] One way of reducing antagonism toward the other side is by empathy training,[22] especially when antagonists are younger[23] and this can be done quickly, within a few short days, by immersion in group interaction between opposing factions.[24] A survey of over five hundred studies revealed that empathy training is more effective than only learning facts about the other group, but that dealing with any anxiety about meeting the other group is also effective.[25] And since eleven-year-olds tend to be more compassionate toward outside groups than fifteen-year-olds,[26] it would seem obvious that empathy training might involve the younger children when possible.

By and large, parental attitudes are very important in determining prejudice but having friends from "the other side" can help mitigate this influence.[27] Once training to reduce intolerance to the other side is successfully completed, researchers reveal that these children will have more tolerance for other groups that are different from them, even when the differences are dissimilar from the original group in the training.[28] In other words, once children are taught to accept one group that differs from them, they are more likely to accept other groups with different values on a separate scale.

What about attitudes toward conspiracy theories? On that issue, the research reveals that those groups that have secure feelings about their own group identities are much less likely to attribute conspiracy theories to other groups than are those that are less secure about their social identities, e.g., possibly QAnon members.[29]

So, when all is said and done, there is hope, but not if we sit on our haunches and expect things to take care of themselves. We can take some initiative, and this would most likely take place within the educational system. Of course, this would require some degree of cooperation between the parents of both political leanings. Is this just a dream? "Ay there's the rub," as Shakespeare put it.

> The possibility to improve the lives of our children is there if we, as loving parents, at least test the waters.

Well, you and I have traversed the terrain of the Big Split, from belief-dependent realism of the tribal mind battling with more rationally assertive Democrats, through the questionable ethics of social media and its seductive algorithms, to the fascinating dynamics of QAnoners and their influence on the ultimate January 6 insurrection.

I trust you've learned a bit, discovered some effective communication skills that will last you some time after you put this book down and, hopefully, enjoyed the ride. If I can be of service in any way, please feel free to reach me at David.bigsplit@gmail.com.

ACKNOWLEDGMENTS

Architects, attorneys, and acrobats all work without depending on their friends for feedback. But authors are different. We crave feedback from anyone in our network who can make some sense out of fresh drafts.

I was lucky enough to have such friends. Among them, in alphabetical order, were: wellness master coach Martin C. Becker, a former student and eventual colleague, who assiduously offered his incisive opinion on the content and value of the book; rheumatologist, musician, and wood craftsman Dr. Gary Botstein, with whom I spent time working through some concepts and how they might be articulated with greater sensitivity to the reader's eyes; Dr. Janet Colvin, associate dean at Utah Valley University, who assisted with editing; Dr. Steve Hamby, who was there just as the book was being conceptualized; senior editor Becky Hilliker, who did an excellent job at improving the copy for the book; educator and avid bridge player Joan Kottler, who helped select the best titles as they transformed over time; biochemist Dr. Bren Morse, who gallantly shared a number of creative ideas and title possibilities; best-selling author Dr. Mike Norwood of Sedona, AZ, whose encouraging endorsement is very much appreciated; educational consultant Dr. Steve Preston, who read through chapters with dedicated thoroughness; my nephew Kenny Ryback, whose direct and candid feedback was as dramatic as it was highly original; author Dr. Dorothy Simpson, professor at New Mexico Highlands University, who was generous with her time to offer her opinion on the benefits of the book; my one-time editor, Suzanne Staszak-Silva of Rowman & Littlefield, who insisted on ensuring that every footnote found its proper place; social scientist

Dr. Esther Sumartojo, who incisively helped me work through some challenging passages; sales director David Surrency, who discussed the progress of the book with me at every step of the way; executive administrator Maria Taro, who assisted with all the painstaking formatting; psychotherapist Leslie Van Toole, another student who became a good friend and who saw the depth of soul hidden between the lines; and executive consultant Mike Wittenstein, whose quick and brilliant take on what worked well was always welcome.

And a heart-felt shout-out to my wonderful agent, Kimberley Cameron, who was always there to lift my spirits when they were low and who celebrated every move ahead as we plodded through the challenging path toward ultimate publication. Also, to publisher John Koehler, who quickly recognized what this book had to offer and took it under his wing of support.

REFERENCES

Notes for Introduction:

1. Krugman, P. We're going to miss greed and cynicism. *The New York Times,* online, Jan. 2, 2023.

2. Frank, T. *What's the Matter with Kansas?* NY: Henry Holt, 2004

3. Whipple, C. *The Fight of His Life.* NY: Simon & Schuster, 2023.

4. Draper. R. *Weapons of Mass Delusion.* NY: Penguin Press, 2022.

5. Roche, D. Marjorie Taylor Greene reveals details of investigation into Joe Biden. *Newsweek,* online, Jan. 23, 2023.

Notes for Chapter One:

1. Shermer, M. *The Believing Brain.* NY: St. Martin's Press, 2011.

2. Ford, M. We regret to inform you that Republicans are talking about secession again. *The New Republic,* online, Jan. 22, 2021.

3. Slisco, A. 47% of West coast Dems, 66% of Southern Republicans want to secede from U.S. *Newsweek,* online, July 14, 2021.

4. Khavin, D., Willis, H., Hill, E., Reneau, N., Jordan, D., Engelbrecht, C., Triebert, C., Cooper, S., Browne, M. and Botti, D. Capitol riot investigations. *The New York Times,* online, Mar. 23, 2022.

5. Walker, R. The shifting symbolism of the Gadsden flag. *New Yorker,* online, Oct. 2.

6. Reuters staff. Trump says, 'We will never give up, we will never concede'. *Reuters,* online, Jan. 6, 2021.

7. Giuliani, R. 'Let's have trial by combat' over election. *Reuters,*

8. https://www.reuters.com/video/watch/idOVDU2NS9R posted Jan. 6, 2021.

9. Hermann, P. and Hsu, S.S. Capitol police officer Brian Sicknick, who engaged rioters suffered two strokes and died of natural causes, officials say. *The Washington Post,* online, Apr. 19, 2021.

10. Treisman, R. Prosecutors: Proud Boys gave leader 'war powers,' planned ahead for Capitol riot. *NPR,* online, Mar. 2, 2021.

11. Fink, J. Full text of Mitch McConnell's speech before 'most important' vote of his career. *Newsweek,* online, Jan. 6, 2021.

12. Jeffery, A. and Bhattacharjee, R. Photos show violent clashes as Trump supporters storm the U.S. Capitol. *CNBC,* online, Jan. 6, 2021.

13. Rev.com Ted Cruz senate speech on election certification transcript. https://www.rev.com/blog/transcripts/ted-cruz-senate-speech-on-election-certification-transcript-january 6, 2021.

14. ABC News Live. Inside the Capitol Hill riot, https://www.facebook.com/watch/?v=282369063493932. Feb. 22, 2021.

15. Rodriguez, J. and Shabad, R. Trump defends Jan. 6 rioters' 'hang Mike Pence' chant in new audio. *NBC News,* online, Nov. 12, 2021.

16. CNN Special Reports The faces of the Trump insurrection, https://transcripts.cnn.com/show/csr/date/2021-01-24/segment/01, Jan. 24, 2021.

17. Goldwater, B. *Conscience of a Conservative.* Wilder Publications, Inc., Blacksburg, VA, 2009.

18. Manning, R. Extremism in the defense of liberty is still no vice. *The Hill,* online, July 16, 2014.

19. Margolin, E. 'Make America great again'—who said it first? *NBC News,* online, Sept. 9, 2016.

20. Yglesias, M. Donald Trump's epic meltdown, explained. *Vox,* online, Oct. 15, 2016.

21. Stecula, D.A. and Pickup, M. Social media, cognitive reflection, and conspiracy beliefs. *Frontiers in Political Science, 8,* online, June 8, 2021.

22. Gallup Three in four Americans believe in paranormal. Gallup. com/poll/16915, online, June 16. Harris, 2009. Harris poll reveals what people do and do not believe, harrisinteracative.com, online, 2005.

23. Porterfield, C. This year's five most distressing poll results. *Forbes,* online, Sept. 14, 2020.

24. Henley, J. and McIntyre, M. Survey uncovers widespread belief in 'dangerous' Covid conspiracy theories. *The Guardian, US Edition,* online, Oct. 26, 2020.

25. Walker, W.R. *et al.* Science education is no guarantee of skepticism. *Skeptic, 9(3),* 24-25, 2002, p. 25.

26. Hawking, S. and Mlodinow, L. *The Grand Design.* NY: Bantam Books, 2010, p. 7.

27. Hayes, C. Transcript: All in with Christ Hayes, 10/29/21. *MSNBC,* online, 2021.

28. Nickerson, R.S. Confirmation bias. *Review of General Psychology, 2(2),* 1998, 175-220.

29. Krikko, P. 'Confirmation bias'. *Power 3.0,* online, Jan. 15, 2019.

30. Docherty, K. 'Totally lost control' What REALLY happened during Capitol riots: Unseen clips show mob taking drugs and officers losing limbs & being tasered. *The Sun,* online, Oct. 20, 2021.

31. Schmidt, B. *et al.* I can't wait! Neural reward signals in impulsive individuals exaggerate the difference between immediate and future rewards. *Psychophysiology, 54,* 2017, 409-415.

32. Mischel, W. *The Marshmallow Test.* NY: Little, Brown/Hachette, 2014.

33. Jansen, B., Wu, Nicholas, Hayes, C. and King, L. 'Bring out Pence.' Managers at Trump trial reveal new video of Capitol riot that shows threat to VP, lawmakers. *USA Today,* online, Feb. 10, 2021.

34. Hermann, P. and Hsu, S.S. Buffalo man charged with stealing radio, badge from D.C. officer pulled into crowd during Capitol riot. *The Washington Post,* online, Mar. 12, 2021.

35. Keller, A. Lawyer for 'guy with the horns and the fur' claims his client finally realizes he's been 'duped' by Trump. *Law & Crime,* online, Jan. 22, 2021.

36. Associated Press Man sentenced to jail in Capitol riot case; judge hopes it sends message. *WEAU 13 News,* online, Oct. 9, 2021.

37. Peters, S. *The Chimp Paradox.* NY: Jeremy P. Torcher/Penguin, 2011.

38. Kahneman, D. *et al. Noise.* NY: Hachette, 2021.

39. Mencken, H.L. *Prejudices: Second Series.* From third chapter, *The Divine Afflatus.* NY: Library of America, 1920.

40. Huntington, S.P. *Political Order in Changing Societies.* New Haven, CT: Yale University Press, 1968.

41. Bloom, M. and Moskalenko, S. *Pastels and Pedophiles: Inside the Mind of QAnon.* Stanford, CA: Redwood Press, 2021.

42. Adams, H. *The Education of Henry Adams.* NY: Modern Library, 1907.

43. Hunnicutt, T., Zengerle, P. and Renshaw, J. 'We must end this uncivil war,' Biden says, taking over a U.S. in crisis. *Reuters,* online, Jan. 19, 2021.

44. Bersoff, D.M. *et al. Global Report.* Edelman Trust Barometer, 2021.

45. Sabato, J.K. *et al.* (Eds.) New initiative explores deep, persistent divides between Biden and Trump voters. Charlottesville, VA: UVA Center for Politics, 2021.

46. Cherry, K. How psychology explains the Bystander Effect. *Verywellmind,* online, Feb. 23, 2020.

47. Orlowski, J. *et al.* The Social Dilemma. *Netflix,* Sept. 9, 2020.

48. Cherry, K. What is a Skinner box? *Verywellmind,* online, Apr. 23, 2021.

49. Eligon, J. *et al.* U.S. authorities warn of threat by extremists. *The New York Times,* Jan. 14, 2021, p. 1.

50. Stelter, B. *Reliable Sources, CNN,* Jan. 23, 2021.

51. Stelter, B. *Reliable Sources, CNN,* Jan. 17, 2021.

52. Leibovich, M. *Thank You for Your Servitude.* NY: Penguin/Random House, 2022.

53. Chung, A.W. Justice Thomas temporarily blocks Graham election case testimony. *Reuters,* Oct. 4, 2022.

54. Pfeiffer, D. *Battling the Big Lie. How Fox, Facebook, and the MAGA media are destroying America.* NY: Twelve Publishing Company, 2022.

55. Pazzanese, C. How an authoritarian wields social media. *The Harvard Gazette,* online, Nov. 18, 2021.

56. Carney, J. On *GPS, CNN,* Jan. 23, 2021.

57. Ischinger, W. *World in Danger.* Washington, DC: Brookings Institution Press, 2021.

58. Corasaniti, N. *et al.* Most voters say U.S. democracy is under threat. *The New York Times,* Oct. 18, 2022, p. 1.

59. Myers, S.L. & Frenkel, S. Exploding online, disinformation is now a fixture of U.S. politics. *The New York Times,* Oct. 21, 2022, p. 1.

60. Brosnan, S.F. and De Waal, F.B. Monkeys reject unequal pay. *Nature, 425(6955),* 2003, 297-299.

61. Woodall, C. Replacement theories, hunting RINOs. *USA Today*, online, July 9, 2022.

62. Broadwater, L. and Feuer, A. Trump rebuffed aides over loss, denying reality. *The New York Times*, June 14, 2022, p. 1.

63. Southall, A. *et al.* Before attack, solitary teen caused alarm. *The New York Times*, May 16, 2022, p. 1.

64. Schmidt, M.S. A Jan. 6 panel member says Trump raising money off bogus election claims was 'the big rip-off.' *The New York Times*, online, June 13, 2022.

65. Haberman, M. and Broadwater, L. Advisers knew Trump electors would be fake. *The New York Times*, July 28, 2022, p. 1.

66. Grant, N. and Hsu, T. Google finds 'inoculating' people against misinformation helps blunt its power. *The New York Times*, online, Aug. 24, 2020.

67. Susaria, A. *et al.* Misinformation remains a force in 2022. *The Atlanta Journal-Constitution*, Jan. 4, 2022, p. A15.

68. Weisman, J. Amid Jan. 6 revelations, election lies still dominate in the G.O.P. *The New York Times*, online, June 17, 2022.

Notes for Chapter Two:

1. Nickerson, R.S. Confirmation bias: A ubiquitous phenomenon in many guises. *Review of General Psychology*, online, June 1. https://doi.org/10.1037/1089-2680.2.2.175. 1998.

2. Harris, T. Frances Haugen: Exposing the truth. *Time*, Jun 23, 2022, p. 52.

3. Smith, S. QAnon and the definitive awakening. *Youcanprint* publishers, 2021.

4. Orlowski, J. *et al.* The Social Dilemma. *Netflix*, Sept. 9, 2020.

5. Kuss, D.J. and Griffiths, M.D. Online social networking and addiction—A review of the psychological literature. *International Journal of Environmental Research Public Health, 8*(9), 2011, 3528-3552.

6. Egolf, B., Lasker, J., Wolf, S. and Potvin, L. The Roseto effect: A 50-year comparison of mortality rates. *American Journal of Public Health*, 82(8), 1992, p. 1089-1092. doi#10.2105/ajph.82.8.1089.

7. Walton, A.G. 6 ways social media affects our mental health. *Forbes*, online, June 30, 2017.

8. Reed, P. *et al.* Differential physiological changes following internet exposure in higher and lower problematic internet users. *PLOS ONE*, online, May 25, 2017.

9. Sagioglou, C. and Greitmeyer, T. Facebook's emotional consequences: Why Facebook causes a decrease in mood and why people still use it. *Computers in Human Behavior, 35,* 2014, 359-363.

10. Dunbar, R.I.M. Do online social media cut through the constraints that limit the size of offline social networks? *Royal Society Open Science*, online, Jan.1, 2016.

11. Tromholt, M. The Facebook Experiment. *Cyberpsychology, Behavior, and Social Networking, 19(11),* 661-666. doi:10.1089/ cyber.2016.0259, 2016.

12. Leetaru, K. What does it mean for social media platforms to "sell" our data? *Forbes,* online, Dec. 15, 2018.

13. King, V. What Netflix's "The Social Dilemma" got wrong. *The Anticapitalist,* online, Oct.28, 2020.

14. Federal Trade Commission. FTC imposes $5 billion penalty and sweeping new privacy restrictions on Facebook. https://www. ftc.gov/news-events/news/press-releases/2019/07/ftc-imposes-5-billion-penalty-sweeping-new-privacy-restrictions-facebook, July 24, 2019.

15. US Government Publishing Office. Algorithms: How companies' decisions about data and content impact consumers. *House Hearing, 115 Congress*, online, https://www.govinfo.gov/content/pkg/CHRG-115hhrg28578/html/CHRG-115hhrg28578.htm, 2017.

16. Dizikes, P. Study: On Twitter, false news travels faster than true stories. *MIT News*, online, Mar. 8, 2018.

17. Quoted in Flood, B. Ex-Facebook honcho Tim Kendall says Big Tech is a 'threat to democracy,' calls for social media reform. *Fox News, Hot Topics*, online, Oct. 13, 2020.

18. Hern, A. Netflix's biggest competitor? Sleep. *The Guardian*, online, Apr. 18, 2017.

19. Silver, C. Patents reveal how Facebook wants to capture your emotions, facial expressions and mood. *Forbes*, online, June 8, 2017.

20. Zuboff, S. *The Age of Surveillance Capitalism*. NY: Hachette, 2019.

21. Mitchell, A. and Diamond, L. China's surveillance state should scare everyone. *The Atlantic*, online, Feb. 2, 2018.

22. Anderson, R. The panopticon is already here. *The Atlantic*, online, Sept. issue, 2020.

23. Marineau, S. Fact check US: What is the impact of Russian interference in the US presidential election? *The Conversation*, online, Sept. 29, 2020.

24. Editors of Encylopaedia Britannica. Algorithm. *Britannica*, online, Updated, May 6, 2021.

25. Veselov, V. Computer AI passes Turing test in 'world first.' *BBC News*, online, June 9, 2014.

26. Metz, C. Meet GPT-3. It has learned to code (and blog and argue). *The New York Times*, online, Nov. 24, 2020.

27. Zhou L. *et al.* The design and implementation of XiaoIce, an empathetic social chatbot. *Computational Linguistics, 46(1),* 2020, 52-93, p. 53.

28. Ellison, M., Jonze, S. and Landay, V. *Her.* Annapurna Pictures, 2013.

29. Zhou L. *et al.* The design and implementation of XiaoIce, an empathetic social chatbot. *Computational Linguistics, 46(1),* 2020, 52-93.

30. Barth, F.D. Lies and half-truths on social media. *Psychology Today*, online, Feb. 21, 2020.

31. Johnson, J. Thanks to social media, we are in a truth crisis. *The Dallas Morning News, Opinion*, online, Nov. 16, 2019.

32. Wlosik, M. What is search advertising and how does it work? *Clearcode.cc,* online, Jan. 22, 2018.

33. McFarlane, G. How Facebook (Meta), Twitter, Social Media make money from you. *Investopedia.com,* online, Nov. 4, 2021.

34. Manjoo, F. The Capitol was just the start. *The New York Times, Opinion,* online, Jan. 13, 2021.

35. Hawkins, S., Yudkin, D., Juan-Torres, M. and Dixon, T. *Hidden Tribes: A study of America's polarized landscape.* More in Common publishers, NY, 2018.

36. Chen, B.X. Battle for users' privacy will transform internet. *The New York Times,* Sept. 17, 2021, p. 1.

37. Vega, N. Google says it will pay news publishers $1B over the next 3 years. *New York Post*, online, Oct. 1, 2020.

38. McCabe, D. and Kang, C. Lawmakers grill tech C.E.O.s on Capitol riot, getting few direct answers. *The New York Times,* online, March 25, 2021.

39. Orlowski, J. *et al.* The Social Dilemma. *Netflix*, Sept. 9, 2020.

40. Hunt, M.G. *et al*. No more FOMO: Limiting social media decreases loneliness and depression. *Journal of Social and Clinical Psychology, 37(10)*, 2018, 751-768. https://doi.org/10.1521/jscp.2018.37.10.751.

41. Grant, A. There's a name for the blah you're feeling: It's called languishing. *The New York Times*, online, April 19, 2021.

42. Blum, D. The other side of languishing is flourishing. Here's how to get there. *The New York Times*, online, May 4, 2021.

43. Sturm, V.E. *et al*. Big smile, small self. *Emotion*, online, Sept. 21, 2020.

44. Lembke, A. *Dopamine Nation*. NY: Dutton, 2021.

45. Spitzer, M. *Demencia Digital*. Munich, Germany: Droemer Knau, 2012, 312.

46. Buckley, C. China tightens limits for young online gamers and bans school night play. *The New York Times*, online, Aug.30, 2021.

47. Johnson, S. A.I. is mastering language. Should we trust what it says? *The New York Times Magazine*, online, April 15, 2022.

48. Roose, K. We need to talk about how good A.I is getting. *The New York Times*, online, Aug. 24, 2022.

49. Grant, N. and Metz, C. Google sidelines engineer who claims it's A.I. is sentient. *The New York Times*, online, June 12, 2022.

50. Broadwater, L. and Feuer, A. Trump pressured states to comply on fake electors. *The New York Times*, June 22, 2022. p. 1.

Notes for Chapter Three:

1. Conway, K. *Meet the Press*, January 22, 2017.

2. Brownstein, R. Trump leaves America at its most divided since the Civil War. *CNN Politics*, online, Jan. 19, 2021.

3. Prior, M. Media and political polarization. *Annual Review of Political Science, 16,* 101-274, 2013.

4. Kerry, J.F. Tora Bora revisited: How we failed to get bin Laden and why it matters today. *Committee of Foreign Relations US Senate,* online, Nov. 3, 2009.

5. National Commission on Terrorist Attacks Upon the United States. *The 9/11 Commission Report, Final Report of the National Commission on Terrorist Attacks Upon the United States, Executive Summary.* Washington, DC: National Commission on terrorist attacks upon the United States of America, June 16, 2004.

6. Keeter, S. Trends in public opinion about the war in Iraq, 2003-2007. *Pew Research Center,* online, March 15, 2007.

7. Whipple, C. 'The attacks will be spectacular.' *Politico Magazine,* online, Nov. 12, 2015.

8. Skoog, T. *et al.* First person: The CIA's former counterterrorism chief on the lead up to 9/11. *WBUR,* online, Oct. 13, 2020.

9. O'Hallroran, M. and Salamy, E. Condoleezza Rice reflects on 9/11: 'Every plane had become a missile.' *KUTV,* online, Sept. 11, 2021.

10. Stahl, J. The pre-9/11 warnings Bush's team ignored were way more intense than we thought. *Slate,* online, Nov. 13, 2015.

11. Thompson, P. They tried to warn us: Foreign intelligence warnings before 9/11. *History Commons,* online, Feb. 27, 2002.

12. Arkin, W.N. Inside the briefing where George Bush heard, 'Bin Laden is determined to strike.' *Newsweek,* online, Nov. 11, 2021.

13. Bush, G.W. President Bush addresses the nation. *The Washington Post,* online, Sept. 20, 2001.

14. Newport, F. Americans still think Iraq had weapons of mass destruction before war. *Gallup News Service,* online, June 16, 2003.

15. Powell, C. *U.S. Secretary of State Colin Powell addresses the U.N. Security Council.* Washington, DC: The White House, Feb. 5, 2003.

16. Taylor, P. Iraq, *BBC News*, online, March 18, 2013.

17. BBC News. Iraq war sources name revealed, online, Nov. 2, 2007.

18. Drogin, B. *Curveball.* London, UK: Ebury Press, 2007, p. 70.

19. Helmore, E. US relied on 'drunken liar' to justify war. *The Observer*, online, April 3, 2005.

20. Linzer, D. Panel: US ignored work of U.N. arms inspector. *The Washington Post,* online, April 15, 2005.

21. Slevin, P. How Colin Powell saw his role—and that of another famous non-quitter. *The New Yorker,* online, Nov. 5, 2021.

22. Cohen, S. Iraq's WMD programs. *CIA Press Releases and Statements*, online, Nov. 28, 2003.

23. Hartig, H. and Doherty, C. Two decades later, the enduring legacy of 9/11. *Pew Research Center*, online, Sept 2, 2021.

24. Newport, F. Americans still think Iraq had weapons of mass destruction before war. *Gallup News Service,* online, June 16, 2003.

25. Wolffe, R. Rumsfeld's much-vaunted 'courage' was a smokescreen for lies, crime and death. *The Guardian,* online, July 1, 2021.

26. Cohen, A. The Torture Memos, 10 Years Later. *The Atlantic,* online, Feb. 6, 2012.

27. Beaumont, P. Stanley McChrystal. *The Guardian*, online, Sept. 26, 2009.

28. Youssef, N. A. *et al.* Obama's Afghan strategy remains plagued by problems. *McClatchy DC Bureau*, online, Sept. 25, 2013.

29. Prokop, A. Why Biden was so set on withdrawing from Afghanistan. *Vox*, online, Aug. 18, 2021.

30. Malkasian, C. Why didn't we leave Afghanistan before now? *TIME*, online, Sept. 19, 2021.

31. Jenkins, B.M. President Obama's controversial legacy as counterterrorism-in-chief. The

32. RANDBLOG, online, Aug. 22, 2016.

33. Friedersdorf, C. Obama's weak defense of his record on drone killings. *The Atlantic*, online, Dec. 23, 2016.

34. Zenko, M. Obama's final drone strike data. *Council on Foreign Relations*, online, Jan. 20, 2017.

35. Cavallaro, J. and Sonnenberg, S. *Living Under Drones.* Stanford, CA: International Human Rights and Conflict Resolution Clinic and Global Justice Clinic, September, 2012, 99-101.

36. De Luce, D. Obama's drone policy gets an 'F'. The Cable, online, Feb. 23, 2016.

37. Timm, T. Obama is bullish on war, no matter how you spin it. *The Guardian*, online, May 16, 2016.

38. President Obama's legacy is endless war. *TIME*, online, May 5.

39. Bush administration ignored clear warnings. NBC News, online, Dec. 1, 2008.

40. Morin, R. Behind Trump's win in rural white America. *Pew Research Center*, online, Nov. 17, 2016.

41. Stauffer, B. What's going on with America's White people? *Politicomagazine*, N.D.

42. Reuters. U.S.-China trade war has cost up to 245,000 U.S. jobs: business group study. *Reuters*, online, Jan. 14, 2021.

43. Randall, D. U.S. investors see more automation, not jobs, under Trump administration. *Reuters*, online, Jan. 19, 2017.

44. Leopold, L. A new study reveals the disturbing truth about the base of Trump's support. *AlterNet*, online, June 8, 2021.

45. Gabbatt, A. 'Jews will not replace us': Vice film lays bare horror of neo-Nazis in America. *The Guardian*, online, Aug. 16, 2017.

46. Johnson, J. and Hauslohner, A. 'I think Islam hates us.' *The Washington Post*, online, May 20, 2017.

47. Bolton, J. *The Room Where It Happened*. NY: Simon & Schuster. 2021.

48. Masters. J. Donald Trump says torture 'absolutely works'—but does it? *CNN politics*, online, Jan. 26, 2017.

49. Gibbons-Neff, T. *et al*. Former commanders fault Trump's use of troops against protesters. *The New York Times*, online, June 2, 2020.

50. Bendery, J. Tammy Duckworth: Trump's use of military against protesters is 'disgusting.' *Huffpost*, online, June 4, 2020.

51. Wike, R. *et al*. U.S. image suffers as publics around world question Trump's leadership. *Pew Research Center*, online, June 26, 2017.

52. Lahoud, N. Bin Laden's catastrophic success. *Foreign Affairs*, online, Sept./Oct., 2021.

53. Masters. J. Donald Trump says torture 'absolutely works'—but does it? *CNN Politics*, online, Jan. 26, 2017.

54. Cohen, L. Explainer-What charges could Trump face over efforts to overturn the 2020 election? *Reuters*, online, Jun 23, 2022.

55. Broadwater, L. and Benner, K. Trump strong-armed Justice Dept. to subvert vote. *The New York Times*, June 24, 2022, p. 1.

56. Confessore, N. and Yourish, K. Creeping into the mainstream, a theory turns hate into terror. *The New York Times*, May 16, 1, 2022.

Notes for Chapter Four:

1. Memmott M. 75 Years Ago, 'War of The Worlds' started a panic. *The Two-Way*, online, Oct. 30, 2013.

2. Blanke, O. Multisensory brain mechanisms of bodily self-consciousness. *National Review of Neuroscience, 13*, 556-571, 2012.

3. Casad, B. J. *Confirmation bias. Encyclopedia Britannica.* https://www.britannica.com/science/confirmation-bias. October 9, 2019.

4. French, C. Why do some people believe in conspiracy theories? *Scientific American Mind*, online, July 1, 2015.

5. Casad, B.J. *Confirmation bias. Encyclopedia Britannica.* https://www.britannica.com/science/confirmation-bias. October 9, 2019.

6. Pennycook, G. *et al.* Prior exposure increases perceived accuracy of fake news. *Journal of Experimental Psychology: General, 147(12)*, 2018, 1865-1880.

7. Rogers, K. *et al.* Trump's suggestion that disinfectants could be used to treat coronavirus prompts aggressive pushback. *The New York Times*, online, April 24, 2020.

8. Erman, M. Malaria drug touted by Trump fails to prevent COVID-19 in high profile study. *Reuters,* online, June 3, 2020.

9. Collins, B. *et al.* Clamoring for Ivermectin some turn to a pro-Trump telemedicine website. *NBC News*, online, Aug. 26, 2021.

10. Walsh, C. Young adults hardest hit by loneliness during pandemic. *The Harvard Gazette*, online, Feb. 17, 2021.

11. Necka, E. After COVID, research on social isolation and loneliness is needed more than ever. *National Institute on Aging, COVID-19*, online, June 2, 2021.

12. Weir, K. Why we believe alternative facts. *APA Monitor on Psychology, 48(5),* May 24, 2017.

13. Kleinfeld, R. The rise of political violence in the United States. *Journal of Democracy, 32(4),* 2021, 160-176.

14. Kleinfeld, R. The rise of political violence in the United States. *Journal of Democracy, 32(4),* 2021, 160-176.

15. Jones, S.G. The rise of far-right extremism in the United States. *Center for Strategic & International Studies,* online, Nov. 7, 2018.

16. Swift, A. Americans' trust in mass media sinks to new low. *Gallup,* online, Sept. 14, 2016.

17. Salmon, F. Media trust hits new low. *Axios,* online, Jan. 21, 2021.

18. Totty, M. How to make artificial intelligence less biased. *The Wall Street Journal,* online, Nov. 3, 2020.

19. Brown, S. A new study measures the actual impact of robots on jobs. It's significant. *MIT Management Sloan School,* online, July 29, 2020.

20. Feldman, D.B. Why do people believe things that aren't true? *Psychology Today,* May 12, 2017.

21. Pringle, Z.I. Harnessing emotions to fuel creativity. *Psychology Today,* online, Jan. 3, 2020.

22. Morton, A. *Imagination and Emotion.* Cambridge, UK: Polity Press, 2013.

23. Van Prooijen, J-W. and van Vugt, M. Conspiracy theories: Evolved functions and psychological mechanisms. *Perspectives on Psychological Science, 13(6),* 2021, 770-788.

24. Riggio, R.E. Why do people believe strange things? *Psychology Today,* online, Aug. 18, 2020.

25. Festinger, L. *A Theory of cognitive dissonance.* Stanford, CA: Stanford University Press, 1957.

26. Casad, B.J. *Confirmation bias. Encyclopedia Britannica.* https:// www.britannica.com/science/confirmation-bias. October 9, 2019.

27. Donegan, M. QAnon conspiracists believe in a vast pedophile ring. The truth is sadder. *TheGuardian.com.* online, September 20, 2020.

28. Leman, P.J. and Cinnirella, M. Beliefs in conspiracy theories and the need for cognitive closure. *Frontiers in Psychology,* 27, doi. org/10.3389/fpsyg201300378, June 27, 2013.

29. Ubel, P.A. Why we cannot trust political pundits, or ourselves. *Psychology Today,* online, Oct. 1, 2014.

30. Blanke, O. Multisensory brain mechanisms of bodily self-consciousness. *National Review of Neuroscience, 13,* 2012, 556-571.

31. French, C. Why do some people believe in conspiracy theories? *Scientific American Mind,* online, July 1, 2015.

32. Temming, M. How many galaxies are there in the universe? Online, July 18, 2014.

33. Peshin, A. Why do we fall for conspiracy theories? *Science ABC,* online, January, 2022.

34. Fox, M. Fake news: Lies spread faster on social media than truth does. *NBC News,* online, March 8, 2018.

35. Bump, P. Donald Trump will be president thanks to 80,000 people in three states, *The Washington Post,* online, Dec. 1, 2016.

36. Bump, B. A remarkable GOP admission. *The Washington Post,* online, Jan. 4, 2021.

37. Mayer, J. The big money behind the Big Lie. *The New Yorker,* online, Aug. 2, 2021.

38. Piacenza, J. Media credibility perceptions are down, due to Republicans. *Morning Consult,* online, April 9, 2019.

39. Watson, A. Credibility of major news organizations in the United States from 2017 to 2021. *Statista*, online, Aug. 31, 2021.

40. Hollandbeck, A. In a word: Propaganda! *The Saturday Evening Post*, online, October 16, 2019.

41. Nisbet, E.C. *et al.* The presumed influence of election misinformation on others reduces our own satisfaction with democracy. *Harvard Kennedy School Misinformation Review, 1, Volume 1, Special Issue on US Elections and Disinformation*, March 12, 2021.

42. Heilweil, R. How the 5G coronavirus conspiracy theory went from fringe to mainstream. *Vox*, online, April 24, 2020.

43. Michael, T. Russia 'hired 1,000 internet trolls to create fake news sites spreading lies about Hillary Clinton during US election'. *Independent*, online, March 30, 2017.

44. Brattberg, E. and Maurer, T. Russian election interference: Europe's counter to fake news and cyber-attacks. *Carnegie Endowment for International Peace*, online, May, 2018.

45. Trump, D.J. Donald Trump Phoenix, Arizona rally speech transcript July 24. *Rev Transcripts*, online, July 24, 2021.

46. Belvedere, M.J. Fellow real estate mogul: Trump is the real deal as a successful businessman. *CNBC*, online, October 5, 2016.

47. Mayer, J. How Russia helped swing the election for Trump. *The New Yorker*, online, September 24, 2018.

48. McCormick, R. Donald Trump says Facebook and Twitter 'helped him win'. *The Verge*, online, November 13, 2016.

49. Lahut, J. Trump says he might be 'the greatest star maker of all time' but some of his stars 'are actually made of garbage'. *Insider*, online, Dec. 3, 2021.

50. Shinkman, P.D. How Vladmir Putin won the U.S. election. *US News and World Report*, online, Nov. 9, 2016.

51. Vosoughi, S. *et al.* The spread of true and false news online. *Science, 359(6380),* 2018, 1146-1151.

52. Langin, K. Fake news spreads faster than true news on Twitter—thanks to people, not bots. *Science,* online, March 8, 2018.

53. Goebbels, J. Der Rundfunk als achte Großmacht, *Signale der neuen Zeit. 25 ausgewählte Reden von Dr. Joseph Goebbels* (Munich: Zentralverlag der NSDAP), 1938, 197-207.

54. Miller, C.R. and Edwards, V. The intelligent teacher's guide through campaign propaganda. *The Clearing House, 11(2),* 1936, 69-77.

55. Lee, A.M. and Lee, E.B. *The Fine Art of Propaganda: A Study of Father Coughlin's Speeches.* The Institute for Propaganda Analysis. NY: Harcourt, Brace, 1939.

56. Shepardson, D. and Bartz, D. Facebook 'operating in the shadows' says whistleblower, lawmakers demand probes. *Reuters,* online, Oct. 6, 2021.

57. Isaac, M. Power of likes puts Facebook in a quandary. *The New York Times,* Oct. 26, 2021.

Notes for Chapter Five:

1. Wilke, C. and Macias, A. Trump threatens to deploy military as George Floyd protests continue to shake the U.S. *CNBC,* online, June 1, 2020.

2. Berzon, A. and Rubin, R. Trump's father helped GOP candidate with numerous loans. *The Wall Street Journal,* online, September 23, 2016.

3. Converse, P.E. Change in the American electorate, in A. Campbell and P.E. Converse (Eds.), *The Human Meaning of Social Change,* NY: Russell Sage, 1972, pp. 263-337.

4. Campbell, D.E. What is education's impact on civic and social engagement? *Symposium on Social Outcomes of Learning*, held at the Danish University of Education (Copenhagen) on 23-24 March 2006, p. 59.

5. Trump, D. Pledge from Trump to 'Make American Great Again.' *Associated Press*, online, January 20, 2017.

6. Barrett, P., Hendrix, J. and Sims, G. How tech platforms fuel U.S. political polarization and what government can do about it. *Techtank*, online, September 27, 2021.

7. Fisher, M. Putin's case for war, annotated. *The New York Times*, online, Feb. 24, 2022.

8. Rathi, A. Kerry lines up pledges to scrub emissions from carbon-heavy industries. *Bloomberg*, online, Oct. 5, 2021.

9. Costello, I. One year later: The lasting effects of the Jan. 6 attack. *Koin*, online, January 6, 2022.

10. Gregorian, D. Trump told Bob Woodward he knew in February that COVID-19 was 'deadly stuff' but wanted to 'play it down.' *NBC News*, online, September 9, 2020.

11. Hais, M., Ross, D. and Winograd, M. Protecting democracy and containing autocracy. *Fixgov*, online, May 10, 2021.

12. Reimann, N. QAnon marked Friday as Trump 'Reinstatement' Day—Here are other flop predictions of Trump's return. *Forbes*, online, August 13, 2021.

13. Desilver, D. Turnout soared in 2020 as nearly two-thirds of eligible U.S. voters cast ballots for president. *Pew Research Center*, online, January 28, 2021.

14. Smith, T. They believe in Trump's 'Big Lie.' Here's why it's been so hard to dispel. *NPR*, online, January 5, 2022.

15. Cameron, C. There are people who died in connection with the Capitol riot. *The New York Times*, online, January 6, 2022.

16. Brockell, G. Historians just ranked the presidents. Trump wasn't last. *The Washington Post*, online, June 30, 2021.

17. Leonnig, C. and Rucker, P. *I Alone Can Fix It*. London, UK: Bloomsbury Publishing, 2021.

18. Zhao, C. Donald Trump blames election loss on Pence certifying Biden's win: 'Disappointed.' *Newsweek*, online, June 21, 2021.

19. Frey, W.H. Biden's victory came from the suburbs. *Brookings*, online, November 13, 2020.

20. Frenkel, S. and Kang, C. *An Ugly Truth*. NY: Harper, 2021.

21. *The University of California Institute for Prediction Technology*. The social dilemma: Should your thoughts be monetized? online, Dec. 2020.

22. McNamee, R. *Zucked*. NY: Penguin Random House, 2021, p. 2.

23. Levy, S. *Facebook*. NY: Penguin Random House, 2020.

24. Hern, A. and Wong, J.C. Facebook employees hold virtual walkout over Mark Zuckerberg's refusal to act against Trump. *The Guardian*, online, June 1, 2020.

25. Levy, S. *Facebook*. NY: Penguin Random House, 2020.

26. Salam, E. Majority of Covid misinformation came from 12 people, report finds. *The Guardian*, online, July 17, 2021.

27. Rosen, G. Moving past the finger pointing. *Facebook Blogpost*: Combating Misinformation, online, July 17, 2021.

28. Kennan, G.F. Memorandum by the Counselor of Embassy in the Soviet Union. Washington, DC: *Foreign Relations of the United States: Diplomatic Papers, 1944, Document 826*, 1944, p. 913.

29. Yarrow, D. From fact-checking to value-checking: Normative reasoning in the new public sphere. *The Political Quarterly*, online, May 6, 2021.

30. Krow, A.J. How does Facebook benefit from your data collection? *Technology Hits*, online, (n.d.).

31. Meta Platforms: Number of Employees 2009-2021/FB. *Macrotrends*, online, 2021.

32. Hall, M. Facebook. *Encyclopedia Britannica*, online, November 9, 2021.

33. Ashton, N.A. and Cruft, R. Rethinking the post-truth polarization narrative: Social roles and hinge commitments in the plural public sphere. *The Political Quarterly*, online, July 3, 2021.

34. Bradshaw, S. *et al.* Industrialized disinformation. University of Oxford: *Demtech Newsletter, Programme on Democracy & Technology*, 2021.

35. Morbin, R. *Helsinki Declaration*, International Communications Consultancy Organization. Munich: Germany, April 1, 2002.

36. Silverman, C. *et al.* Disinformation for hire: How a new breed of PR firms is selling lies online. *BuzzFeed News*, online, January 6, 2020.

37. Otis, C.L. *True or False.* NY: MacMillan, 2020.

38. Brownstein, R. Trump leaves America at its most divided since the Civil War. *CNN politics*, online, January 19, 2021.

39. Rhodes, J. Fake radio war stirs terror through US: Orson Welles' War of the Worlds turns 70. *Smithsonian Magazine*, online, October 31, 2008.

40. Dixon, G. Fake radio 'war' strikes terror through U.S. *Daily News*, October 31, 1938.

41. Rutenberg, J. Trump's fraud claims died in court, but the myth of stolen elections lives on. *The New York Times*, online, October 11, 2021.

42. Frenkel, S. and Kan, C. *An Ugly Truth*. NY: Harper, 2021.

43. Roberts, D. Why conspiracy theories flourish on the right. *Vox*, online, September 13, 2016.

44. Horwitz, J. The Facebook whistleblower, Frances Haugen, says she wants to fix the company, not harm it. *The Wall Street Journal*, online, October 3, 2021.

45. Simon, S. and Stevenson, J. How can we neutralize the militias? *The New York Review*, online, August 19, 2021.

46. Kissinger, H.A. *et al. The Age of AI*. NY: Hachette, 2021.

47. Holm, L. Bullying, social psychology, and mob mentality. *Owlcation*, online, September 23, 2018.

48. Paul, K. 'Congress will be taking action': key takeaways from the Facebook whistleblower hearing. *The Guardian*, online, October 5, 2021.

Notes for Chapter Six:

1. Shermer, M. The conspiracy theory detector. *Scientific American, Mind*, online, Dec. 1, 2010.

2. Settle, J.E. *et al.* Friendships moderate an association between dopamine gene variant and political ideology. *The Journal of Politics, 72(4)*, 2010, 1189-1198.

3. Alford, J. *et al.* Are political orientations genetically transmitted? *American Political Science Review, 99(2)*, 2005, 153-167.

4. Hatemi, P.K. and McDermott, R. The genetics of politics. *Trends in Genetics, 28(10)*, 2012, 525-533.

5. Puttonen, S., Ravaja, N. and Keltikangas-Jarvinen, L. Cloninger's temperament dimensions and affective responses to different challenges. *Comprehensive Psychiatry 46 (2)*, 2005, 128–34.

6. Lewis, G.J. and Bates, T.C. Common heritable effects underpin concerns over norm maintenance and in-group favoritism:

Evidence from genetic analyses of right-wing authoritarianism and traditionalism. *Journal of Personality, 82,* 2013, 297–309.

7. Hufer, A. *et al.* Genetic and environmental variation in political orientation in adolescence and early childhood. *Journal of Personality and Social Psychology,* 2019, 1-15.

8. Leary, M.R. and Baumeister, R.F. The nature and function of self-esteem: Sociometer theory. *Advances in Experimental Social Psychology, 32,* 2000, 1–62.

9. Greenberg, J., Pyszczynski, T. and Solomon, S. The causes and consequences of a need for self-esteem: A terror management theory. In R. Baumeister (Ed.), *Public Self and Private Self* (pp. 189–212). New York: Springer, 1986.

10. Routledge, C. and Vess, M. *Handbook of Terror Management Theory.* London, UK: Academic Press, 2019.

11. Hogg, M.A. Uncertainty–identity theory. *Advances in Experimental Social Psychology, 39,* 2007, 69–126.

12. Choi, E.U. and Hogg, M.A. Self-uncertainty and group identification: A meta-analysis. *Group Processes & Intergroup Relations, 23(4),* 2020, 483-501.

13. Pettypiece, S. Trump on QAnon conspiracy theory: 'Is that supposed to be a bad thing?' *NBC News,* online, Aug. 19, 2020.

14. Grunwald, M. Trump's love affair with coal, *Politico Magazine,* online, Oct. 15, 2017.

15. Breuninger, K. Trump says he'll cut off foreign aid to countries that send 'not their best' people. *CNBC,* online, June 19, 2018.

16. Douglas, K. Speaking of Psychology: Why people believe in conspiracy theories, with Karen Douglas, Episode 124, *American Psychological Association,* online, 2021.

17. Abalakina-Paap, M., Stephan, W.G., Craig, T., and Gregory, W.L. Beliefs in conspiracies. *Political Psychology*, 20, p. 637–647. doi:10.1111/0162-895X.00160. 1999.

18. Douglas, K.M., Sutton, R.M. and Cichocka, A. The Psychology of Conspiracy Theories. *Current Directions in Psychological Science*, 26(6), 2017, 538–542.

19. Stecula, D.A. and Pickup, M. "Social Media, Cognitive Reflection, and Conspiracy Beliefs." *Frontiers in Political Science*, 3. 2021.

20. Hutchison, A. New research shows that 71% of Americans now get news content via social platforms. *Social Media Today*, online, Jan. 12, 2021.

21. Roose, K. What is QAnon, the viral Pro-Trump conspiracy theory? *New York Times*, online, Sept. 3, 2021.

22. Edsall, T.B. White riot. *The New York Times*, *Opinion*, online, Jan. 13, 2021.

23. McAdams, D.P. The appeal of the primal leader: Human evolution and Donald J. Trump. *Evolutionary Studies in Imaginative Culture*, 1, 2018, 1–14.

24. Smith, D. Trump hails 'good man' Boris Johnson and says of UK: 'They like me over there.' *TheGuardian.com*, online, July 23, 2019.

25. Zitser, J. Donald Trump claimed he played Elton John's 'Rocket Man' to North Korea dictator Kim Jong Un, video shows. *Businessinsider.com*, online, Dec. 12, 2021.

26. Woody, C. Trump lies Mexico's new president so much that he apparently calls him 'Juan Trump.' *Businessinsider*, online, July 9, 2018.

27. Mortosko, D. Trump rips 'phony' *New York Times* columnist Tom Friedman for calling him a racist and nicknames him 'the chin' as he reveals that the Pulitzer Prize winner 'kissed my a**' in a recent phone call. *Dailymail.com*, online, July 19, 2019.

28. Nelson, L. Trump slams CNN's 'Crazy Jim Acosta' in shutdown victory lap tweet. *Politico.com,* online, Jan. 23, 2018.

29. Goldiner, D. and Greene, L. Trump says Chris Cuomo is too angry to own a gun after anti-Italian 'Fredo' confrontation. *NYDailyNews.com,* online, Aug. 13, 2019.

30. Greenwood, M. Don Lemon: Trump's nickname for me is 'sour Lemon.' *Thehill.com,* online, Mar. 2, 2018.

31. Keneally, M. 'Sloppy Steve' Bannon becomes Trump's latest example of name-calling. *ABCNews,* online, Jan. 5, 2018.

32. Lee, B.X. *The Dangerous Case of Donald Trump.* NY: St. Martin's Press, 2019.

33. Panning, J.C. Trump anxiety disorder. In *The Dangerous Case of Donald Trump,* NY: St. Martin's Press, 2019, 228-236.

34. Cheng, J.T., Tracy, J.L. and Henrich, J. Pride, personality, and the evolutionary foundations of human social status. *Evolution and Human Behavior, 31,* 334–347, 2010, p. 334.

35. Lewis, N. Here's a list of people Trump has fired or threatened to fire. *WashingtonPost.com,* online, July 25, 2017.

36. Lord, J. Trump setting stage for Supreme Court battle over executive privilege. *The Epoch Times,* online, Nov. 29, 2021.

37. Ocobock, C. Yes, we should correct misinformation; we also need to teach others how to spot it. *University of Notre Dame, sites.nd.edu/cara-ocobock/2020/05/04,* online, May 4, 2020.

38. Matyla, K. Jerome Corsi has uncovered irrefutable proof of the authenticity of 'QAnon.' *Right Wing Watch,* online, Jan. 11, 2018.

39. Mak, A. Does HBO's QAnon documentary reveal who Q is? *Slate.com,* online, Apr. 4, 2021.

40. Hoback, C. (Director). *Into the Storm.* HBO, March 21, 2021.

41. Berkowitz, R. A game designer's analysis of QAnon. *Curiouserinstitute,* online, Sept. 30, 2020.

42. McDonough, F. *The Gestapo.* NY: Skyhorse. 2017.

43. Wilde, R. Hitler's rise to power. *ThoughtCo,* online, Jan. 21, 2020.

44. Sonmez, F. Trump again jokes about staying on as president for more than two terms. *The Washington Post, Election 2020,* online, April 18, 2019.

45. Mencken, H.L. Bayard vs. Lionheart. *Baltimore Evening Sun,* July 26, 1920.

46. Fandos, N. Trial strategy aims to rekindle Capitol outrage. *The New York Times,* Feb. 8, 2021.

47. Feuer, A. and Hong, N. We just followed Trump's cue, several accused in rioting say. *The New York Times,* Jan. 18, 2021.

48. Edmondson, C. *et al.* G.O.P. leader criticizes freshman for remarks but doesn't punish her. *The New York Times,* Feb. 4, 2021.

49. Edmonson, C. Vote by House ejects Greene from two panels. *The New York Times,* Feb. 5, 2021.

50. Rothschild, M. *The Storm Is Upon Us.* Brooklyn, NY: Melville House, 2021.

51. Office of the Director of National Intelligence. Domestic violent extremism poses heightened threat in 2021, online, March 1, 2021.

52. Packer, G. How America fractured into four parts. *The Atlantic,* online, July/August, 2021.

53. Ludlow, R. 'I wish Republican members would show some spine': Ohio Sen. Sherrod Brown says GOP colleagues fear Trump, his base. *Dispatch.com,* online, Feb. 10, 2021.

54. Menninger, B. *Mortal Error: The Shot That Killed JFK.* Kansas City: Hunter's Moon Press, 2013.

55. Ojjdp.gov/ojstatbb/publications/statbb.a

Notes on Chapter Seven:

1. Hulse, C. The respectful supreme court hearing that wasn't. *The New York Times,* online, March 24, 2022.

2. Assemblee Nationale de France. *Proposition de loi relative a la lutte contre la manipulation de l'information,* November 20, 2018.

3. Matzko, P. The sordid history of the fairness doctrine. *CATO Institute,* online, Jan. 30, 2021.

4. Flynn, D.J., Nyhan, B. and Reifler, J. The nature and origins of misperceptions. *Political Psychology, 38(S1),* 2017, 127-150.

5. Korteling, J.E., Brouwer, A-M. and Toet, A. A neural network framework for cognitive bias. *Frontiers in Psychology,* online, Sept. 3, 2018. https://doi.org/10.3389/fpsyg.2018.01561

6. Bates, T. Editor's letter. *The Week,* 2016, p. 3.

7. Abramowitz, A.I. *The Great Alignment.* New Haven: Yale University Press, 2018.

8. Martin, G.J. and Yurukoglu, A. Bias in cable news. *American Economic Review, 107(9),* 2017, 2565-2599.

9. Abramowitz, A.I. *The Great Alignment.* New Haven: Yale University Press, 2018.

10. Miroff, N. Where Trump's border wall left deep scars and open gaps Biden plans repair job. *Washington Post,* online, Feb. 19, 2022.

11. Lipton, E. 'The coal industry is back,' Trump proclaimed. It wasn't. *New York Times,* online, Oct. 18, 2020.

12. Stein, J. Trump's 2016 campaign pledges on infrastructure have fallen short creating opening for Biden. *Washington Post,* online, Oct. 18, 2020.

13. Cusick, J. Less coverage and higher costs: The Trump's administration's health care legacy. *American Progress,* online, Sept. 25, 2020.

14. Smith, D. Trump's promise to 'drain the swamp' proves false even with Scott Pruitt out. *The Guardian*, online, July 5, 2018.

15. Dennis, B. and Eilperin, J. Former Pruitt aide alleges wasteful spending, extravagant travel by EPA chief. *The Washington Post*, online, Apr. 12, 2018.

16. Holden, E. Trump weakens Obama-era rules on toxic wastewater from coal plants. *The Guardian*, online, Aug. 31, 2020.

17. Bruni, F. Scott Pruitt, gone but not forgotten. *The New York Times*, online, July 5, 2018.

18. Radnofsky, L. Embattled Scott Pruitt resigns as EPA administrator. *Wall Street Journal*, online, July 5, 2018.

19. Fund, J. John Fund: Why EPA's Scott Pruitt had to go (and what to expect from the EPA now). *Fox News*, online, July 5, 2018.

20. Schneider, B. *Standoff.* NY: Simon & Schuster, 2018.

21. Kessler, G. Trump made 30,573 false or misleading claims as president. Nearly half came in his final year. *The Washington Post*, online, Jan. 23, 2021.

22. Gramlich, J. 5 facts about Fox News. *Pew Research Center*, online, April 8, 2020.

23. Trump, D.J. and Scwartz, T. *The Art of the Deal.* Ballantine Books, New York, NY, 1987.

24. Parker, K. Fearing the worst and it finally happened. *Houston Chronicle, July 2.* Also reported in *The Atlanta Journal-Constitution,* July 8, 2018.

25. Bolton, J. *The Room Where It Happened.* NY: Simon & Schuster, 2020.

26. Trump. M. *Too Much and Not Enough.* NY: Simon & Schuster, 2020.

27. Anderson Cooper 360 Degrees. *CNN Transcripts,* July 17, 2018.

28. Panetta, L. Leon Panetta: How to save America from President Trump's foreign policy hell: Opinion. *Newsweek,* online, March 28, 2018.

29. Balluck, K. Trump rips 'Fake news media': Many of the stories are 'total fiction'. *The Hill,* online, July 19, 2018.

30. Reints, R. New York Times correspondent Maggie Haberman says Trump'. *Fortune,* online, July 23, 2018.

31. Boot M. Trump always puts Putin's interests first. Quoted in *The Week, 20(988),* Aug. 14, 2020, p. 14.

32. Robb, A. Anatomy of a fake news scandal. *Rolling Stone,* online, Nov. 16, 2017.

33. Helm, B. Pizzagate nearly destroyed my restaurant. Then my customers helped me fight back. *Inc.com,* online, July/August, 2017.

34. King, C. and Goldman, A. In Washington pizzeria attack, fake news brought real guns. *New York Times,* online, Dec. 5, 2016.

35. Pasley, J.L. Articles on conspiracy theory in early American history. In P. Knight, (Ed.), *Conspiracy Theories in American History: An encyclopedia.* ABC-CLIO, Santa Barbara, CA, 2003.

36. Goodykoontz, B. Stumping with Trump, Sean Hannity calls reporters covering rally 'fake news'. *The Republic,* online, Nov. 6, 2018.

37. Zadrozny, B. Alleged victim is a no-show for news conference claiming Mueller 'sex assaults'. *NBC News,* online, Nov. 1, 2018.

38. Cummings, W. Jack Burkman: The conspiracy theorist accused of offering money for Mueller allegations. *USA Today,* online, Nov. 1, 2018.

39. Rossi, A. *After Truth,* HBO Documentaries, 2020.

40. Heffernan, V. Op-Ed: Alex Jones belongs to a long line of shrill, right-wing male hysterics. *Los Angeles Times,* online, July 7, 2018.

41. Silva, D. Alex Jones 'resolves' lawsuit with Chobani Yogurt, issues retraction. *NBC News,* online, May 17, 2017.

42. Robb, A. Anatomy of a fake news scandal. *Rollingstone,* online, Nov. 16, 2017.

43. Merlan, A. *Republic of Lies.* NY: Metropolitan/Henry Holt, 2019, pp. 4-5.

44. Buzbee, S. *Frontline: United States of Conspiracy,* M. Kirk *et al.,* producers, Aug. 2, 2020.

45. Trump, D.J. At White House press briefing on Aug. 14, 2020.

46. Rondeaux, C. The digital general. *The Intercept,* online, June 27, 2021.

47. Schaeffer, K. A look at the Americans who believe there is some truth to the conspiracy theory that COVID-19 was planned. *Pew Research Center,* online, July 24, 2020.

48. Douglas, K.M., Sutton, R.M. and Cichocka, A. The psychology of conspiracy theories. *Current Directions in Psychological Science,* 26(6), 2017, p. 538-542.

49. Buttigieg, P. Interviewed on *Real Time with Bill Mahrer,* HBO, Aug. 14, 2020.

50. Marwick, A. QAnon goes mainstream. Quoted in *The Week, 20(988),* Aug. 14, 2020, p. 13.

51. Rosenberg, M. and Haberman, M. More in G.O.P. speak the language of QAnon. *The New York Times,* Aug. 21, 2020, p. 1.

52. Mazzetti, M. Senate panel ties Russian officials to Trump's aides. *The New York Times,* Aug. 19, 2020, p. 1.

53. Wolfe, J. A second wave in Iran. In *The New York Times' Coronavirus Briefing,* online, Aug. 19, 2020.

54. Sanger, D.E. Baseless attacks threaten process in place since 1788. *The New York Times,* Oct. 1, 2020, p. 1.

55. Reid, T. *et al.* Backer of Trump's false fraud claims seek to control next elections. *Reuters*, Sept. 27, 2021.

56. Corasaniti, N. False election claims in California reveal a new normal for G.O.P. *The New York Times*, online, Sept. 12, 2021.

57. Stetler, B. 'We went so far right we went crazy:' How Fox News was radicalized by its own viewers. *CNN Business*, June 8, 2021.

58. 1tv.ge. Trump: We were winning everything, and all of a sudden it was just called off. April 4, 2020. https://1tv.ge/en/news/trump-we-were-winning-everything-and-all-of-a-sudden-it-was-just-called-off/

59. CNN Special Reports. "Trumping democracy: An American coup. Nov. 6, 2021.

60. Fuchs, H. and Cameron, C. Highlights of Trump's call with Georgia Secretary of State. *The New York Times*, online, Jan. 3, 2021.

61. Duncan, G. *GOP 2.0*. Nashville, TN: Forefront Books, 2021.

62. Woodward, B. and Costa, R. *Peril*. NY: Simon & Schuster, 2021.

63. CNN Special Reports. Trump supporters attack U.S. Capitol. *Transcripts.cnn.com*, online, Nov. 5, 2021.

64. English Times. Adam Kinzinger tears Trump has no regrets that he stood alone with Liz Cheney. *English Times*, online, Jan. 7, 2022.

65. Woodward, B. and Costa, R. *Peril*. NY: Simon & Schuster, 2021.

66. Lemon, J. GOP Rep. Gonzalez issues warning on Trump: U.S. 'Can't survive torching the constitution.' *Newsweek*, online, Nov. 6, 2021.

67. Tapper, J. *Trumping Democracy: An American Coup*. CNN, Nov. 6, 2021.

68. Breuninger, K. House Republicans elect Trump loyalist Elise Stefanik as conference chair after ousting Liz Cheney. *CNBC*, online, May 14, 2021.

69. Zhao, C. Retiring GOP lawmaker warns Trump will try to 'steal' 2024 election. *Newsweek*, online, Nov. 16, 2021.

70. Marche, S. *The Next Civil War*. NY: Avid Reader Press/Simon & Schuster, 2022.

71. Barrett, D. *et al.* FBI searches Trump safe at Mar-a-Lago for possible classified documents. *The Washington Post*, online, Aug. 8, 2022.

72. Collins, B. and Reilly, R.J. After Mar-a-Lago search, users on pro-Trump forums agitate for 'civil war'—including a Jan. 6 rioter. *NBC News*, online, Aug. 9, 2022.

73. Blest, P. Politician investigated by the FBI denounce FBI investigation. *Vice News*, online, Aug. 9, 2022.

74. Folkenflik, D. and Dreisbach, T. 'Off the rails': New Tucker Carlson project for Fox embraces conspiracy theories. *NPR*, online, Nov. 3, 2021.

75. Griffin, D. *Megaphone for Conspiracy: The Alex Jones Story*. Atlanta, GA: CNN, Feb. 27, 2022.

76. Kapur, S. Did Trump hurt Republicans in the 2022 elections? The numbers point to yes. *NBC News*, online, Nov. 13, 2022.

77. Pew Research Center. Two years after election turmoil, GOP voters remain skeptical on elections, vote counts. Online, Oct. 31, 2022.

78. Epstein, R.J. *et al.* Key allies are inching away from Trump. *The New York Times*, online, Nov. 16, 2022.

79. Goldmacher, S. Crowded G.O.P. field could take on Trump, and help him, too. *The New York Times*, Nov. 21, 2022, p. 1.

80. Leonard, K. Top Florida lawmakers want to change state law so DeSantis can run for president in 2024 without resigning as governor. *Business Insider*, online, Nov. 22, 2022.

81. Friedman T.L. America dodged an arrow. *The New York Times,* online, Nov. 9, 2022.

82. Haberman, M. and Rogers, K. Trump's trusted ploy: Spreading distrust. *The New York Times,* online, Sept. 4, 2020.

Notes for Chapter Eight:

1. Suttie, J. Life stages of trust. *Greater Good Magazine,* online, September 1, 2008.

2. Jones, R. The white supremacist 'Great Replacement Theory' has deep roots. *TeenVogue,* online, November 15, 2021.

3. Pappas, S. Are flat-earthers being serious? *LiveScience,* online, December 16, 2021.

4. Davidson, M. Vaccination as a cause of autism—myths and controversies. *Dialogues in Clinical Neuroscience,* Dec. 19(4), 2017, pp. 403-407.

5. Reiss, Julian and Jan Sprenger, "Scientific Objectivity", *The Stanford Encyclopedia of Philosophy* (Winter 2020 Edition).

6. Abbas, A.H. Politicizing COVID-19 vaccines in the press: A critical discourse analysis. *International Journal of Semiot Law,* online, July 201, p. 1-19, doi: 10.1007/s11196-021-09857-3.

7. Palm, R., Bolsen, T. and Kingsland, J.T. The effects of frames on COVID-19 vaccine resistance. *Frontiers in Political Science,* online, May 13, 2021.

8. Parikh, S. Why we must rebuild trust in science. Pewtrusts.org, online, Winter, 2021.

9. Lindzon, J. Why executives don't trust their own data and analytics insights. *Fast Company,* online, November 4, 2016.

10. Miller, J. Education is a bigger factor than race in desire for COVID-19 vaccine. *USC News,* online, February 25, 2021.

11. Ravenelle AJ, Newell A, Kowalski KC. "The Looming, Crazy Stalker Coronavirus": Fear Mongering, Fake News, and the Diffusion of Distrust. *Socius*. January, 2021. doi:10.1177/23780231211024776

12. Bloomberg, M.R. Commencement address at the University of Maryland, 2019.

13. Von Eschenbach, W. Western societies can't ignore the 'crisis of trust' we're experiencing. *Americamagazine.org*, online, February 20, 2019.

14. Sprunt, B. Trump pressed the Justice Department to reverse the election results, documents show. *NPR*, online, June 15, 2021.

15. The House Impeachment Managers and the House Defense. Prosecution of an insurrection: The complete trial transcript of the second impeachment of Donald Trump. *The New Press*. 2022.

16. Broadwater, L. Once a foe of Trump, Cruz leads a charge to reverse his election loss. *The New York Times*, online, February 18, 2021.

17. Durkee, A. More than half of Republicans believe voter fraud claims and most still support Trump, poll finds. *Forbes*, online, April 5, 2020.

18. Putnam, R.D. *The Upswing*. NY: Simon & Schuster, 2020.

19. Wallace, G.C. Inaugural address of Governor George C. Wallace, 1963. https://digital.archives.alabama.gov.

20. https://history.house.gov/People/Detail/13850

21. Rogers, D. Ex-GOP leader Bob Michel, face of decency and public service, dies. *Politico*, online, February 17, 2017.

22. Grimaldi, J.V. Playing to empty house, speakers get tight focus. *Washington Post*, online, April 6, 1994.

23. Hobson, J. How Newt Gingrich shaped the Republican party. *Wbur*, online, July 7, 2020.

24. Gillon, S. GOPAC strategy and instructional tapes (1986-1994). https://www.loc.gov. 2010.

25. Kenes, B. Rupert Murdoch: A populist emperor of the fourth estate. *Populismstudies.org,* December 22, 2020.

26. Lauer, D. Facebook's ethical failures are not accidental; they are part of the business model. *AI Ethics* 1, p. 395–403. https://doi.org/10.1007/s43681-021-00068-x. 2021.

27. Ray, M. Tea party movement. *Britannica*, online. (n.d.).

28. https://www.census.gov

29. Hobson, J. How Newt Gingrich shaped the Republican party. *Wbur*, online, July 7, 2020.

30. Miller, S. The coast vs. the heartland. *The Democracy Network*, online, October 29, 2016.

31. Shribman, D. Nixon's 'silent majority' speech, 50 years later. *The Detroit News*, online, Oct. 30, 2019.

32. Garland, M.B. Statement from Attorney General Merrick B. Garland on the 27th anniversary of the Oklahoma City Bombing. *The U.S. Dept of Justice, Office of Public Affairs*, April 19, 2022.

33. Wolf, Z.B. The 5 key elements of Trump's Big Lie and how it came to be. *CNN Politics*, online, May 19, 2021.

34. Dickson, E.J. Former QAnon followers explain what drew them in—and got them out. *Rollingstone*, online, September 23, 2020.

35. Doward J. 'Quite frankly terrifying': How the QAnon conspiracy theory is taking root in the UK. *The Guardian*, online, September 20, 2020.

36. The Times Editorial Board. Editorial: Liz Cheney isn't the only victim of the Republican Party's Trump cult. Los Angeles Times, online, May 6, 2021.

37. Benner, K. Trump pressed Justice Dept. to declare election results corrupt. *The New York Times*, online, July 30, 2021.

38. Gurlan, M. Reality cloaking: A new social disease? *Psychology Today*, online, January 9, 2021.

39. Stephens-Davidowitz, S. *Everybody Lies.* NY: Dey St./Morrow/ HarperCollins, 2017.

40. Altman, I. and Taylor, D. *Social Penetration.* NY: Holt, 1973.

41. Lemay, E.P. Jr., Ryan, J.E. and Teneva, N. Pursuing interpersonal value: An interdependence perspective. *Journal of Personality and Social Psychology, 120*(3), 716–744, 2021. https://doi-org. ezproxy.uvu.edu/10.1037/pspi0000289.supp (Supplemental)

42. Swenson, A. and Seitz, A. AP fact check: Trump tweets a tall tale of 'deleted' votes. *AP News*, online, November 12, 2020.

43. Froehlich, T. A disinformation-misinformation ecology: the case of Trump. *IntechOpen*, online, November 11, 2020. doi:10.5772/ intechopen.95000.

44. Wanta, S. The 5 key elements of trust. *Just Media*, online, February 25, 2021.

45. Myers, C.D. and Tingley, D. The influence of emotion on trust. *Political Analysis, 24(4)*, 2016, 492-500.

46. Selig, M. Know yourself? *Psychology Today*, online, March 9, 2016.

47. O'Malley, C. Trust: Begins and ends with self. Outlander Executive Services, 2020.

48. Selig, M. Know yourself? *Psychology Today*, online, March 9, 2016.

49. Barron, R., Kurtzer-Ellenbogen, L. and Yaffe, M. Middle East peace: What can we learn from Camp David 40 years later? *United States Institute of Peace*, online, March 25, 2019.

50. Stracqualursi, V. Trump says Kim 'trusts me, and I trust him.' *CNN Politics*, online, June 12, 2018.

51. Kende, A., Adrienn, U., Van Zomeren, M. and Lantos, N.S. The social affirmation use of social media as a motivator of collective action. *Journal of Applied Social Psychology*, 46(8), 2016, p. 453-469, doi:10.1111/jasp.12375.

52. Wilcox, W.B. *A Scientific Review of Abstinence and Abstinence Programs.* Arlington, VA: Under Contract Number GS-10F-0311K between Pal-Tech, Inc. and the Family and Youth Services Bureau Administration for Children, Youth, and Families Administration for Children and Families, 2008.

Notes for Chapter Nine:

1. Mounk, Y. *The Great Experiment*. NY: Penguin, 2022.

2. Ben-Ghiat, R. *Strongmen*. NY: Norton, 2020.

3. Stanley, J. *How Fascism Works*. NY: Random House, 2018.

4. Snyder, T. *The Road to Unfreedom*. NY: Tim Duggan Books, 2018.

5. Applebaum, A. *Twilight of Democracy*. NY: Doubleday, 2020.

6. Levitsky, S. and Ziblatt, D. *How Democracies Die*. NY: Crown, 2018.7.

7. *One Year Since the Jan. 6 Attack on the Capitol.* Washington, DC: US Dept. of Justice, online, 2022.

8. Samuels, B. Trump explodes at special counsel appointment. *The Hill*, online, Nov. 18, 2022.

9. Bernstein, B. Bill Barr: It would be a 'tragedy' if Trump is GOP's nominee. *National Review*, online, Nov. 18, 2022

10. Schwartz, H.A. Examining extremism: QAnon. *Center for Strategic & International Studies*. Washington, DC, June 10, 2021.

11. Kidwai, A. 'Facebook destroyed democracy,' says the U.S. government's former head of technology. *Fortune,* online, June 7, 2022.

12. Duffy, C. Here's how US lawmakers could finally rein in Facebook. *CNN Business*, online, Jan. 17, 2022.

13. Sun, Y and Zhang, Y. A review of theories and models applied in studies of social media addiction and implications for future research. *Addictive Behaviors, 114,* March 2021.

14. Akbari, M. *et al.* Metacognitions as a predictor of problematic social media use and internet gaming disorder. *Addictive Behavior, 137,* Feb. 2023.

15. Ren, R. XiaoIce, the IA chatbot spinoff of Microsoft, raises $138.4 million. *Ping West,* online, Nov. 9, 2022.

16. Cinelli, M. *et al.* Conspiracy theories and social media platforms. *Current Opinion in Psychology, 47,* Oct. 2022.

17. Van Prooijen, J-W. Psychological benefits of believing conspiracy theories. *Current Opinion in Psychology, 47,* Oct. 2022.

18. Sutton, R.M. and Douglas, K.M. Rabbit Hole Syndrome. *Current Opinion in Psychology, 48,* Dec. 2022.

19. Klepper, D. Choose your reality, *Associated Press*, online, July 9, 2022.

20. Insel, A. *et al.* Tolerated but not equal. *Philosophy and Social Criticism, 45(4),* Feb. 2019.

21. Rutland, A. and Killen, M. A developmental science approach to reducing prejudice and social exclusion. *Social Issues and Policy Review, 9(1),* Jan. 2015, pp. 121-154.

22. Beelmann, A and Heinemann, K.S. Preventing prejudice and improving intergroup attitudes. *Journal of Applied Developmental Psychology, 35(1),* Jan.-Feb. 2014, pp. 10-24.

23. Bobba, B. and Crocetti, E. "I feel you!" *Journal of Youth and Adolescence, 51*, Oct. 2022.

24. Rogers, C.R. and Ryback, D. One alternative to nuclear planetary suicide. In R.F. Levant & J.M. Shlien (Eds.), *Client-centered Therapy and the Person-centered Approach.* NY: Praeger.

25. Pettigrew, T.F. and Tropp, L.R. How does intergroup contact reduce prejudice? Meta-analytic tests of three mediators. *European Journal of Social Psychology, 38(6),* Sept./Oct. 2008, pp. 922-934.

26. Peplak, J. and Malti, T. Toward generalize concern. *Journal of Adolescent Research, 37(6),* April 2021.

27. Miklikocka, M. Development of anti-immigrant attitudes in adolescence. *British Journal of Psychology, 108(3),* Aug. 2017, pp. 626-648.

28. Vezzali, L. *et al.* Secondary transfer effect among children. *British Journal of Social Psychology, 57(3),* July 2018, pp. 547-566.

29. Cichocka, A. *et al.* 'They will not control us.' *British Journal of Psychology, 107(3),* Aug. 2017, pp. 556-576.

www.ingramcontent.com/pod-product-compliance
Lightning Source LLC
Chambersburg PA
CBHW020535030426
42337CB00013B/863